INDIVIDUAL COUNSELLING THEORY AND PRACTICE

A Reference Guide

DOULA NICOLSON
AND
HARRY AYERS

David Fulton Publishers

London

David Fulton Publishers Ltd
2 Barbon Close, London WC1N 3JX

First published in Great Britain by
David Fulton Publishers 1995

British Library Cataloguing in Publication Data

A catalogue record for this book is available from the British Library

ISBN 1–85346–373–6

Typeset by Ian Hall
Printed in Great Britain by Bell & Bain Ltd., Glasgow

CONTENTS

PREFACE

The idea for this book arose from the experience of counselling where practice suggested the need for a guide that is both easy to use and informative.

It is a reference book that provides a basic grounding in counselling theory and practice.

The aim is practicality and accessibility in order to meet the needs of over-burdened readers who would appreciate a minimalist text that avoids elaboration. The text consists of brief definitions and succinct explanations along with illustrative diagrams.

It will serve as a specialist dictionary, a means of revision, a primer and a basis for further study.

Doula Nicolson and Harry Ayers
London
January 1995

COMPARISON OF COUNSELLING THEORIES (Figure 1)

COUNSELLING THEORY	CONCEPT OF PERSON	ORIGINS OF PROBLEMS	FORMULATION OF THE PROBLEM	COUNSELLING TECHNIQUES	KEY CONCEPTS	ASSESSMENT TECHNIQUES
Behavioural: ideas of I. Pavlov and B.F. Skinner.	Person's behaviour acquired through learning processes: classical / operant conditioning. Behavioural is overt, observable and measurable.	Problem behaviour is the result of maladaptive or inadequate learning.	Problems will be decreased or extinguished through client's learning or unlearning.	Conditioning: operant-reinforcement of behaviour. Classical-systematic desensitization. Exposure. Assertiveness / social skills training.	Classical / operant conditioning. Reinforcement. Extinction. Contingencies.	Establish baseline. Observation. Checklists. Rating scales.
Cognitive-behavioural: ideas of A. Ellis: Rational-emotive therapy. A. Beck: Cognitive therapy.	Person's behaviour is associated with their own particular cognitive processes: beliefs, expectations, attitudes.	Problems are associated with maladaptive thinking processes.	Problems will be reduced or resolved through changing client's cognitive processes.	Rational-emotive / Cognitive therapy: changing irrational, erroneous or unrealistic thinking.	Irrational thinking. Cognitive restructuring. Self-efficacy. Re-attribution.	Self-monitoring. Checklists. Rating scales. Sociogram.
Person-centred counselling: ideas of C. Rogers.	Person's self-concept influences behaviour. People have potential for growth: self-actualization.	Problems arise from trying to fulfil conditions of worth and discrepancy between actual and ideal self.	Problems will be reduced or resolved through the client developing positive self-concept and through self-actualization.	Person-centred: empathy, congruence, unconditional positive regard.	Phenomenology. Actualization. Subception. Conditions of worth. Self-concept.	Q-Sort. Actual / ideal self.
Psychodynamic counselling: ideas of S. Freud.	Person's behaviour is determined by unconscious processes.	Current problems arise from unresolved unconscious conflicts originating in early childhood i.e. Oedipus complex.	Problems will be reduced or resolved through the client attaining insight / increasing ego strength.	Use of the transference / counter-transference. Interpretation of resistances and defences. Dream analysis. Free association.	Structural: id, libido, ego, superego. Psychosexual stages. Unconscious. Transference / Counter-transference. Defences. Oedipus complex.	Interpretation of transference / counter-transference / defences. Dream analysis. Free association. Projective tests.
G. Egan's eclectic model of counselling.	Person's behaviour depends on skills acquisition.	Problems arise from lack of skills.	Problems will be reduced or resolved through the client goal setting / acquiring knowledge / skills.	Use of empathy, respect, genuineness. Three-stage helping model: clarification, forming new perspectives, devising strategies.	High level functioning helpers. Social influence. Learning theory. Goal setting. Skills deficit.	Assessing client's skills, stages and key messages.

FIVE THEORIES OF COUNSELLING

BEHAVIOURAL COUNSELLING

CONCEPT (BASED ON CLASSICAL AND OPERANT CONDITIONING; FIGURE 2)

Behaviours are described as overt, specific, observable and quantifiable and are considered to be specific actions which can be directly observed and measured. Criticism of this concept of behaviour resulted in the development of the **cognitive - behavioural** approach which focuses on the client's beliefs, attitudes and expectations as well as overt behaviour.

Behavioural counselling is based on the ideas of **classical conditioning** (originating in **Pavlov's** work) and **operant conditioning** (originating in **Skinner's** work).

Classical conditioning is a form of learning where behaviour, a conditioned response (salivation) is brought about by a conditioned stimulus (bell) that draws its power through its connection with an unconditioned stimulus (food).

Operant conditioning is where behaviour operates on the environment to increase the probability of certain consequences and that behaviour is itself modified by those consequences. Behaviour is dependent or contingent upon a particular response. The environment is pivotal in shaping and determining behaviour.

The **behavioural approach** uses the principles of classical and operant conditioning to modify a client's behaviour. This occurs after a behavioural assessment and analysis of the client's personal and interpersonal problems in terms of conditioning processes.

THE MODEL OF THE PERSON

Behaviour is seen as the product of learning processes and people are seen as capable of learning appropriate and unlearning inappropriate behaviour. Environmental responses determine peoples behaviour and given this, it is possible to manipulate the environment to change behaviour. People are also seen as pleasure seeking and pain avoiding and as a result their behaviour can be changed by the use of reinforcement or punishment. The emphasis is on people's learning behaviour as being amenable to empirical analysis through the use of observational techniques.

THE NATURE OF PERSONAL AND INTERPERSONAL PROBLEMS

Personal and interpersonal problems are seen as resulting from learning inappropriate behaviour or failing to learn appropriate behaviour. There is no place in this approach for the unconscious, repressed conflicts or any underlying disease or syndrome.

It is assumed that the main aim of any person is to adapt effectively to their environment. A person can achieve this goal on the basis of the application of the principles of learning. The aim is for the client to increase desirable behaviours and decrease undesirable ones. As there are no underlying conflicts once the problem behaviour is extinguished or replaced by the desired behaviour, the client's problem is deemed solved, therefore symptom-substitution is not possible.

BEHAVIOURAL ASSESSMENT AND ANALYSIS:

Behavioural assessment seeks to observe and measure behaviours until the observed behaviour is seen as being a representative sample of the client's behaviour. During assessment attention is focused on how the behaviour varies in particular settings and under specific conditions.

Functional analysis attempts to discover precise relationships between changes in stimulus conditions and changes in behaviour using the ABC model.

THE ROLE OF THE BEHAVIOURAL COUNSELLOR

The counsellor has a number of different roles:

- The counsellor undertakes *behavioural assessment* - The counsellor observes the client's behaviour in the counselling setting and also acquires knowledge of the client's behaviour in other settings through using various assessment instruments such as behaviour checklists, questionnaires, self-monitoring reports and interviews. The assessment process should lead to the establishment of *baseline* of the problem behaviour, i.e. its current *intensity, frequency* and *duration* so that it can serve as a reference point for future comparison.

- The counsellor undertakes *behavioural analyses* - The counsellor analyses the client's presenting problems on the basis of his or her assessment and seeks ways in which the problem behaviour has been maintained. The counsellor hopes to identify the specific stimuli that currently trigger the problem behaviour, its *intensity, frequency and duration*. The counsellor can use the **ABC model** to analyse the client's behaviour. The counsellor should be able to construct an hypothesis ,that is, **formulate** as to why the problem behaviour is maintained and on the basis of this hypothesis produce a **formulation** of the client's problem. The formulation ought to lead to a planned *intervention* that specifies targets and objectives which are themselves testable.

The **ABC model** is a method of analysing a client's behaviour based on observation in a setting where the problems arise:

(A) Refers to the *antecedents*, events which occur before the problem behaviour.

(B) Refers to the problem *behaviour itself.*

(C) Refers to the *consequences* of the problem behaviour.

The client as well as the counsellor is able to use this form of analysis to identify situations, events, incidents and actions that occur prior to the onset of a given problem behaviour and also to note what consequences result from that behaviour.

This can enable both counsellor and client to think of ways in which the antecedents can be changed so that the problem behaviour is reduced or **extinguished.** Alternatively the consequences of the behaviour may be changed so reducing or eliminating the problem behaviour.

- **The counsellor as modeller** - The counsellor can successfully demonstrate a desired behaviour for the client or they can jointly and gradually perform a particular repertoire of behaviour through **behaviour rehearsal.**

The counsellor has also to be aware that he or she can unintentionally reinforce the client's problem behaviour through their own behaviour towards the client.

- **The counsellor as reinforcer** - The counsellor can be seen as a person who intentionally reinforces a client's desired behaviour by the use of praise, warmth, empathy and acceptance in the counselling situation.

The counsellor can also help the client to identify people and situations that provide *positive reinforcement* for the desired behaviour and conversely help identify people and situations that lead to the client maintaining the problem behaviour.

- **The counsellor undertakes to draw up a behavioural contract** - The counsellor in collaboration with the client and possibly significant others designs a contract that specifies the client's target behaviours and the behavioural techniques to be used in achieving those behaviours. It also outlines the role of the counsellor and the client and the nature of the counselling relationship.

BEHAVIOURAL TECHNIQUES OR STRATEGIES

- *Contingency management* - A counsellor can suggest to the client ways of changing their behavior through the management of particular contingent responses. This can be achieved through encouraging the client to replace the reinforcers that maintain his or her difficulties with ones that increase the desired behaviours. Additionally the client can suggest to others ways in which they can reinforce the desired behaviours.

- *Positive reinforcement* - The counsellor can directly reinforce or reward the client's desired behaviour or suggest ways in which the client can arrange for others to reinforce their behaviour. The client can also self-reinforce.

- *Shaping* is a gradual process of producing new behaviours by successively reinforcing behaviours that approximate the desired behaviour.

- *Contingency contract* - A contract is drawn up with the client and significant others who are seen as making a positive or negative contribution to the client's problems. The aim is to get all participants to agree on collaboration in achieving specific, behavioural goals that will ameliorate the client's problems. Each participant ought to gain reinforcement from achieving those goals.

- *Rapid exposure or flooding* - A technique to reduce acute anxiety or phobic behaviour by encouraging the client to confront the stimulus conditions directly without dilution.

- *Slow exposure or systematic desensitization* requires an approach that arranges for the client to work gradually through an anxiety-producing hierarchy until the client feels able to cope with the full impact of the stimulus conditions.

Elements of the Cognitive-Behavioural Model of Counselling (Figure 2)

Cognitive - Behavioural Counselling

- Assessment: Identification of Problem: When Where Frequency Duration
  - Problem Solving Approach. Setting Targets / Goals
    - Contract
  - Using Counselling Techniques.
    - Challenging Negative Self-Statements and Beliefs Reframing Perceptions
    - Encouraging the use of Positive Self-Statements in the Imagination and in Real Situations
    - Systematic Desensitization
    - Thought Stopping
    - Assertiveness and Social Skills Training
    - Rapid & Slow Exposure (in vivo)
    - Use of Reinforcement and Self Reinforcement
    - Monitoring and Evaluation of Progress Measurement

Cognitive Processes
- Beliefs Expectations Attitudes & Perceptions

Cognitive Distortion
- Over-Generalization
  - Dichotomous Thinking
    - Personalization

Meta-Cognition Reflection Cognitive Processes
- ABC Functional Analysis

Cognitive Contents
- Negative Self-Statements / Beliefs
  - Self-Defeating Behaviour

COGNITIVE-BEHAVIOURAL COUNSELLING

CONCEPT (FIGURE 2)

Cognitive - behavioural counselling integrates thought with behaviour. Cognition can be thought of in terms of **information-processing**. Information is processed differently by different people and people as a consequence hold different beliefs, attitudes and expectations about the world and others. Peoples' information about others and the external world can become distorted. People have the ability to reflect on their own thought processes, this is known as **metacognition**. This in turn enables them to interpret what is happening to them in a variety of ways. These interpretations can become associated with different types of behaviour. Changing those interpretations can lead to behavioural change.

Cognitive-behavioural counselling subscribes to three basic ideas: that **thinking affects behaviour,** that **thinking processes may be monitored and changed,** and that **changes in behaviour can occur through changes in thinking processes.**

Thinking is seen as knowable, accessible and assessable. Peoples' thought processes are seen as mediating their responses to the external world and others and, where distortion occurs, can lead to problems in personal and interpersonal relationships. People are seen as taking responsibility for their own problems and that they have within themselves potential control over their own thought and behaviour. Clients are seen as active participants who learn the elements of the cognitive-behavioural approach to counselling and use it to change their thinking processes in a way that leads to improved functioning in the world and in their relationships.

THEORETICAL CONCEPTS

Information-processing - People interpret or process information about the world and others in a specific way. They develop constructs, hypotheses and beliefs about themselves, others and the external world.

People can develop **negative and unrealistic beliefs** about themselves and others which in turn leads to personal and interpersonal problems.

Automatic thoughts - Some thought processes are 'automatic' or involuntary, persisting, even though the client attempts to terminate them. If this negative thinking is prolonged then problems arise. If those thoughts are threatening then anxiety occurs, if loss or separation then depression may be the outcome.

Irrational beliefs are ones of irrational self-evaluation, for example in terms of attaining perfection in one's life. These beliefs are expressed in extreme terms and make it impossible for people to achieve their goals.

THE PROBLEM-SOLVING APPROACH

This approach advocated by **D'Zurilla and Goldfried** looks at how problems are perceived, to what they are attributed to,how they are appraised as a problem, the level of perceived personal control, and the time and effort perceived as necessary for problem solving.

The problem has to be clearly and specifically defined, information about the problem has to be collated, realistic goals need to be established, and the problem has to be appraised in relation to personal potential.

Alternative solutions have to be evaluated and the optimum one selected. The solution selected has to be tested in real-life situations.

Problem-Solving Training

The aim of this type of training is to help the client identify and clarify their problems and to train them in skills that enable them to deal with future problems. Training employs direct verbal instruction and **dialogical (Socratic)** instruction. The client is encouraged to formulate their own solutions.

Other training procedures include **coaching, modeling, rehearsal, feedback** and **positive reinforcement.**

The Problem-Solving Process

Decision-Making - The client thinks of alternative solutions and their risks and the skills and resources required. The client is asked to consider the positive and negative consequences (immediate, long-term, social and personal) of each solution.

Implementing the Solution - After selecting the solution the client performs the appropriate activities and monitors them through self-observation. When the client achieves success, the client uses **self-reinforcement.**

The counsellor provides positive reinforcement and feedback, monitors the client's cognitions, generalizes the client's solution to other problems and situations and anticipates future difficulties and problems.

THE SELF-MANAGEMENT APPROACH

This approach assumes that people are controlled through their responses to their own inner world and the external environment and that they also try to control their responses in such a way as to realize their goals. Self-management requires the client to learn new controlling strategies.

Approaches to Self-Management

*   ***Self-efficacy (A. Bandura)*** - Perceived self-efficacy is a client's estimation as to whether they can initiate and maintain a given behaviour. Interventions are designed to raise a client's perceived self-efficacy. Clients also make incorrect attributions about the causes of their problems. Through **attribution retraining** clients can learn to make accurate attributions which enable them to help resolve their problems.

*   ***Self - instructional training (D. Meichenbaum)*** - Assumes that a client's self-instruction can bring about behaviour change. Self-instruction can lead to recall of appropriate behaviours and the correction of mistakes. The client monitors their thoughts associated with their presenting problems. This should lead to agreement between the counsellor and client as to how the problem should be defined. The client learns to adopt **positive self-statements** in place of negative thoughts.

*   ***Feedback - loop (F. Kanfer)*** - Requires the client to undertake a process of self-monitoring, self-evaluation and self-reinforcement. The client observes their thoughts, feelings and behaviour and evaluates them in terms of a standard of performance. The client on attaining a desired level of performance self-administers positive reinforcement and punishment where performance is unsatisfactory. The client must be committed to self-correcting their behaviour and believe that their behaviour is in fact under their control.

RATIONAL EMOTIVE BEHAVIOURAL THERAPY

Rational emotive behavioural therapy *(A. Ellis)* assumes that thought processes play an important part in personal development and thought, feelings and behaviour are all seen as interconnected. The main tenet is that there are **rational** and **irrational beliefs** which influence a client's behaviour. There is a tendency for people to think irrationally and also to think in absolute rather than relative terms. However, people are also able to think about their beliefs and change them. Rationality is defined relatively as that which brings about the realization of the client's goals. Conversely irrationality is that which frustrates the client in reaching their goals. Irrational thinking is seen as inherent in people but this type of thinking can be challenged and changed.

People tend to make absolute generalizations and absolute demands on themselves and others. This *absolutistic thinking* impedes personal development. It takes the form of people evaluating their lives and that of others in terms of unconditional *"musts"* , this being called *"musturbation"*.

Some ways in which absolutistic thinking is manifested:

- *Awfulizing* - Meaning what is happening to the client is rated by the client as bad as it could possibly be.

- *I-can't-stand-it-itis* - The client believes that it is impossible to experience any happiness no matter what happens in their life.

- *Damnation* - A tendency for the client to see him or herself and others as totally undeserving because they do or fail to do something seen by the client as necessary.

These forms of absolutistic thinking need to be altered in order to modify behaviour and resolve problems :

- The way to change behaviour is through the logical and empirical challenging of irrational beliefs. Clients can be helped to find alternatives to awfulizing, I-can't-stand-it-itis and damnation by asking them to scale down their evaluations and expectations or by pursuing new goals.

- Clients are helped to detect their own irrational beliefs. Then the truth or falsity of those beliefs is challenged. Clients are also helped to distinguish rational from irrational beliefs and to accept that at times psychological discomfort is inevitable when change is required.

- Clients are therefore seen as contributing to their own problems by the way they view them and they continue due to the client maintaining that viewpoint. It is only through the client's efforts to jettison their irrational beliefs that their problems will be resolved.

- Ellis has produced an ABC model (**see diagram**) that enables a counsellor to illustrate how problems can be analysed and it can also be used by the clients themselves to analyse their problems.

The ABC Model (Ellis) illustrates how problems can be analysed:

- (A) an Activating event which leads to emotional and behavioural Consequences (C)

- (C) those emotional and behavioural consequences being mediated by Beliefs (B)

- (A) = Activating event (can be an actual incident, a memory, anticipation or emotion)

  Client fails to get a job

- (B) = Clients beliefs:

  inferences   the interviewer dislikes me

  self-evaluation   the interviewer dislikes me
  because I am unintelligent

- (C) = Consequences of the client's beliefs:

  emotional response   depression

  behavioural reaction   avoids applying for other jobs

COGNITIVE THERAPY

Cognitive therapy *(A. Beck)* makes the assumption that in order to understand a client's feelings or emotional problems it is necessary to concentrate on their cognitive reactions to their problems. The counsellor ought to examine the client's thoughts and feelings about him or herself, about the external world and the future - called the *"cognitive triad."*

This approach focuses on the client's beliefs, values and the way causality or responsibility is attributed. The client is encouraged to consider their beliefs as hypotheses that require testing. If their current beliefs are found wanting hopefully the client will be able to acquire new beliefs that are emotionally more satisfying. Through working with the client the counsellor may be able to detect patterns of thinking or schemata that underlie the client's recurrent emotional problems. *Schemata* are ways in which an individual organizes his or her experience and errors or distortions in thinking can arise from these schemata. Once identified the value and validity of these schemata can be assessed.

The client can be helped to detect specific *cognitive errors* listed by Beck and others in their own thinking:

- *Arbitrary inference* - Refers to a client making an inference without backing it up with evidence or alternatively ignoring conflicting evidence.

- *Selective abstraction* - The client takes a fact out of context whilst ignoring other significant features and then proceeds to base their entire experience on that isolated fact.

- *Over-generalization* - Refers to the client forming a general rule from a few instances and applying this rule to all situations no matter how inappropriate.

- *Magnification and Minimization* - The client magnifies or minimizes events out of all proportion to their actual significance.

- *Personalization* - The client relates incidents to him or herself where such incidents have no personal bearing or significance.

- *Dichotomous thinking* - Refers to the client thinking about events in terms of opposite extremes

The *role of the counsellor* is one where the client is encouraged to collaborate with the counsellor and both assume an equal responsibility. The client is seen as having an intimate knowledge and understanding of their own thoughts and feelings and as a result the counsellor depends on the client to convey their meaning. The client is also encouraged to take an active part in the counselling process, it is assumed that the client is the only one who has intimate knowledge of their problems and is therefore privileged. As a result the client is required to take on greater responsibility for testing and changing their patterns of thinking.

The **role of the client** is to engage in various **behavioural tasks**:

- **Self-monitoring,** i.e. keeping a record of activities and associated feelings. With this record the counsellor obtains knowledge of how the client is using their time; it also enables the client to test their beliefs or hypotheses. Additionally it affords the client a way of seeing how certain feelings are associated with particular activities. Finally it provides a baseline for future comparison.

- Another task is for the counsellor to suggest activities to the client that he or she would normally avoid; this also enables the counsellor to see what activities are avoided. The client can be asked to undertake new activities and the counsellor can assist by anticipating internal and external hurdles. The counsellor will the be able to gauge the client's reactions to those activities and futher possibilities.

- Finally these tasks can be broken down into small steps and graded in difficulty thereby making them more attainable.

Beck's CognitiveTheory of Depression (an application of cognitive therapy to an emotional problem)

Depressed clients have a predisposition to depression through negative cognitive schemas which are activated by stressful life events. The schema exacerbates hopelessness, pessimism and apathy in the client and as a result the client becomes inactive compounding the depression. The client excludes positive but includes negative information. Cognitive distortions e.g. arbitrary inference, selective abstraction, over-generalization, magnification and minimization, personalization and dichotomous thinking maintain the client's negative schema.

Cognitive therapy for depression involves the counsellor in identifying the client's thoughts particularly ones that the client avoids and examining the client's beliefs about their self in terms of their validity.

Elements of the Person-Centred Model of Counselling (Figure 3)

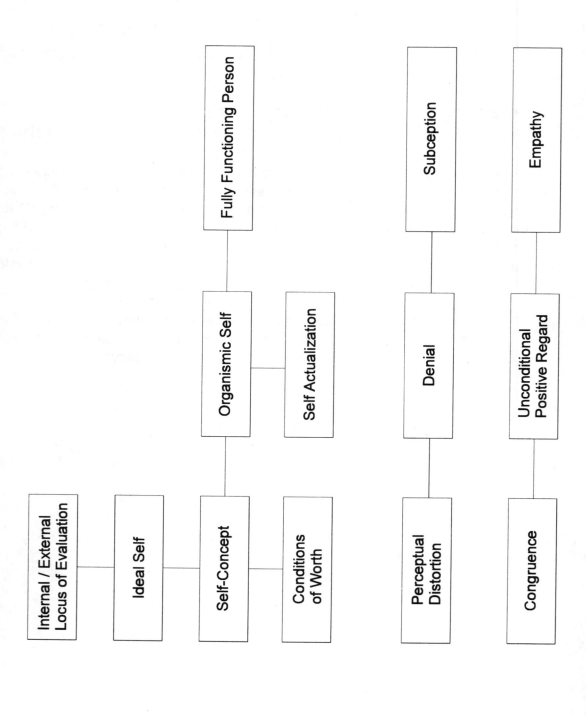

PERSON-CENTRED COUNSELLING

CONCEPT (FIGURE 3)

The person or client-centred approach *(Rogers)* is one where a person's experience and their *phenomenological* or subjective appraisal of the world is seen as having validity in itself. It also sees people as having responsibility for their own lives and being able to draw on their own inner resources as a means of personal growth and development.

THEORETICAL CONCEPTS

The *self-concept* is the idea or conceptualization that people have of themselves. This self-concept can be positive or negative or a combination of both. A person's behaviour can be seen as a reflection of the way they think and feel about their self and the world around them. Behaviour reflects the way people evaluate themselves.

> The *conditions of worth* refers to the conditions that are laid down by others in order for a person to think and feel that they are accepted. A person's sense of worth becomes conditional on them winning the approval of others and avoiding any beliefs, feelings and behaviour that leads to disapproval.

> The *organismic self* refers to the true or genuine self that is aware of its needs for personal development both from others and from the external world. The organismic self can come into conflict with the desire for the approval of others and where this arises the person may develop a self-concept that is alien to their true self. The person comes to doubt the reliability of the promptings of the organismic self and this leads to guilt and self-denigration.

> The *fully-functioning* or *self-actualizing person* is a person who has achieved a self-concept which reflects their organismic self. This state is one where a person is open to experience and is able to have trust and confidence in their self and others. The fully-functioning person who is confident in their own judgment and decision-making is said to have an *internal locus* of *self-evaluation*.

> The process of *subception* occurs where a person's experience is outside of their direct awareness but nonetheless has an impact on their behaviour and is manifested in a particular behaviour or reaction.

Emotional conflict - A person who finds that their self-concept is in conflict with their organismic self will develop an impoverished self-concept, **a false self**, and therefore experience unhappiness. Even in the case of apparently self-assured people the self-concept may be a front which, through an unexpected trauma, may collapse. The self-confident person may maintain their false self-concept by continually seeking the approval of others. However, if this false self-concept is at all threatened then through fear the person will resort to two types of defence, perceptual distortion or denial.

Perceptual distortion occurs where a person distorts a message perceived as threatening so that it does not damage their self-concept.

Denial is a process whereby a person avoids any contact with thoughts or feelings that might threaten their self-concept.

Conditions for personal growth are the conditions that are necessary for people to experience personal growth and it is further believed that everybody has within them this potential to grow and develop into a fully-functioning person.

There are three conditions for growth:

- *Congruence* - The counsellor has to display genuineness, that is avoid erecting a professional demeanour and to renounce the role of expert so as to empower people to find strength from within themselves. The counsellor has to encourage people to believe in themselves.

- *Unconditional positive regard* is where the counsellor accepts the person, non-judgementally. The person then feels able to talk freely and honestly about their negative thoughts and feelings.

- *Empathy* is where the counsellor is able to understand how people are thinking and feeling about themselves and others and their perspective on the world. The counsellor is also able through successful empathy to communicate understanding and acceptance to the person. It is then possible for the person to grow and develop positively without feeling alienated.

THE COUNSELLING RELATIONSHIP

The counsellor's core beliefs about people:

- Every person has the capacity for positive personal growth by calling on their inner resources.

- Through the counsellor showing congruence, empathy and unconditional positive regard a person will be able to better use their inner resources in order to grow.

- People are seen as fundamentally positive, truth seeking, sociable and as needing self-regard.

- Personal development will be enhanced by the counsellor relating to the person holistically and by recognizing that the person will feel empowered.

- People are capable of developing without the counsellor presenting him or herself as an expert or guru.

The counsellor - client relationship:

- The counsellor explains clearly and openly the counsellor's role in relation to the client.

- The counsellor outlines their commitment and responsibility to the person but does not assume responsibility for the person's choices and decisions.

- The counsellor affirms that the client has to arrive at his or her own choices with the help of the counsellor but the counsellor cannot decide what is best for the client.

EMPATHY

This is central to the counselling relationship. It is defined as the counsellor putting him or herself in the place of the person. It is a process of understanding the person's expressed feelings and thoughts and is called **accurate empathy**. Another more encompassing definition is where the counsellor understands underlying feelings that are below the person's level of awareness.

By empathizing with the person the counsellor communicates their understanding o f their feelings, which by itself can have a positive affect on the person. It also enables the person to focus more clearly on their overt and underlying feelings and to become aware of incongruence between the two. From this awareness it is possible for the person to move forward and make progress.

The counsellor may find that they are having difficulties in empathizing with the person and this can be due to particular **blocks**. One block arises from the counsellor having a particular model of human nature which leads to bias in their perceptions of the person.

Another block arises where the counsellor's own needs, wishes, problems and anxieties get in the way of empathizing with the person.

UNCONDITIONAL POSITIVE REGARD

This phrase refers to the counsellor showing and communicating effectively acceptance and warmth towards the person and not allowing any of the person's behaviours to influence adversely the counsellor's regard.

By accepting the person as they are the counsellor shows that this regard does not depend on the person meeting conditions of worth. The person comes to realize that he or she is accepted unconditionally and does not have to worry about behaving in a particular way towards the counsellor. The person no longer has to be defensive and can express their thoughts and feelings openly without fear. This helps the person to increase their self-esteem.

The counsellor needs to prepare for the possibility that the person may reject the counsellor's acceptance out of a mistrust of others. Alternatively the person may interpret the counsellor's acceptance as offering friendship or a more intimate relationship.

CONGRUENCE

Congruence is a state in which the counsellor's overt responses and reactions consistently reflect his or her inner thoughts and feelings. The counsellor does not pretend or simulate responses towards the person. The person must feel that the counsellor is being sincere towards him or her and the counsellor must ensure that this congruence is effectively communicated.

The counsellor's congruence should be one that is a sincere and relevant response to the person's significant and persistent feelings.

Incongruence can occur where the counsellor is unaware of feelings that he or she has towards the client and which remain covert or where the counsellor is conscious of those feelings but chooses not to communicate them.

Congruence is important as it enables the person to feel that they are taken seriously by the counsellor and that the counsellor can be trusted. This in turn enables the person to become more congruent with their own self. The counsellor must be wary of imposing his or her own needs on the person in claiming congruence with the person.

Elements of the Psychodynamic Model of Counselling (Figure 4)

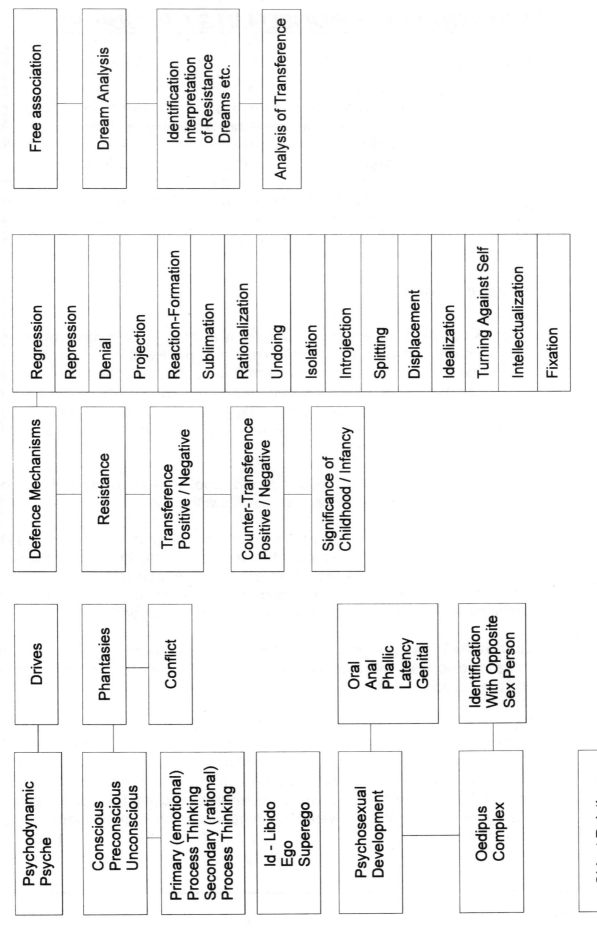

PSYCHODYNAMIC COUNSELLING (FREUDIAN)

CONCEPT (FIGURE 4)

The mind or psyche is perceived as having **unconscious**, active processes taking the form of **dynamic** forces or impulses seeking expression and satisfaction. A person also relates to other selves but also to itself, to parts of itself and to symbols of these, all being called **objects.** This means that we can love or hate parts of our selves or the selves of others. These objects have originated in early childhood through relationships especially with one's father and mother. The mind has **phantasies** about such objects which persist into adult life and reappear particularly at times of personal stress when the mind can regress or return to infantile methods of coping.

STRUCTURAL CONCEPTS

Unconscious - This is a source of emotional and traumatic conflicts of which the person is unaware and which give rise to particular symptoms in the form of personal and interpersonal emotional problems. The unconscious expresses itself in terms of unacceptable sexual desires, aggressive and other anxiety, shame or guilt-producing impulses. The contents of the unconscious can be explored through dreams, free association, art and slips of the tongue and the pen.

Preconscious - Refers to thoughts and emotions which are below the conscious threshold but that are accessible with effort.

Id - Primitive sexual and aggressive impulses that arise from the deepest part of the unconscious and that demand immediate and unconditional satisfaction. The id obeys the **pleasure principle** and engages in **wish-fulfilment** through **primary process thinking** which demands instant gratification regardless of the constraints of time and space.

Libido - Refers to energy derived from the id which is primarily sexual but came to be equated with a generalised life energy, a force that drives physical and mental processes.

Ego - The self that attempts to or asserts conscious control over the id and its impulses while at the same time coping with the demands of the external environment. It tries to to find tension-reducing objects. The ego observes the **reality principle** and tests reality through **secondary process thinking** which adapts to the demands of the external world using logic and reason. The ego tries to mediate between the demands of the id, the superego and the external world.

Superego - The injunctions and inhibitions that have been **internalized** through one's parents and which censor the unconscious and one's thoughts and actions in terms of an ego ideal. It develops at first through fear and subsequently through **identification** with one's parents. The superego's demands can become severe, compulsive punitive and overwhelming.

DEFENCE MECHANISMS

The defences erected by the ego in order to control the direct expression of sexual and aggressive desires and other anxiety, gulit and shame producing impulses that are a threat to the self and which originate in the unconscious.

The main defences are:

- **Regression** - Returning to an earlier, more immature or childhood stage of functioning in order to avoid anxiety. A person may have become **fixated** in the past on some person or object as in the case of mother or father fixation and this is deemed to affect that person's current relationships.

- **Repression** - Where sexual and aggressive impulses and other anxiety-producing impulses are kept in the unconscious thus enabling a person to avoid conscious guilt or anxiety.

- **Denial** - Denying thoughts, feelings and desires that might cause anxiety if released into consciousness.

- **Projection** - Unacceptable impulses are attributed to another person thus enabling the person having those impulses to avoid experiencing guilt or anxiety.

- **Reaction formation** - Unacceptable impulses are controlled by replacing them with their opposite extremes.

- **Sublimation** - Unacceptable desires are redirected and refined into creative and artistic activities which are more socially acceptable.

- **Rationalization** - Making unacceptable impulses acceptable by attributing them to more acceptable reasons which hide ulterior motives.

- **Undoing** - A person tries to reduce anxiety by a ritual re-enactment of events which then leads to a more acceptable outcome.

- **Isolation** - Separating an unacceptable impulse from the original memory of it so that although the original event is not forgotten its emotional charge is lost.

- *Introjection* - Parental values are taken in and accepted and form the superego. This process helps a person to avoid the anxiety that arises from separation from significant others.

- *Splitting* - A person divides their self and/or others into good and bad objects and avoids anxiety and guilt by this process of separation.

- *Displacement* - Positive and/or negative feelings are directed away from a person that they are really intended for, on to another often safer target.

- *Intellectualization* - Refers to the process of looking at an emotional or relationship difficulty as an intellectual, problem-solving exercise thus trying to avoid its emotional implications.

- *Asceticism* - An attempt to isolate feelings through abstinence, that is through avoiding them completely.

- *Idealization* - A way of coping with ambivalence towards a person by idealizing them and so not recognizing any negative feelings for them.

- *Turning against self* - A person redirects negative feelings away from others on to him or herself to avoid the negative feelings they have for others.

- *Fixation* - A person remains emotionally static at a particular developmental stage for fear of what the next stage might threaten or because they have not fulfilled the emotional demands of the current stage.

PSYCHOSEXUAL DEVELOPMENT

There are **five stages** of psychosexual development which are seen as occurring through the interaction of biological impulses and the external world. These stages have to be successfully completed in order to attain adulthood. If transition at the various stages is not satisfactorily achieved then fixations occur. Emotional conflicts are associated with the various fixations and if not resolved continue into adulthood.

In the first 5 years:

- The **oral stage** is characterized by pleasure derived from the mouth, this being incorporative through sucking, biting and chewing. People fixated at this stage are said to have the following tendencies: dependency, generosity, optimism or pessimism, depression or aggression.

- The **anal stage** is characterized by pleasure derived from the anus, this being achieved through the retention or expulsion of faeces. People fixated at this stage are said to have the following tendencies: if anal **retentive** they show obstinacy, miserliness, orderliness and a preoccupation with cleanliness; if anal **expulsive** they display untidiness or generosity.

- The **phallic stage** is characterized by a strong interest in the genitals and leads to the **Oedipus complex**, that is the unconscious desire on the part of a child to have sex with the opposite-sexed parent and at the same time the desire to get rid of the same-sexed parent. It is said to arise between the ages of 3-5 and it is claimed that it is common to all cultures. This complex is resolved through the child identifying with the parent of the same sex.

- A boy suffers from **castration** anxiety, the fear that he might lose his penis as paternal punishment for sexual desire for his mother, this fear leads him to identify with his father to avoid being punished. Girls are said to experience this complex in the form of feeling that they have lost their penis and as a result seek an appropriate symbolic substitute for the penis.

- The **latency stage** commences around the age 4 or 5 and ends at puberty. During this stage the child is said to repress their memories of unacceptable impulses experienced during infancy.

- The **genital stage** is where a person can show love for others and achieve an heterosexual relationship with another adult.

PSYCHODYNAMIC MODEL OF CLIENT FUNCTIONING AND CLIENT PROBLEMS

Clients are seen as struggling with internal unconscious conflicts originating in infancy which prevents them having fulfilling personal and interpersonal relationships in later life.

Unacceptable sexual, aggressive and other anxiety-producing impulses originate in the unconscious and threaten the client's self.

A fully functioning client has been able to attain an equilibrium between the demands of the id, ego and superego. Ideally the ego gains control over unacceptable and anxiety-producing impulses by being strengthened through insight into the origin and nature of unconscious conflicts.

Client problems arise where defences are erected to protect the ego but which collapse or are insufficient when under stress.

Memories may be revived from the past that interfere with a client's fully functioning in the present.

Symptoms and the defences used by a client often represent underlying difficulties which are the result of internal psychodynamic conflicts and which are also the product of external relationships in childhood with parents, siblings and significant others in the client's life.

AIM

The aim is to interpret the transference, resistances and defences displayed by the client. This requires making the conscious self aware of unconscious conflicts. This insight should enable the client to unblock emotionally and so develop into a fully functioning person.

For a client to achieve this aim they have to meet the following criteria: be motivated, have a sufficiently strong ego, be patient with slow progress, have the potential to develop the necessary degree of insight, sufficient finance and external support.

STYLE

The counsellor is **neutral,** i.e. does not deliberately reveal their own attitudes and feelings towards the client or aspects of their private life and also observes boundaries by not becoming friendly or intimate with the client. This enables the client to perceive the counsellor as they wish and express any fantasies they may have and in doing so disclose ways in which the client related to significant others in the past.

The counsellor forms a working relationship with the client and offers **interpretations** to the client where appropriate. These interpretations depend on the establishment of transference between counsellor and client. Such transference can be positive or negative. Conflicts from the past are re-experienced during the transference with the counsellor. The transference enables the counsellor to interpret how the client related to significant others in the past and how they relate to others at present. The re-emergence of conflicts often leads to resistance by the client to further exploration of their problems due to the anxiety and guilt that they evoke.

The counsellor ought to be aware of the counter-transference where the counsellor can become emotionally involved in the counselling relationship as a result of the displacement of feelings from past relationships on to the client. The counsellor should be aware of their own preconceptions and feelings in relation to the client. These feelings may provide useful clues as to the kinds of relationships the client has experienced with significant others in the past, or as they currently relate to others.

TECHNIQUES:

- **Free association** - The counsellor encourages the client to express thoughts and emotions as they spontaneously arise in a conducive situation. The idea is for the counsellor to facilitate this free flow of thought and feeling by appropriate reflection, paraphrasing, periods of silence and interpretations which can break down the client's resistance to discussing painful thoughts and feelings. The client may resist in order to avoid painful feelings, to evade the transference and to maintain the **primary** and **secondary gains** that arise from relieving anxiety and which also result from the problem itself.

- **Interpretation** - The counsellor interprets the client's defences, free associations and resistances. The meaning the counsellor ascribes will be different from the client's interpretations. The aim of interpretation is to increase the client's self-awareness or insight and by doing so strengthen the ego and personal integration. The material for interpretation comes from the results of free association, slips of the tongue and pen, dreams and the transference. These enable the counsellor to unravel the content of the client's unconscious conflicts and so facilitate the client's insight into their problems.

- **Dream interpretation** is seen as a way of penetrating to the unconscious and revealing conflicts and traumas that afflict the client. The **manifest** content of the dream is its surface meaning whereas the **latent** content is its underlying meaning revealed through interpretation. The dream can be seen as a **wish-fulfilment** which undergoes censorship through the client's dream-work. This dream-work employs certain processes: **condensation**, combining two or more images into one and **displacement** where one image can stand for another.

- The **transference relationship** occurs when the client behaves as if the counsellor is their mother, father, sibling or significant other from the past. Feelings and problems experienced in childhood with these significant figures are transferred on to the counsellor. The client can transfer on to the counsellor positive or negative feelings and phantasies arising from parent-childhood relationships. With **positive transference** the client sees the counsellor as if they were the wished for parent or as embodying the positive aspects of past relationships with parents, this can lead to the client having confidence in the counsellor. However the client can also transfer strong feelings, seeing the counsellor as someone who will transform their life or as a person who arouses suspicion, these being examples of **negative transference**. The counsellor uses the client's transference to help the client work through their positive and negative feelings and phantasies towards the counsellor as a means of resolving past and present conflicts with significant others.

- The **counter-transference** exists where the counsellor has positive and negative feelings towards the client which can either result from the counsellor's attitude towards the client or are evoked by the client. The counter-transference can be productive through enabling the counsellor to experience the feelings the client evokes in others. This can help to confirm an interpretation given to the client. It can also be unproductive where the counsellor's feelings are positive (e.g. over-involvement) as well as negative (e.g. hostility).

- **Resistance** - At times the client may refuse or be reluctant to communicate thoughts or feelings because of resistance to making unconscious conflicts, conscious. The counsellor will find it useful to identify the client's defences as a way of enabling the client to understand the reason for their defences. Resistance can also be due to a refusal on the part of the client to accept the counsellor's interpretations.

- **The fundamental rule** - The counsellor should encourage the client to express whatever comes into their mind no matter how embarassing, trivial or irrelevant it might seem.

- **The rule of abstinence** - The counsellor observes the rule of abstinence by undertaking a role that enables the client to express their thoughts and feelings without interruption while at the same time not satisfying them.

PRINCIPLES AND PROCESSES

The counsellor does not reveal anything about their personal life and beliefs. The client is likely to project on to the counsellor their own particular conception of the counsellor.

The counsellor listens carefully to the client's verbal and non-verbal communications, the contents of dreams, as well as the client's resistances as all these indicate the nature of the transference. The counsellor also listens to their own thoughts and feelings about the client and through empathy tries to understand what the client is experiencing.

The counsellor reflects back to the client their words by paraphrasing what the client has said. This enables the counsellor to check that they have heard accurately, so conveying to the client that the counsellor is listening and ready to carry forward communication.

The counsellor maintains boundaries so the client is aware that there are certain constraints on the counsellor-client relationship for instance with regard to time allocation, breaks, endings, friendship and sexual relationships

The counsellor is particularly concerned with the client's past and how it relates to the presenting problems. The client's current problems are seen as originating in past relationships and conflicts with significant others particularly in the family.

The counsellor will focus on what the client brings as the presenting problem but through a process of selection will concentrate on certain aspects that appear significant in terms of the client's problems.

The counsellor facilitates the development of the transference through listening to the client so that the client has space to express the transference. Through becoming aware of the transference the client gains insight into their problems and the underlying conflicts. The client's insight enables them to increase control over their feelings. The opportunity also arises for the client to display strong feelings in the counselling relationship and to realize that the expression of these feelings do not adversely affect the relationship. As a result the power of such feelings to disturb the client can diminish.

An appropriate client for this approach will be one who has:

*   Had long-term problems over many years.

*   The necessary communication skills.

*   Developed resistances to communication.

*   Had a close relationship with another person.

*   The willingness to co-operate with the counsellor.

*   Realized that they contribute to their problems and that ready-made solutions are not available.

*   An ego sufficiently strong to control contrary impulses or demands.

Elements of Egan's Model (Figure 5)

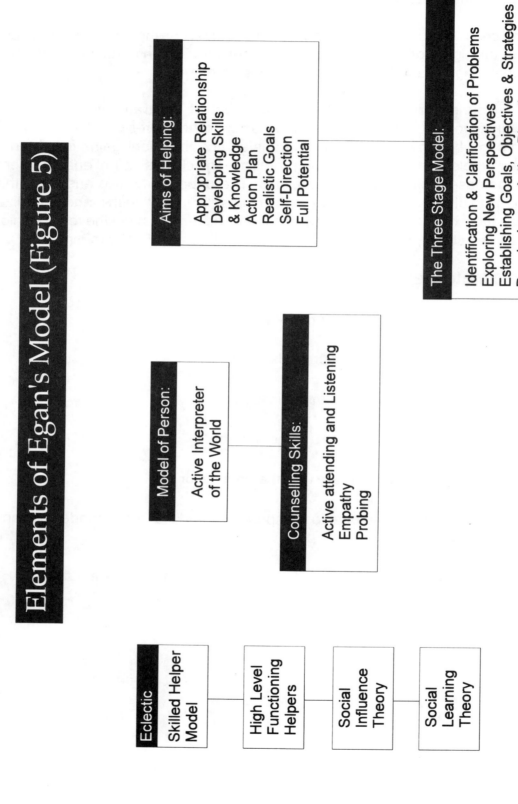

Aims of Helping:

Appropriate Relationship
Developing Skills
& Knowledge
Action Plan
Realistic Goals
Self-Direction
Full Potential

The Three Stage Model:

Identification & Clarification of Problems
Exploring New Perspectives
Establishing Goals, Objectives & Strategies
Developing an Action Plan

Model of Person:

Active Interpreter
of the World

Counselling Skills:

Active attending and Listening
Empathy
Probing

Eclectic

Skilled Helper
Model

High Level
Functioning
Helpers

Social
Influence
Theory

Social
Learning
Theory

EGAN'S MODEL OF COUNSELLING

Egan's **Skilled helper model** of counselling is an *eclectic* approach which draws on three main strands :

- The *theory of high-level functioning helpers (Carkuff)* - Those having the following skills: empathy, respect, concreteness, congruence, self-disclosure, confrontation and immediacy.

- *Social influence theory (Strong)* - Helping is seen as a process whereby clients are influenced by others because they perceive counsellors as having particular attributes. Influence lies along a continuum, the helper should avoid the opposite extremes of coercion and laissez-faire by ensuring that they are collaborative, empowering and democratic.

- *Learning theory (Bandura)* - Clients are seen as acquiring skills through understanding the processes of learning, particularly *self-efficacy expectations* where people expect to achieve their goals through learning relevant behaviours.

THEORETICAL CONCEPTS (FIGURE 5)

Model of a person - People are seen as *active interpreters* of the world, giving meanings to actions, events and situations. They are also active in the sense of facing challenges and in initiating challenges for themselves. They are also proactive in exploring problems, seeking opportunities and establishing goals. The aim of a person should be to become more active in terms of initiating action and developing problem-solving strategies.

The Helping Process - The *core skills* required by a counsellor are based on *Carkhuff's* idea of the high-level functioning helper, a person who uses the communication skills of empathy, regard, concreteness, congruence, self-disclosure, confrontation and immediacy. These skills need to be communicated to the client and in achieving this the counsellor gains the client's confidence and trust.

THE AIMS AND SKILLS OF HELPING

The **main aims** are to help the client to develop the skills and the knowledge necessary for solving their problems. To achieve these goals the counsellor ought to:

- Establish an **appropriate relationship** with the client based on warmth and acceptance and one in which there is a collaborative partnership.

- Enable the client to formulate an **action plan** .

- Ensure that the client develops their own **inner resources** and accepts **responsibility** for becoming a more effective person.

- Help the client to **transfer** newly acquired skills and knowledge to fresh situations.

Specifically the counsellor ought to:

- Help the client establish appropriate and realistic **goals** which will match the client's problem-solving skills.

- Encourage the client to become **self-directive** and develop the skills and knowledge that are needed for problem-solving.

- Enable the client to build on their inner strengths and take advantage of **external resources** and support groups.

- Encourage the client to realize their **full potential**.

- Help the client set goals which are **specific, measurable, achievable, realistic, ethical** and **reasonable** in terms of solving their problems.

SKILLS OF HELPING

The counselling skills required are in essence communication skills that facilitate communication between counsellor and client. The counsellor should use the following skills:

- **Effective Attending and Listening** - These consist of various **microskills** which Egan describes using the acronym *SOLER*, facing the client *S*quarely, having an *O*pen posture, *L*eaning towards the client, maintaining appropriate *E*ye -contact and being *R*elaxed. The counsellor should also be aware of their non-verbal signals to the client.

- **Active Listening** - The counsellor should concentrate on the client's *non-verbal* and *verbal communication* and relate them to the client's contexts. Non-verbal communication includes body language, facial expressions, physical responses, and appearance. Verbal communication will articulate the client's experience, behaviours and feelings. When listening, counsellors should beware of drifting off the point, being judgemental, being prejudiced, labelling the client, dwelling on facts rather than the client, rehearsing responses and being sympathetic rather than empathic.

- **Empathy** - The counsellor through empathy understands the client's world or perspective, what they are thinking and feeling. It requires the counsellor to be accurate in their perceptions and understanding of the client's perspectives on their problems. The counsellor's empathy must be communicated to the client and the counsellor at the appropriate moment must also assert him or herself and challenge the client if thought necessary. To achieve empathy the client should look for the client's *key messages* and relate them to contexts. Empathy is useful in establishing the counsellor-client relationship and in encouraging the client to explore their problems in a focused way whilst feeling supported. The counsellor should avoid the following pitfalls when trying to be empathic e.g. not responding, responding with platitudes, giving advice inappropriately and merely repeating what the client says.

- **Probing** - Where the client appears reluctant it will be necessary to prompt him or her to engage in communication with the counsellor. Question, statements or interjections can be used to prompt clients.

THE THREE-STAGE MODEL

Egan's client-centred model has three main stages which are not necessarily followed by the client in a linear way as the client may move backwards and forwards between the different stages. It is intended to be flexible and should not be implemented rigidly or in a formulaic way. The aim is to empower the client to utilize their own inner resources and to enable the client to accept self-responsibility. The emphasis is also on the client's present situation not the past.

Stage 1: Looking at the client's existing situation

The helper assists the client in identifying and clarifying their problems and opportunities that might exist. An assessment process is undertaken to find out the client's resources. Some clients may appear reluctant or resistant at this stage. The counsellor helps the client to explore new perspectives by challenging the client's negative mode of thinking. The counsellor constructively challenges the client's excuses, evasiveness, distortions and negative self-statements. The helper also assists the client in establishing prorities. Arising out of the counselling sessions should be action plans that put into practice productive strategies.

Stage 2: Helping the client to establish goals and objectives

The helper assists the client in exploring options and goals that the client wants to achieve. The counsellor should establish from the outset what the client really wants and needs. The client is encouraged to consider new possibilities and perspectives and choose ones that are realistic, consistent with their values and for which there are adequate incentives. The counsellor helps the client to develop rational decision-making in the form of data collection, analysis and action planning. It is helpful to use ***brain-storming***, ***divergent thinking*** and a ***balance-sheet approach*** and ***force-field analysis*** with the client in order to faciliate choices between different goals and strategies. These techniques enable the client to consider a range of options for goals and strategies as well as constraining and facilitating factors.

Stage 3: Helping the client to devise strategies

The helper assists the client in finding ways of achieving their goals. At first the counsellor should assist the client in arriving at many strategies as possible and then focus on those that are viable in terms of the client's needs, wishes, resources and environment. The aim is for the client to move from the current situation to one the client prefers. This transition period may make the client feel vulnerable. Small steps right from the beginning can increase the client's confidence. Strategies are best implemented in incremental stages within a realistic timetable. The counsellor should be supportive by helping the client to look out for possible obstacles, presenting challenges and mobilizing the client's resources, including social support and self-help networks.

FUNDAMENTAL ASPECTS OF THE COUNSELLING RELATIONSHIP

SELF-DISCLOSURE

CONCEPT

Self-disclosure is the process of communicating thoughts and feelings about one's self to other people. This communication can be intentional or unintentional and verbal and non-verbal. It can be positive or negative. **Positive self-disclosure** is the communication of positive thoughts and feelings to others; **negative self-disclosure** conveys negative thoughts and feelings. Positive self-disclosure is effective in initiating and maintaining warm, genuine and empathic relationships. It can be the case that both positive and negative self-disclosure can have negative and positive consequences.

THE PROCESS

- Verbal and non-verbal communication about one's thoughts, feelings, moods and attitudes are disclosed to others.

- This information can be expressed directly and indirectly.

- Inflection of the voice, pauses and silences can communicate significant information about the person.

- Facial expressions, gaze, gestures, body language, mannerisms are further means of self-disclosure.

- Selective disclosure can determine the self-disclosing responses of others.

- Disclosure must be genuine in order to avoid the appearance of contrived or scripted disclosure.

- Disclosure is most effective when both verbal and non-verbal communication is used.

- Disclosure is valuable because it increases the chances of positive communication and interaction between people.

COUNSELLOR SELF-DISCLOSURE

In restricted circumstances the counsellor can self-disclose in order to move the client on in a session but for this to be appropriate the counsellor should consider whether self-disclosure meets the needs of the client, whether it is appropriate for the stage and whether the client can cope with self-disclosure.

NON SELF-DISCLOSURE OR INSUFFICIENT SELF-DISCLOSURE

The absence or insufficiency of self-disclosure can prevent relationships from forming and developing through:

• Conveying secretiveness, an unwillingness to confide and trust in others.

• Erroneous perceptions of other people, i.e.assuming other people will think and feel exactly the same as oneself. Fitting others into pigeon-holes. Basing one's image on first impressions or superficial judgements.

FACILITATING CLIENT SELF-DISCLOSURE

The counsellor:

• Greets the client warmly, exchanging names.

• Chooses a neutral aspect of oneself or the client to talk about.

• Decides on what stage the client is at in terms of the range and depth of self-disclosure.

• Ensures they are aware of the differences between their own thoughts and feelings about the client and those disclosed by the client.

• Is aware of the client's non-verbal self-disclosure as well as verbal disclosures and of any self-disclosure that they might make in response to the client's.

• Encourages the client to increase self-disclosure by responding appropriately.

• Responds in ways to reduce any ambiguities in the client's self-disclosure.

TRANSFERENCE

CONCEPT

Transference is the process whereby **positive** and **negative thoughts** and feelings derived from the past are conveyed from the client to the counsellor. Those thoughts and feelings arise in relationships with significant others, e.g. parents. It can be positive or negative. It also refers to the client regarding the counsellor as if they were a significant other from the client's past.

> **Positive** transference occurs where a client displays positive feelings such as love, affection, trust and desire towards the counsellor.

> **Negative** transference occurs where a client displays negative feelings such as hate, dislike and distrust towards the counsellor.

THE PROCESS

Transference is a major source of personal growth and change. This arises through the client's problems being given a chance to work themselves out through the counselling relationship. The counsellor neither satisfies those fellings nor rejects them but engages with them in order to enable the client to become aware of those feelings and their source.

> The client during the transference may perceive the counsellor in ways that diminish the client's responsibility for growth and change. The client may see the counsellor as:

- An **idealized** person who they should imitate.

- An omniscient **expert** who will magically provide instant solutions to the clien's problems.

- A **benefactor** who will look after the client containing all their anxieties and fears.

- An **obstructionist** who prevents the client from expressing their feelings.

- An impersonal **automaton** who has no feelings for the client.

COUNTER-TRANSFERENCE

CONCEPT

Counter-transference is the process whereby **positive** and **negative thoughts** and feelings are conveyed from the counsellor to the client. It can be positive or negative.

> **Positive counter-transference** occurs where the counsellor displays positive feelings for the client and **negative counter-transference** where the counsellor displays negative feelings. The counsellor will transfer feelings onto the client that stem from relationships with significant others in the counsellor's past.
>
> The counsellor may over - or under - identify with the client. This will result in a lack of objectivity or bias. In the case of over-identification the counsellor will become protective or parental towards the client shielding the client from the client's own thoughts and feelings. In the case of under-identification the counsellor will see the client as being over-needy and the counsellor will, as a result, be remote and detached.
>
> Counter-transference can be productive as it enables the counsellor to understand the reactions of significant others in the client's life through the counsellor experiencing the client's thoughts and feelings.

EMPATHY, CONGRUENCE AND UNCONDITIONAL POSITIVE REGARD

Empathy, congruence and unconditional positive regard are qualities the counsellor should possess and which are necessary for facilitating the counselling relationship with the client, enabling the client to experience personal growth.

THE CONCEPT AND PROCESS OF EMPATHY

Empathy occurs where a counsellor understands a client's thoughts and feelings about their self and their world from the *client's perspective* and it is important because it:

- Contributes to effective counselling.

- Facilitates the client's awareness of their own feelings and experience.

- Encourages the client to explore their feelings in greater depth.

The counsellor in communicating empathy:

- Puts aside their own preconceptions about the client's perspective on the world and strives to understand the client's perceptions and experiences from the client's viewpoint.

- Takes on the client's perspective.

- Senses the feelings of the client 'as if' they were their own.

- Ensures that they convey accurate understanding of the client's feelings and experience.

- Should focus on underlying feelings that the client is only dimly aware of and which need to be brought to the surface.

- Should be aware of *blocks to empathy*, e.g. having preconceived ideas about human nature; being self-preoccupied, antagonistic, directive or sympathetic; becoming emotionally involved; labelling and interrogating the client and monopolizing sessions.

THE CONCEPT AND PROCESS OF CONGRUENCE

Congruence is where a counsellor conveys genuine thoughts and feelings towards the client and it is important because it:

- Conveys to the client that the counsellor's inner feelings about the client match the counsellor's public feelings.

- Enables the client to see the counsellor as being sincere and authentic and not as duplicitous.

- Encourages the client to trust the counsellor and express their own inner feelings.

The counsellor in communicating congruence responds:

- To the client appropriately and genuinely but avoids self-disclosure except in certain rare circumstances.

- In a way that is relevant to the client.

- To the client's significant and persistent concerns.

The counsellor should avoid incongruence by becoming aware of:

- Underlying feelings towards the client remaining unexpressed because the counsellor is not in touch with them.

- Feelings of which they are conscious but which are not communicated to the client.

- Simulated responses.

THE CONCEPT AND PROCESS OF UNCONDITIONAL POSITIVE REGARD

Unconditional positive regard is where a counsellor accepts the client unconditionally and it is important because it:

- Avoids imposing conditions of worth thus enabling the client to feel valued for the person they are rather than for being compliant.

- Breaks down the client's defensiveness, the client avoids displaying negative feelings and behaviour.

- Enables the client to experience personal growth.

The counsellor in communicating unconditional positive regard shows the client:

- Warmth, respect and acceptance.

- Positive regard without requiring that conditions of worth be met.

The counsellor should be aware of difficulties in:

- Showing unconditional positive regard to certain kinds of clients e.g. a child abuser.

- Displaying the appropriate level of warmth that the client finds acceptable.

- Meeting the expectations of clients regarding warmth.

- Observing boundaries.

BEGINNING AND ENDING THE COUNSELLING RELATIONSHIP

BEGINNINGS

CONCEPT

The beginning of the counselling relationship is the crucial phase where the foundations of trust and mutuality are established between counsellor and client.

ISSUES

The counsellor should be aware that the client may arrive:

- Having preconceptions or expectations about counselling and the counsellor.

- In a crisis state, with feelings of powerlessness and helplessness.

- In a state of unreadiness due to: uncertainty about goals, distrust of people, a dislike for accepting responsibility and difficulties with self-disclosure.

- Having experienced a variety of caring agencies, becomes cynical and defensive.

BEGINNINGS AND THE ROLE OF THE COUNSELLOR

The counsellor should:

- Convey that the counselling relationship is based on an equality with the client.

- Sensitively pace the session and establish the time limits, a contract could specify number of sessions, frequency and length.

- Show the client unconditional positive regard.

- Encourage the client to begin to think of the relationship as one of mutuality, both having their own defined roles and responsibilities.

- Establish with the client that the counsellor is not an expert or guru, providing solutions to the client's problems.

- Patiently establish trust with the client.

- Recognize that the client in the beginning may engage in evasion or blocking.

- Be aware when the time has arrived for the client to move forward, depending on the level of client trust.

ENDINGS

CONCEPT

The end of counselling is meant to be a developmental stage rather than an abrupt or sudden finish. The client is ready for closure and transference and emotional issues have been resolved. Sometimes, however, the client wishes to end the relationship even if those issues remain unresolved.

ISSUES

Indications that the counselling relationship is near or at an end:

- Counsellor and client agree that conflicts have been resolved.

- Client expresses a wish for it to end or indicates to the counsellor that the counsellor should end it.

- Onset of the end may be expressed through the client's unpunctuality, irregular attendance, indifference and over-dependence.

- The counsellor feels that they have achieved as much as they can with the client.

Indications that the client is ready for the end are if the client has:

- Partially or fully resolved their presenting problems.

- Developed coping strategies.

- Increased insight and self-esteem.

- Improved social skills.

- Achieved at work or college.

- Better interpersonal relationships.

- Become more independent.

The client may have a variety of reasons for ending counselling which may be unexpressed. They may:

- Deny they have any problem.

- Claim they are cured.

- Feel their defences have been breached.

- Reached a crisis or transition point which they are unwilling to confront.

ENDINGS AND THE ROLE OF THE COUNSELLOR

The counsellor should ask the client to:

- List changes in their life.

- Compare earlier sessions with the current session.

- Find out the views of significant others on their progress.

- Explore feelings arising from the prospect of ending the relationship.

- Reflect on their expectations for the future.

- Consider phasing out sessions.

- Consider if the sessions have now achieved the client's goals.

APPROPRIATE , INAPPROPRIATE AND UNRESPONSIVE CLIENTS FOR INDIVIDUAL COUNSELLING

Individual counselling is particularly useful as it:

- Facilitates transference.
- Enables the client to proceed at their own pace.
- Allows the counsellor to focus completely on the client, particularly a confused, uncertain, inhibited or anxious client.

APPROPRIATE CLIENTS

It is necessary to consider those clients who would be appropriate or inappropriate for individual counselling. **Individual counselling will benefit those clients who:**

- Wish to disclose their thoughts and feelings confidentially and who would feel uncomfortable in a group.

- Are isolated and reticent and who need to develop a relationship with one other person.

- Have unstable personal and social relationships and need to experience stability in a relationship.

- Have problems arising mainly from low self-esteem.

INAPPROPRIATE CLIENTS

Individual counselling will not benefit those clients who:

- Would become over-dependent on the counsellor.

- Find one-to-one relationships threatening.

- Wish to dominate or manipulate situations.

- See their difficulties as impersonal, abstract problems to be solved intellectually.

THE UNFOCUSED CLIENT

CONCEPT

The unfocused client is **confused**, **uncertain** or **ambivalent** about the nature of the problem they are currently experiencing. The client finds it difficult to focus on the issues and lacks clear goals and priorities.

THE ISSUES

The unfocused client may seek counselling uncertain as to their problems. They may also be unsure about the nature of counselling and the respective roles of counsellor and client. **The unfocused client may express these uncertainties through:**

- Confused thoughts and feelings.

- Uncertainty as to what they think or feel.

- Ambivalence about their problems.

- Feeling that significant others perceive them as having problems.

DIFFICULTIES

Difficulties in the counselling relationship can arise through the unfocused client:

- Continually presenting new or irrelevant material.

- Jumping or gliding from one area to the next.

- Evading their responsibility in the counselling relationship.

- Perpetually going over the same problems with the counsellor.

- Not observing boundaries and thereby maintaining confusion.

- Continually expressing uncertainty about whether there is progress.

COUNSELLING

The counsellor should help the client to focus by encouraging them to:

- Concentrate on one problem at a time.

- To identify and prioritize short and long -term goals.

- To identify feelings.

- Express any hidden agenda.

- Clarify and observe boundaries.

- To accept their role and responsibility in the relationship.

- Be realistic and avoid wishful thinking.

THE RELUCTANT CLIENT

CONCEPT

A client who presents him or herself as unwilling or who finds it difficult to present or communicate problems.

REASONS FOR CLIENT RELUCTANCE

The client may be:

- Angry with him or herself or the counsellor and find their anger interferes with or frustrates self-disclosure.

- Fearful of self-disclosure because of shame, guilt or embarassment.

- Inarticulate and fear that they will be tongue-tied.

- Blocking i.e. the client feels defensive about revealing particular problems or feelings.

- Sceptical about the nature and aims of counselling and their doubts may prevent them from entering into the counselling relationship.

- Misunderstanding the roles of client and counsellor and because of uncertainty feel reticent in becoming a client.

COUNSELLING

To gain the client's confidence the counsellor should:

- Communicate empathy, congruence and unconditional positive regard.

- Observe the client's behaviour closely and provide accurate feedback.

- Encourage the client to communicate non-verbally and ensure that the client is aware that this form of communication is helpful.

- Use questionnaires and checklists with the client if they find verbal communication difficult or painful.

- Ask the client to visualize him or herself in the role of client in order to develop self-confidence.

- Encourage the client to keep a diary or log which will facilitate communication.

- Match the stage which the client has reached.

- Explain the nature and aims of counselling to the client to clear up any preconceptions or prejudices.

COMMONLY OCCURRING CLIENT PROBLEMS

ADOLESCENTS

CONCEPT

Adolescence is a period of transition from childhood to adulthood characterized by physical, emotional and intellectual development. For some adolescents that period is a time of emotional stress and conflict leading to chronic psychological and psychiatric problems.

THE PROCESS

PHYSICAL DEVELOPMENT AND BODY IMAGE

- Anxieties over physical and hormonal changes generate concerns over physical appearance particularly to peers.

- Preoccupation with ideals of masculinity, femininity and sexual orientation.

EMOTIONAL DEVELOPMENT

- Emergence of moodiness, self-consciousness, depression, self-depreciation, social anxiety, hero-worship and intense sexual feelings.

- Having thoughts and feelings that appear shameful or disturbing; ignoring or pretending that they do not exist.

- Specific anxieties over exams and employment.

- Acting out behaviour, e.g. aggression.

- Idealism.

- Establishing a personal and sexual identity and identifying with peer groups.

- Rebellion, e.g. belonging to particular youth cults and substance abuse.

- For some adolescents the onset of **anorexia, bulimia, phobias, anxiety states, schizophrenia** and **substance abuse**.

EARLY WARNING SIGNALS

- Truancy, school avoidance, compulsive stealing and lying.

- Extreme withdrawal, depression and social isolation.

- Conflict with parents, carers and siblings.

- Substance abuse.

- Learning and behavioural difficulties.

- Communication difficulties.

- Sexual experimentation and obsessions.

- Eating problems and over-concern with body image.

COMMON DIFFICULTIES

- Reverting to child-like dependency on parents.

- Fear of changing behaviour.

- Fear of losing control.

- Choosing younger friends in order to feel one is in control.

- Finding it difficult to form personal relationships due to over-dependency on parents.

- Finding it difficult to articulate or express feelings.

- Finding it difficult to distinguish between others' thoughts and feelings and their own imaginings.

- Regarding feelings as threatening or uncontrollable, a fear of going mad.

- Seemingly unconcerned about the future or seeing it as threatening.

SELF-DISCLOSURE ISSUES

- Whether the client has strategies to cope with self-disclosure regarding:

- Physical / sexual changes.

- Moodiness, specific and non-specific anxieties.

- Independence from family.

- Interpersonal and work relationships.

- Choosing and forming a sexual identity.

- Studying and passing exams.

- Choosing a career.

Points on self-disclosure:

- The language used by adolescents during self-disclosure may not reflect the full meaning of what they are experiencing.

- In addition adolescents may make some self-disclosing statements which should not too readily be taken at face value, they may distort reality

- It is necessary for the counsellor to develop a common language with the adolescent to facilitate accurate communication between them.

- If adolescents have experienced rejection in the past it might take time before they are prepared to self-disclose.

MOODS, FEARS AND ANXIETIES

The counsellor:

- Actively listens to accounts of mood changes and specific and non-specific anxieties.

- Provides descriptions and explanations of common mood changes, fears and anxieties in relation to physical / hormonal factors and body image.

- Enables the adolescent to express thoughts and feelings regarding moods, fears and anxieties in a non-judgemental setting.

INDEPENDENCE

The counsellor:

- Actively listens to the adolescent's perceptions of their relationships with parents, carers, siblings, friends and significant others and facilitates the expression of concerns over those relationships.

- Facilitates discussion of anxieties over the choice and formation of a self-identity in relation to: family members, choosing friends, experimenting with dress, choosing leisure time activities, choosing and expressing a sexual orientation, making educational and career choices and observing developmental and cultural norms.

INTERPERSONAL RELATIONSHIPS

The counsellor:

- Actively listens to interpersonal difficulties as expressed by the adolescent, e.g. the family, rows with family members, choosing a peer group, sexual orientation, engaging in sexual experimentation, feelings of personal inadequacy with regard to body image, self-concept and social interactions.

- Facilitates personal growth through encouraging: acceptance of things that cannot be changed, alternative ways of seeing a situation, development of capacity to negotiate and discharge of emotion.

PHILOSOPHICAL AND SPIRITUAL MATTERS

The counsellor:

- Actively listens to the adolescent's reflections on the meaning and purpose of life, not endorsing their viewpoint but respecting their right to express it.

- Facilitates the expression of idealism, religious and political beliefs in a non-judgemental setting.

STUDYING

The counsellor:

- Actively listens to the adolescent's concerns over: organizing and maintaining a study schedule, relating to particular teachers and teaching styles, continuing or discontinuing a course of study and progression routes.

- Describes effective methods of study and organisation.

- Facilitates reflection on the adolescent's reasons for experiencing difficulties with particular teachers, continuing or discontinuing courses and progression routes.

CAREER CHOICE

The counsellor:

- Actively listens to the adolescent's expression of thoughts and feelings about choosing a career.

- Facilitates reflection on how personal needs and aspirations would be met by a career choice.

- Engages with the adolescent in reflecting on concern over existing academic attainment and potential.

- Encourages referral to an appropriate agency.

COUNSELLING ADOLESCENTS

ADOLESCENTS AND PARENTS OR CARERS

THE FAMILY

The family can be understood as a **system of interconnecting parts** or **subsystems** all of which influence each other e.g. parents and siblings.

FAMILY TYPES

- Some families have **rigid internal** and **external boundaries** and as a result are relatively inflexible to change, whilst families with **loose boundaries** are in perpetual flux.

- Within the family parents and adolescents can be **enmeshed** i.e. over-dependent on each other to the exclusion of others. This can lead to problems at times of separation or individuation.

- Alternatively parents and adolescents can be **disengaged** i.e. uninvolved and remote from each other. This can lead to problems of family members being insensitive to each others needs.

PARENTS AND ADOLESCENT PROBLEMS:

Adolescents can experience various family problems in **separating from parents:**

- Adolescents develop a self-identity which is different from that of their parents and which may lead to conflict over cultural, religious, political beliefs and practices as well as conflict over choice of friends, sexual experimentation and drug use.

- Adolescents in striving for independence form relationships with others that exclude their parents and seek to engage in activities without parental permission or supervision leading to possible conflict.

PSYCHOLOGICAL / PSYCHIATRIC PROBLEMS

Adolescents may be experiencing psychological or even psychiatric problems e.g. **anorexia, bulimia, anxiety states, phobias, depression, suicidal ideation** and **schizophrenia.** These problems impact on the family. Where these problems arise it will be necessary to ask the adolescent to seek specialist advice.

COUNSELLING THE ADOLESCENT WITH RESPECT TO FAMILY RELATIONSHIPS

The counsellor should:

- Actively listen to the viewpoints of parents or carers, significant others and the adolescent.

- Consider all viewpoints in order to determine the areas of agreement as well as conflict.

- Ask the adolescent to describe their patterns of behaviour.

- Consider what kind of communication is occuring between the adolescent and the family members and whether it is appropriate.

- Find out the needs of all the family members in relation to the adolescent.

- Understand the roles ascribed to or adopted by the adolescent in relation to family members.

- Discover areas that need to be negotiated between the adolescent and family members.

COUNSELLING STRATEGIES WITH RESPECT TO ADOLESCENTS AND THE FAMILY

The counsellor should ask the adolescent how they would:

- Resolve the problem if they were all powerful or needed to advise a friend.

- Express their thoughts and feelings to an invisible third person.

- Think and feel if they were in the place of others in their family.

Should ask significant others how they would:

- Perceive the adolescent's problem.

- Resolve the conflict if they were the adolescent.

- Communicate with the adolescent if they thought they were very sensitive and easily hurt.

- Deal with the situation if the problem occurred in a professional relationship.

- Determine if it would be helpful to draw up a contract that incorporates all points of views.

DRUGS AND ALCOHOL PROBLEMS

THE CONCEPTS OF DEPENDENCY, ABUSE AND ADDICTION

- **Dependency** - Excessive use of drugs and alcohol leading to psychological or physiological problems.

- **Abuse** - Less severe use but still significant in terms of harmful effects.

- **Addiction** - Tolerance has developed and withdrawal reactions occur if use is decreased or stopped.

- The effects of dependency, abuse and addiction threaten health, work, finances, social and personal relationships.

FACTORS RELATING TO DEPENDENCY, ABUSE AND ADDICTION

There are a number of factors that may relate to people who have drug and alcohol problems:

- Problems may run in families through the client modelling their behaviour on parents and siblings who engage in drug and alcohol abuse.

- Client may imitate members of their peer group.

- Certain clients might be vulnerable, e.g. early maturers who want adult status, but lack the necessary skills and experience.

- The client has easy access to drugs and alcohol, e.g. publicans.

- Stress, anxiety and depression may lead the client to resort to drugs and alcohol to alleviate those problems.

- Enables the client to override inhibitions so allowing then to engage in activities they would normally avoid.

- The client may be influenced by the positive status given to drinking and drug taking among certain social groups.

COUNSELLING CLIENTS WITH DRUGS AND ALCOHOL PROBLEMS

The counsellor should:

- Identify and find out information about the particular substance the client is using and provide that information to the client so they can make informed choices about controlling the problem.

- Clarify and explore the nature of the problem: the forms it takes, its effects in terms of work, health, family and personal relationships.

- Explore with the client the costs and benefits of continuing, modifying or stopping.

- Communicate empathy, congruence and unconditional positive regard to the client.

- Ask the client if there are any predisposing or precipitating factors.

- Recognize that clients who have drug problems have similarities as well as differences to other clients but that the counselling process is the same.

- Help empower the client so they can feel responsible for the changes they might need to make especially in life-style.

Discuss with the client a variety of possible coping strategies:

- A diary or log for monitoring their thoughts, feelings and behaviour.

- Recognizing early warning signs and high-risk situations.

- Anxiety management skills, e.g. relaxation techniques.

- Social skills and assertiveness training.

- For family and relationship difficulties.

- Fnding alternative distractions.

- Obtaining help from significant others or from support groups.

- For dealing with relapses.

ASSERTIVENESS

CONCEPT

Assertion or assertiveness is a process whereby a person stands up for their rights and affirms their beliefs, values and feelings in a direct, open and honest way that does not infringe the rights of others.

ASPECTS

Assertiveness is:

- An acquired or learned social skill.

- A functional interaction between people.

- An expressive skill in verbal and non-verbal communication.

- A process that needs to consider social and cultural contexts.

- Neither a passive nor an aggressive process.

THE ASSERTIVE PERSON

The assertive individual will:

- Try to discover the rights of all participants.

- Influence others without threatening or damaging their self-esteem.

- Be aware of negative feelings aroused in others.

- Explain their reasons for being assertive and arrive at a compromise where people are considered equally.

THE PROCESS

The process is composed of a variety of elements:

- **Content:**

  - what is stated;

  - expression of rights;

  - refusal to accept unreasonable demands;

  - logical explanations;

  - acknowledgement of others' feelings;

  - search for compromise;

- **Verbal** - Fluent speech, moderate in tone but firm;

- **Non-verbal** - Relevant aspects of body language are eye-contact, proximity, facial expressions, gestures, mannerisms and posture.

- **Social** - Use of assertiveness in appropriate social contexts and reinforcing appropriate responses.

- **Cognitive** - Use of positive self-statements and the avoidance of negative self-statements.

COUNSELLING CLIENTS ON ASSERTIVENESS

Assessment:

- *Interviews* - Finding out from the client their definition of the problem, their past history, their reasons for lack of assertiveness, the situations where assertiveness is desired or absent and the effects on their life.

- *Self-monitoring* - The client records those situations where they lack assertiveness and the effects.

- *Observation* - The client's actual behaviour may be observed in specific situations where assertiveness is absent or deficient.

Developing **self-efficacy:** i.e. having belief in being able to achieve one's goals through different *strategies:*

- Cognitive restructuring i.e. replacing perfectionism, self-blame, the blaming of others and fatalism with realistic and positive thoughts.

- Understanding the impact on assertiveness of cultural differences, gender and social class.

- Developing empathy with others and alternative perspectives.

- Direct instruction or coaching of assertive behaviour.

- Modelling the assertive behaviour for the client and the client practising and rehearsing that behaviour *in vivo.*

- Self-monitoring and self-instruction by the client.

DEATH AND BEREAVEMENT

CONCEPT

The client facing their own death or those of significant others or the loss or end of a relationship.

RESPONSES TO DYING AND BEREAVEMENT

Recognition of imminent or actual loss can result in:

- Shock: disruption of routines, feelings of unreality, numbness and denial.

- Anger and pain directed at significant others.

- Feelings of guilt and self-blame.

- Feelings of punishment

Acceptance of reality where there is realization that the loss is permanent, feelings of emptiness, loneliness and hopelessness may occur.

> A dying client may feel they are losing their roles and independence, or becoming socially isolated.

> Grief can lead to reminiscing: reflection on the loss, longing to turn the clock back.

Recovery is heralded by:

- Realization that prolonged grief is ultimately intolerable.

- The desire to make a new start in life.

- Finding satisfaction in other areas of one's life

THE DYING CLIENT

The counsellor should:

- Actively listen to thoughts and feelings expressed in grief.

- Provide support aimed at preventing or breaking down social isolation and facilitating communication between the client and others.

- Supply information about support groups.

- Help the client to find meaning in their situation.

- Explore with the client their expression of thoughts and feelings with regard to the process of dying and their communication with significant others e.g. the course of the disease, whether and how much to disclose, dependency, and changing roles.

The counsellor also needs to be in a position to:

- Absorb the client's expressions of grief.

- Understand the client's physical and psychological changes.

- Consider what the client needs to express to significant others.

- Explore the client's feelings and reactions to medical treatment and the course of the disease.

- Understand the client's perceptions of their changing roles.

- Work through the client's fears, guilt, shame, anger and denial.

THE BEREAVED CLIENT

The counsellor should:

- Actively listen to the client's thoughts and feelings about the bereavement e.g. expressions of numbness, shock, denial, hallucinations, guilt and anger.

- Provide space and time for the client to express grief.

- Help the client to talk through their fears, anger, guilt, denial and despair.

- Reassure about eventual recovery from grief.

- Provide information about support groups.

- Assess how far the client is recovering and whether the rate of recovery is appropriate given the age of the client, the past relationship and the nature of the bereavement.

- Consider whether the client is in danger of depression.

The client will show signs of recovery if he or she :

- Accepts the loss.

- Experiences and tolerates grief.

- Revives relationships and interests.

- Develops new interests and relationships.

ANXIETY

CONCEPT

Anxiety Is composed of three elements:

- **Cognitive** - e.g. anxious or fearful thoughts; dread of the future and anticipation of physical and social threats to ones self.

- **Physiological** - e.g. increased heart and pulse rate, palpitations, sweating, raised blood pressure and hyperventilation (over-breathing).

- **Behavioural** - e.g. avoidance of people, open spaces, public places and social situations.

TYPES

Commonly occurring types of anxiety are:

- **Free-floating** - Unattached to a particular situation, incident or event.

- **Specific** - Attached to a particular situation, incident or event.

- **Anticipatory** - Fear of impending danger or threat.

- **Separation** - Fear of loss or separation.

- **Phobic** - Fear of a particular thing, place, situation or event e.g. animal, social situation, public place, disease or death.

Panic attacks are sudden strong feelings of anxiety associated with:

- An overwhelming desire to escape the situation or place.

- A fear of being trapped.

- Physiological reactions e.g. hyperventilation, palpitations and sweating.

- Feelings of unreality of the self and the external world.

- Fear of appearing foolish in public.

FUNCTIONS

- **Biological** - Prepares for fight or flight.

- **Learning** - Increases concentration, attention and vigilance up to an optimal level as long as the anxiety is not too severe.

ORIGINS

Anxiety problems can relate to:

- *External factors* - Actual or threatening e.g. of unemployment, breakdown of relationships, financial difficulties, phobic feelings in public places.

- *Internal factors* - e.g. irrational beliefs about one's state of physical and psychological health, a deficiency or lack of problem-solving and social skills, a past trauma and a feeling that one has or is about to lose control.

COUNSELLING ANXIOUS CLIENTS

With a psychodynamic approach the counsellor explores:

- Reasons for its onset in the past.

- The particular form and content of the anxiety.

- How it fits into the client's life plan.

- Resistances to change.

- Unresolved unconscious conflicts or traumas originating in the client's past.

With a cognitive-behavioural approach the counsellor assesses the client through:

- *Interviews* - Brief account of the anxiety, the background history and information on the frequency, duration and intensity of the anxiety.

- *Self-monitoring* - The client monitors the occurences of their anxiety and its antecedents and consequences leading to a *functional analysis* and *formulation.*

The counsellor can use the following techniques:

- **Desensitizing** the client to anxiety through *rapid* or *slow exposure* to the anxiety-producing situation.

- **Modelling** the anxiety-reducing behaviour for and with the client *in situ* or *in vivo* and then asking the client to practise the behaviour (*behaviour rehearsal* and *role play*).

- **Assertiveness training** - The client can be trained to be more assertive in social situations.

- **Cognitive restructuring** - The client is required to re-evaluate the probability of a threat occuring and review what strategies they possess in coping with the anxiety. The client can be asked to examine the reality of their fears through a behavioural test, criticize their irrational beliefs and learn to re-attribute their fears to less threatening factors.

- **Relaxation techniques** enable the client to learn to relax in order to decrease the likelihood of anxious responses to an anxiety-producing place or situation.

EXAM ANXIETY

CONCEPT

Exam anxiety is made up of two elements:

- **Cognitive** - having fearful thoughts before and during the exam.

- **Physiological** - having physical responses e.g. palpitations, rapid heart beat and pulse, muscle tension, sweating and hyperventilation (over-breathing).

ANXIETY AND AROUSAL

Arousal is the state of being alert, vigilant, attentive and prepared. Anxiety can, when extreme, be disabling, reducing or preventing optimum performance. However, if moderate, it can increase performance.

COUNSELLING CLIENTS WHO EXPERIENCE EXAM ANXIETY

PRIOR TO THE EXAM

The counsellor should encourage the examinee to:

- Engage in physical exercises.

- Make positive self-statements.

- Practise relaxation.

- Avoid **retroactive inhibition** by not learning new material.

- Revise, read through summaries and practise recall.

- Keep away from anxiety-provoking places, situations and people.

- Practise exam papers in the prescribed times.

- Avoid drugs and alcohol which reduce or affect performance.

DURING THE EXAM

The counsellor should encourage the examinee to:

- Read and follow exam instructions.

- Make positive self-statements.

- Use *thought-stopping.*

- Use *visualization*.

POSITIVE COPING STRATEGIES

Behavioural - The counsellor can help the client to use:

- *Systematic desensitization* - Identify triggers that cause the client's exam anxiety and place them in a hierarchy with the most anxiety-provoking at the top and the least-provoking at the bottom. Encourage the client to practise relaxation commencing with the least anxiety-producing situation, proceeding to the exam itself.

Cognitive - The counsellor can help the client to use:

- *Cognitive restructuring* - The examinee identifies negative self-statements about exams and constructs alternative positive self-statements which they practise.

- *Thought-stopping* - The examinee summons up anxious thoughts and images of exams and shouts "stop!" out aloud to interrupt the negative thinking process. This can also be performed sub-vocally.

- *Covert-conditioning* - The examine imagines they are performing well in exams and then practises self-reinforcement.

- *Visualization* - The examinee should imagine a clear image of exam anxiety, visualize the fear-provoking situation and then counter it with positive alternatives.

ORGANIZATIONAL SKILLS

The counsellor should encourage the examinee to:

- Set clear and specific targets

- Plan a revision timetable.

- Establish priorities.

- Select likely question areas.

- Use associaitive and visual recall methods.

- Use mnemonics.

EXAMINATION TECHNIQUES

The counsellor should encourage the examinee to know how to:

- Follow exam instructions.

- Revise and organize revision.

- Allocate time in exams.

- Write succinctly, legibly and to the point.

- Identify probable questions.

EATING DISORDERS

CONCEPT

A client with an eating problem may experience persistent anxiety over their body image and eating habits. They may develop **anorexia**, a persistent pursuit of thinness or, **bulimia**, alternating between binge eating and severe dieting. Eating problems and disorders affect females more than males.

THE ISSUES

The client may seek counselling because they:

- Experience eating as a problem.

- Perceive their body or body image as a problem.

- Find physical and sexual development difficult to cope with.

- Realize that others are commenting on their body and eating habits.

TYPES OF EATING DISORDERS

ANOREXIA NERVOSA

Anorexia is where a person pursues their ideal body image of thinness until emaciation or death. **The characteristics are:**

- Restriction to a severe diet.

- Intense physical and social activity.

- Peak onset ages between 14 and 18.

- Mainly females / particularly high-achievers.

- Depression.

- Preoccupation with body size and ideal image of thinness.

Suggested factors:

- **Predisposing** - being female, lacking a sense of control, fears of physical and sexual development and conscientiousness.

- **Interpersonal** - Parents emphasizing achievement.

- **Social, cultural** - media emphasis on thinness as a body image ideal.

- **Precipitating** - Perceived low self-esteem and perceived social and academic failure, fear of new social situations particularly ones relating to sex.

BULIMIA

Bulimia is where a person engages in episodes of binge eating; consuming copious amounts of food in a short time, vomiting and then dieting. **The characteristics are:**

- Being female.

- Onset at 18.

- Weight often normal.

- Preoccupied with thoughts of food, eating and vomiting.

- High achievers.

COUNSELLING ANOREXIC CLIENTS

The counsellor should:

- Recognize that anorexics are highly resistant to counselling and want to avoid confronting their problems.

- Understand that the client has a great need to be in control.

- Focus on helping the client identify and evaluate their attitudes towards eating.

- Give the client time and space to reflect on their life and enable the client to see how and why patterns of eating have developed.

- Ask the client to test out alternative patterns of eating and see what consequences result.

COUNSELLING BULIMIC CLIENTS

The counsellor should help the client by:

- Finding out the client's level of motivation.

- Providing the client with time and space to reflect on controlling the intake of food.

- Enabling the client to monitor their eating.

- Exploring with the client alternative eating patterns.

- Enabling the client to identify crisis points and relevant coping strategies.

- Developing with the client self-reinforcement measures for the avoidance of vomiting or purging.

- Exploring with the client their thoughts, feelings and behaviour towards food and body image.

- Exploring with the client their feelings about the past, childhood experiences and relationships.

CONCLUSION

- Effective counselling in the case of eating disorders depends on the client's motivation to attack the problem.

- Clients need to make links with their past.

- Clients need help in attaining a realistic body image that relates to an understanding and implementation of a balanced diet.

- It is important that clients recognize what triggers their eating habits and they need ways to avoid recurring patterns.

- Referal to a specialist, especially medical supervision, is crucial.

DEPRESSION

CONCEPT

Depression can be manifested in a variety of ways:

- **Cognitive** - e.g. loss of motivation, poor concentration, low self-esteem, excessive anxiety and fears, an overall sense of hopelessness, loss of interest in life, sense of loss or separation, sense of powerlessness mediated through comparison with others and suicidal thoughts.

- **Physiological** - e.g. significant weight loss or gain, decrease or increase in appetite and fatigue.

- **Behavioural** - Psychomotor agitation or retardation and insomnia.

TYPES OF DEPRESSION

There may be a number of external and internal factors that are associated with a client's depression:

- **Internal** - e.g. physical or hormonal reasons (post-natal), during the menopause and pre and post-operation.

- **External** - e.g. loss of a relationship through break-up, divorce or bereavement; separation from a significant other; loss of employment; financial difficulties and failing tests or exams.

SIGNS OF DEPRESSION

Commonly occuring signs of depression are:

- **Low self-esteem** - Expressed in negative self-statements or moods.

- **Attributional style** - A tendency for the client to blame themself for negative events that happen to them or others or to construe events from a negative viewpoint.

- **Learned helplessness** - Where a client thinks that they have no control over a situation and as a result gives up trying, the client then feels depressed.

- **Feeling overwhelmed** or unable to cope through lack of skills or resources.

- Experiencing a lack of enjoyment in life.

- Having recently experienced a major negative life event, e.g. a loss of some kind such as unemployment or a relationship.

- Having sleeping difficulties, e.g. early morning waking.

- Experiencing weight and appetite problems.

- Body language: expressed through fatigue or agitation.

CAUSES OF DEPRESSION

- ***Interpersonal relationship problems*** - Due to a lack or absence of relevant social and personal coping skills in dealing with for example conflict with significant others, the forming and ending of relationships.

- ***Early relationship problems*** - Traumas or conflicts (e.g. emotional neglect, physical and sexual abuse) arising during early relationships with parents, carers and siblings whose effects are felt in current relationships.

- ***Negative cognitive processes*** or ***schemata*** - Having negative beliefs and attitudes towards one's self and significant others and construing events and situations in a negative way e.g. thinking one is worthless and ineffective in relation to other people, regarding one's self as lacking positive qualities or abilities and always looking on the negative side.

COUNSELLING DEPRESSED CLIENTS

The counsellor can:

- Identify and explore the clients thoughts, beliefs, attributions and feelings.

- Explore and work with the client on their beliefs and feelings about past and present relationships and consider with the client how these might be resolved.

- Encourage the client to develop alternative and positive ways of construing, events and situations, (**positive schemata**).

- Work with the client to develop strategies for coping with negative feelings, e.g. anger, resentment, anxiety, guilt, shame, disappointment and envy.

- Help the client to record and monitor their depressive thoughts and feelings, e.g. keeping a diary in order to record when, where and how they occur.

- Suggest to the client ways of avoiding negative thinking, e.g. by challenging perfectionist ideas and notions of lost chances.

- Work with the client on ways of changing their behaviour rather than the client attributing blame to their personality.

- Encourage the client to avoid self-blame and explore ways of coping with their depression by the client looking at their problem from the standpoint of a friend or another person.

- Work with the client on their resistance to change by looking at the gains and losses that result from not changing.

- Encourage the client to develop or maintain physical fitness through exercise and a healthy diet and to avoid resorting to alcohol or drugs to alleviate depression.

- Suggest to the client that assertiveness training would be useful through encouraging the client to initiate positive interactions with others. Alternatively enable the client to assert their rights where those rights are not recognized by others and which contributes to the client's depression.

HIV / AIDS

CONCEPT

HIV is the **Human Immuno-Deficiency Virus** that is transmitted through blood, semen and cervical fluid. It can also be transferred from a pregnant mother to her unborn child. Casual contact does not appear to lead to infection. The immune system produces an antibody, and the infected person can remain in that state (HIV positive) for years without showing any disease symptoms but is able to infect others. The two major risk groups are homosexual men and intravenous drug users in the West, but heterosexuals are also at risk. Heterosexuals are a major risk group in Africa.

AIDS is the **Acquired Immune Deficiency Syndrome** - The body is defenceless against opportunistic bacterial, viral, parasitical, fungal and tumerous infections because the immune system is damaged through the depletion of T-lymphocytes and macrophages. A person who is infected by HIV does not necessarily have AIDS; AIDS is the final stage of the disease process. Some people who are infected with HIV develop **ARC** - (AIDS related complex) which manifests itself through various symptoms such as fatigue, constant fevers, weight loss, diarrhoea, night sweats and sometimes shingles, herpes and thrush in the mouth. Some people who have had HIV for years have not ended up with AIDS.

The symptoms of AIDS are:

- Persistent diarrhoea.

- White spots in mouth.

- Pneumonia - (pneumocystis carinii).

- Oral lesions - (herpes simplex).

- Cough - (tuberculosis).

- Muscular impairment.

- Blindness, dementia.

- Bluish skin rash - (Kaposi's sarcoma)

People who are at high risk are those who engage in:

- Unprotected anal intercourse.

- Sex with a large number of partners.

- Sharing of needles.

THE CLIENT'S PROBLEMS

The client may:

- Feel depressed, angry and guilty.

- Face rejection from parents, partner, friends, employer and colleagues.

- Experience possible insurance problems.

- Lose their job.

- Become stressed and anxious.

- Have suicidal thoughts.

- Engage in denial-unwilling to contemplate the possibility of infection or that they are infected.

- Withdraw and hide away from people.

- Be ambivalent about having a test.

COUNSELLING HIV / AIDS CLIENTS

The counsellor should encourage clients to seek:

- Medical advice regarding pregnancy, symptoms and the course of HIV / AIDS.

- Advice on protective measures, e.g. use of condoms, avoidance of shared needles.

- Specialized counselling if the counsellor is not trained in this area.

- Changes in high-risk behaviours.

The counsellor should:

- Aim to help the client to develop a sense of control.

- Concentrate on opening up communication with the client.

- Encourage the client to acknowledge and express feelings.

- Review with the client that they have accurate information about HIV and AIDS.

- Explore with the client their perceptions of their state of health and their quality of life.

- Encourage them to seek peer-group support.

- Explore with the client coping strategies-depending on the stage at which the client is at.

- Facilitate the client's reflections upon medical treatment, work and relationships.

SEXUAL ABUSE

CONCEPT

Sexual abuse occurs when a child is sexually molested or interfered with by another person, its effects being felt by the client in adulthood.

SHORT-TERM AND LONG-TERM EFFECTS

There are a variety of effects, the most common being:

- *Fear* - Maintaining secrecy, disbelief and shame.

- *Post-traumatic stress* - Powerlessness, hopelessness, mental pain and sense of disintegration.

- *Behaviour difficulties* - Deviant and anti-social behaviour.

- *Sexualized behaviour* - An increased prominence of sexual issues, precocity. and experimentation.

- *Low self-esteem* - Arising from feelings of shame and guilt.

Other possible effects are:

- Depression or hostility, e.g. due to feelings of betrayal.

- Suicidal thoughts, intentions and attempts.

- Substance abuse.

- Anxiety.

- Sexual problems - difficulties with sexual identity and fears of sexual relationships.

- Nightmares.

- Withdrawal.

- Eating disorders.

- Intrusive obsessions.

CLIENT RESPONSES TO REPEATED TRAUMA

The client shows:

- An apparent self-sufficiency which masks pain and trauma.

- Over-compliant behaviour-clingingness.

- Acceptance and clinging to the role of victim.

- Angry identification with the abusing person arising from feelings of powerlessness.

- Flashbacks to the trauma.

- Guilt over what has happened.

- Soiling.

- Disgust.

COUNSELLING THE SEXUALLY ABUSED CLIENT

The counsellor should:

- Provide support enabling the client to feel safe in disclosing and recounting events.

- Facilitate the expression of childhood feelings.

- Give encouragement to the client for tolerating traumatic memories.

- Help the client to work through and control painful feelings.

- Explore any problems the client has within current relationships particularly in terms of avoidance and confusion.

- Consider the client's family context, i.e. the roles of family members in relation to the client's problem.

- Understand the particular transference and counter-transference responses in the counselling relationship with the client e.g. the client's feelings of abuse may be re-experienced and the counsellor's reactions may be perceived as re-enactments of past abuse. The counsellor may experience disturbing phantasies.

- Aim to help the client to work through their problems until they feel that they have attained a sense of control and mastery over the problem.

- Realize that a number of different counselling approaches can be used: psychodynamic, cognitive-behavioural and psycho-educational.

STRESS

CONCEPT

A person's experience of psychological tension frequently associated with physical symptoms.

FACTORS RELATED TO STRESS

Physiological

Stress has physiological accompaniments through the action of the **sympathetic** division of the **autonomic nervous system**, e.g. preparing the organism for **"fight or flight";** increases in heart, pulse and respiratory rate, sweating and dilation of the pupils. Stress is also mediated through the **endocrine** system particularly in the form of increases in **adrenaline** a hormone which produces physical arousal.

Psychological

The person's perception of a situation or event determines stress reactions. It occurs when a person perceives something as threatening or potentially harmful whether real or apparent. It also occurs when a person's perceived or actual capabilities and resources are not sufficient to meet the demands of a given situation.

Stress is more likely to occur when a person feels:

- **Vulnerable** - Perceiving a lack of resources, physical or social.

- **Unable to cope** - Lacking a positive belief that one can cope as well as believing one does not have the skills to cope with personal problems.

EFFECTS OF STRESS CLIENTS

Positive effects:

- Depending on the degree or level of stress it can help people to think more clearly in threatening situations through a greater focus and concentration on tasks.

Negative effects:

- **Cognitive** - e.g: anger, frustration, resentment, worry, loss of commitment, depression, anxiety and poor motivation.

- **Behavioural** - e.g. insomnia, sexual problems, absenteeism, burn-out and fatigue.

- **Physiological** - e.g. headaches, hypertension, ulcers and depressed immune system.

SOURCES OF STRESS

Stress arises from external pressures brought about by:

- **The physical environment** - e.g. overcrowding, pollution, noise and traumatic events.

- **Social and cultural environment** - e.g. social isolation, adverse life events such as bereavement, divorce and separation and conflict with cultural demands.

- **Occupational and study situations** - e.g. jobs with high demands and low levels of control and exam anxiety.

Stress also arises from internal pressure brought about by:

- Low self-esteem.

- Helplessness and powerlessness.

- Physical illness.

INEFFECTIVE CLIENT STRATEGIES

Clients may resort to the following ineffective strategies to avoid or reduce stress:

- Withdraw from or avoid a recurrent, stressful situation.

- Deny that they are stressed.

- Become perfectionist about work.

- Become over-emotional.

- Resort to drugs, drinking and smoking.

COUNSELLING CLIENTS WHO ARE STRESSED

The counsellor should:

- Identify and acknowledge the nature of the client's stress.

- Look at present and potential effects.

- Work out practical measures to reduce client stress.

- Explore with the client to see if they think the situation can be changed.

If the client feels the situation cannot be changed then the counsellor should work with the client to:

- Change the way the client reacts to the problem.

- Reduce the negative effects of the situation.

- Develop coping strategies e.g. relaxation techniques and self-reinforcement.

- Find appropriate support groups.

- Identify short - and long - term goals.

- Organize leisure time to include exercise and other distractions.

RECURRENT ISSUES RESULTING FROM THE COUNSELLING RELATIONSHIP

COUNSELLING AND GENDER

CONCEPT

- **A person's sex** - The biological distinction between male and female.

- **Gender identity** - A person's conception of themself as male or female.

- **Gender role** - A person's conformity to expectations of what society considers as male or female behaviour.

GENDER ISSUES

Gender issues the client may be aware of or concerned about. The client may perceive:

- Others as being defined as male or female in terms of what are considered essential biological and psychological attributes **(essentialism).**

- Males as being superior to women or vice versa.

- Society as being a **patriarchy** i.e. social, economic, cultural and sexual domination of males and their institutions over females.

- Sexual oppression as a particular dominant sexual orientation e.g. **heterosexism** and **homophobia**, in effect inhibiting and limiting the expression of their own sexuality.

- Their gender identity as different from that ascribed by significant others, e.g. **transsexuality**.

- Differential attitudes and treatment towards males and females.

- **Gender stereotypes** as limiting their social, sexual and economic potential.

- The difference between their self-defined gender and what is publicly ascribed to them as personal failure.

- Him or herself as failing to meet the socially defined body image for their gender.

COUNSELLING WITH REGARD TO GENDER ISSUES

The counselling relationship may be perceived as problematic by the client because of the identical or different genders of counsellor and client.

The counsellor should actively listen to the client's expression and concerns over:

- Their gender identity and how they perceive it affecting the counselling relationship and relationships with significant others.

- Gender role expectations and their negative effects.

- Whether to conform or not to gender stereotypes.

- The possibility of exploring alternative gender identities.

The counsellor can help the client develop awareness of:

- Gender stereotyping and its effects.

- Gender power relationships.

- The usefulness of assertiveness in personal, social and work relationships.

TRANSCULTURAL COUNSELLING

CONCEPT

Transcultural counselling occurs where the counsellor and the client have different cultural backgrounds and this difference in cultures has a bearing on the counselling relationship.

ISSUES WITH RESPECT TO TRANSCULTURAL COUNSELLING

The counsellor should consider if they have:

- Sufficient knowledge and understanding and if possible experience of the client's culture.

- Understood and have empathy with the client's cultural beliefs, attitudes and needs.

- Explained the role of the counsellor and the nature of the counselling relationship to the client.

- Avoided cultural bias or **ethnocentrism.**

- Considered the cultural aspects of verbal and non-verbal communication with the client.

THE COUNSELLING RELATIONSHIP

It is necessary to consider the following points with regard to the counselling relationship:

- The client's cultural beliefs and needs may lead them to a different conception of the relationship than that held by the counsellor.

- The counsellor needs to consider how empathy, congruence and unconditional positive regard will be communicated to the client in light of the client's culture.

- The non-directive aspects of the relationship may need to be explained if the client expects the counsellor to offer advice and ready-made solutions.

- The counsellor needs to communicate to the client that their culture is respected.

TRANSFERENCE AND COUNTER-TRANSFERENCE

The following points should be considered:

- Where a client has experienced prejudice and discrimination, feelings surrounding those issues might emerge in the counselling relationship.

- The counsellor needs to reflect on their own feelings about the client's culture and the issues of prejudice and discrimination.

- The counsellor should also think about their own cultural background, particularly in terms of its meaning for the client.

BOUNDARIES

CONCEPT

Boundaries are established within counselling in order to avoid the distortion or collapse of the relationship. When boundaries are adhered to they prevent inappropriate expectations.

THE ISSUES

- **Confidentiality** - Unless there is an overriding reason, e.g. a life-threatening situation then confidentiality must be preserved.

- **Attitudes to the client** - Attitudes to the clients should reflect acceptance, warmth and empathy and avoid value-judgements.

- **Self-Awareness** - Counsellors ought to be aware of themselves, their personalities and how clients react to them. There should be a separation of the counsellor's needs from the client's needs.

- **Power** - Counsellors ought to be aware of their client's perceptions of them and their role. There is also a need to understand the messages conveyed and that if the aim is to empower clients then counsellors should act appropriately.

- **Time** - Counselling sessions must adhere to time constraints. It is important to recognize what it is possible to achieve within those limits. There is also a need to understand that time constraints affect clients.

- **Environment** - Counselling sessions ought to take place in the same surroundings.

- **Goals and Expectations** - Counsellors must have clear aims of what is achievable with clients. Expectations must be explicit. An action plan is a useful way of setting goals and expectations and the means by which they can be achieved.

- **Perceptions** - Counsellors should convey to clients a consistent approach that is fair, neither over-involved or indifferent to them. Counsellors ought to be sensitive to clients' feelings and moods.

- **Significant Others** - Where appropriate it helps to involve others who are in various relationships with clients.

ETHICS

CONCEPT

The counsellor should be aware of their own ethical principles or value system and those of their client. In the counselling sessions ethical issues and moral dilemmas may be raised by the client which the counsellor needs to explore. The counsellor should behave in an ethical way towards the client.

ISSUES

The counsellor should:

- Ensure that the client has given their informed consent to counselling but problems can arise, e.g. in the case of young children or where people suffer from a mental illness.

- Be sure that they have the client's interests at heart and that they do not exceed their competence or fail to maintain that competence through supervision.

- Consider issues of fairness, e.g. in seeing some kinds of clients before others.

- Make sure that they do not resort to deception and that they abide by contracts.

CONFIDENTIALITY

The onus is on the counsellor to preserve confidentiality but problems arise where:

- The client threatens to harm him or herself or others.

- The counsellor has split loyalties to the client and the client's employer.

- The client has another relationship with the counsellor, e.g. a friendship or a commercial relationship.

SEXUAL RELATIONSHIPS:

- The counsellor should not engage in sex with the client.

- Sexual attraction may arise in the course of the counselling relationship. This can be perceived as part of the transference or counter-transference and worked through as an aspect of the counselling relationship.

- Any intentional physical contact with the client should not have sexual overtones.

THE COUNSELLOR'S PROBLEMS:

The counsellor needs to be aware of:

- Counter-transference arising in the counselling relationship.

- Over-identification with the client where the client has a similar problem.

- Violating boundaries by inappropriate touching, offering friendship and inappropriate self-disclosure.

- Maintaining set times.

THE COUNSELLOR'S POWER:

- The counsellor may be in a powerful position as a member of a dominant group in society e.g. white, male, upper / middle class and heterosexual.

- The power that arises from membership of dominant groups may present obstacles in the counselling relationship and the client may feel disempowered as a result.

- The counsellor who perceives the power relationship as likely to affect the relationship may decide to counsel only certain types of clients or by becoming knowledgeable about a client's particular group enhance empathy thus dealing with any guilt or prejudice that may arise.

BIBLIOGRAPHY

Bandura, A. (1969) *Principles of Behavior Modification*, London: Holt, Reinhart & Winston.

Beck, A. (1976) *Cognitive therapy and the emotional disorders*, New York: International Universities Press.

Bootzin, R.B., Acocella, J.R. and Alloy, L.B. Sixth Edition (1993) *Abnormal Psychology: Current Perspectives*, London: McGraw-Hill, Inc.

Brown, D., and Pedder, J., Second Edition (1991) *Introduction to Psychotherapy*, London: Routledge.

Carkhuff, R. & Anthony, W.A. (1979) *The skills of helping: An introduction to counseling*, Amherst, MA: Human Resource Development Press.

Clarkson, P., and Pokorny, M. (editors) (1994) *The Handbook of Psychotherapy*, London: Routledge.

Cowie, H., and Pecherek, A. (1994) *Counselling: Approaches and Issues in Education*, London: David Fulton Publishers.

Cramer, D. (1992) *Personality and Psychotherapy: Theory, practice and research*, Milton Keynes: Open University Press.

D'Ardenne, P. and Mahtani, A. (1989) *Transcultural Counselling in Action*, London: Sage Publications.

Dryden, W., Charles-Edwards, D. and Woolfe, R. (editors) (1989) *Handbook of Counselling*, London: Tavistock/Routledge.

Dryden, W. (editor) (1984) *Individual Therapy in Britain*, Milton Keynes: Open University Press.

Dryden, W. (editor) (1989) *Key Issues for Counselling in Action*: London: Sage Publications.

Dryden, W. (1990) *Rational Emotive Counselling in Action*, London: Sage Publications.

D'Zurilla, T.J. and Goldfried, M.R. (1971) Problem-solving and behavior modification. *Journal of Abnormal Psychology*, **78**, 107-126.

Egan, G. Fifth Edition (1994) *The Skilled Helper*, Pacific Grove, California: Brooks/Cole Publishing Company.

Ellis, A. (1990) *Reason and emotion in psychotherapy*, New York: Citadel Press.

Freud, S. (1986) *The Essentials of Psychoanalysis*, (Collection of writings, selected by Anna Freud), London: Penguin Books.

Hawton, K., Salkovskis, P.M. Kirk, J. and Clark, D.M. (editors) (1993) *Cognitive Behaviour Therapy for Psychiatric Problems*, Oxford: Oxford University Press.

Hough, M. (1994) *A Practical Approach to Counselling*, London: Pitman.

Jacobs, M. (1988) *Psychodynamic Counselling in Action*, London: Sage Publications.

Kanfer, F.H. & Schefft, B.K. (1988) *Guiding therapeutic change*. Champaign, IL: Research Press.

Laplanche, J. and Pontalis, J.B. (1988) *The Language of Psychoanalysis*, London: The Institute of Psychoanalysis, Karnac.

Lindsay, S.J.E. and Powell, G.E. (editors) Second Edition (1994) *The Handbook of Clinical Adult Psychology*, London: Routledge.

McLeod, J. (1993) *An Introduction to Counselling*, Buckingham: Open University Press.

Mearns, D. and Thorne, B. (1988) *Person-Centred Counselling in Action*, London: Sage Publications.

Meichenbaum, D. (1977) *Cognitive-behavior modification*, New York: Plenum.

Mischel, W. Fifth Edition (1993) *Introduction to Personality*, London: Harcourt Brace Jovanovich College Publishers.

Nelson-Jones, R. (1982) *The Theory and Practice of Counselling Psychology*, London: Cassell.

Orbach, S. (1986) *Fat is a Feminist Issue*, London: Arrow.

Orbach, S. (1986) *Hunger Strike*, London: Penguin Books.

O'Sullivan, S. and Thomson, K. (editors) (1992) *Positively Women, Living with Aids*, London: Sheba Feminist Press.

Pavlov, I. (1927) *Conditional reflexes*, (Translation by G.V. Anrep), Oxford: Clarendon Press.

Pervin, L.A. Fourth Edition (1984) *Personality: Theory and Research*. Chichester: John Wiley & Sons.

Rogers, C.R. (1992) *Client-Centered Therapy*, London: Constable.

Skinner, B.F. (1993) *About Behaviorism*, Harmondsworth: Penguin Books.

Strong, S.R. (1968). Counseling: An interpersonal influence process. *Journal of Counseling Psychology*, **15**.

Tavanyar, J. (1992) The Terence Higgins Trust, HIV/AIDS Book, London: Thorsons.

Trower, P., Casey, A. and Dryden, W. *Cognitive-Behavioural Counselling in Action*, London: Sage Publications.

Velleman, R. (1993) *Counselling for Alcohol Problems*, London: Sage Publications.

Ward, B. (1993) *Healing Grief, A Guide to Loss and Recovery*, London:Vermilion.

Warden, J.W. Second Edition (1993) *Grief Counselling and Grief Therapy: A Handbook for the Mental Health Practitioner*, London: Routledge.

Going off the Rails

THE COUNTRY RAILWAY IN WEST SUSSEX

Produced by
Mallard Communications Services,
22 Crofton Close, Ottershaw, Chertsey,
Surrey KT16 0LR
for
West Sussex County Council

Design by Robert Wilcockson

Text © Bill Gage, Michael Harris
and Tony Sullivan

Published by West Sussex County Council 1997

ISBN 0 8626 0 400 1

1 *Petworth stationmaster*

WEST SUSSEX PAPERS
present new research into the county's history
and heritage in a scholarly yet popular format.

It is an occasional series but aims to publish
at least one new title each year.

For details contact:
The County Archivist
West Sussex Record Office
County Hall
Chichester
PO19 1RN

Printed by
Ian Allan Printing Ltd, Coombelands House,
Coombelands Lane, Addlestone,
Surrey KT15 1HY Tel: 01932 855909

CONTENTS

FOREWORD

At one time West Sussex had many picturesque branch lines which connected tiny villages and hamlets to the market towns. The trip on the railway to go shopping was for many a highlight. Railways such as the Selsey Tramway provided access to the ever popular seaside and enabled the fishermen to transport shellfish to the profitable market of Billingsgate.

I remember the Selsey Tram very well indeed; my first memories are of the Peninsula - from 1924 to 1929 we lived in Aldwick, outside Bognor, and up to 1939 we retained a holiday house there.

The Tram was great fun! Of course it wasn't reliable; but it was entertaining, if only because nobody knew what was likely to happen. It was also convenient, and above all it was friendly.

All these country branch lines have passed into history and when the Tram disappeared, in 1935, I was one of many who felt an acute sense of loss. This book aims to record the life of a bygone railway age. Drawing on personal recollections, it provides an insight to some of the activities of the typical country branch line and the Selsey Tram. I am sure this book will be of interest not only to the railway enthusiast but to all who have a longing for an age that has passed into history.

I have always hoped that one day the Tram would be reopened. I suppose this is a pipe-dream, but one can go on hoping!

Dr Patrick Moore

ACKNOWLEDGEMENTS

The authors gratefully acknowledge the many people who have kindly permitted reproduction of their photographs and archival material in this book. The number given below is that given at the start of the caption for each photograph or illustration.

Every effort has been made to reach copyright holders: the publishers would be pleased to hear from anyone whose rights they have unwittingly infringed.

Dr I. Allen, 75;
Arundel Museum, 55;
Mr A. Baker, 92;
Mr T. Burlinson, 134;
Mr G. Bush, 58, 126;
Mr D. Brough, 13, 18, 49, 56, 76, 94;
Mr C. Carpenter, 135;
Governors of Christ's Hospital, 61;
Mr G. Collins, 68, 74, 83, 113, 122;
Mr G. Croughton, 91;
Mr L. Darbyshire, 84, 89, 103, 108;
Lord Egremont, 33, 116, 117;
Horsham District Museum, 5;
Mr G. Howes, 153;
Lens of Sutton, 78;
Mr J. Lisher, 158;
Mr L. Marshall, 24, 35, 44, 58, 118;
Mr K. Marx, 9, 25, 26, 53, 67, 80, 81, 147;
Mr R. Millington, 42;
Mr J. Minnis, 82;
Mr R. Monks, 48;
National Railway Museum, 95;
Railtrack, 15, 16, 27, 43, 64, 128;
Mr D. Trevor Rowe, 32;
Colonel Stephens Museum, 111, 112;
Mr A. Sullivan, 45, 52, 155;
Mr J. Tawse, 12, 14;
Mrs J. Tupper, 85, 104;
D. Wallis, 3, 63;

West Sussex Library Service, 7, 11, 47, 57, 71, 72, 90, 121;
West Sussex Record Office, 1, 2, 4, 6, 10, 17, 19-22, 28-31, 34, 36-41, 45, 46, 50-52, 54, 59, 62, 65, 66, 69, 70, 73, 77, 79, 86-88, 93, 96-102, 105, 106, 107, 109, 114, 115, 119, 120, 123-125, 127, 129-133, 136-146, 148-152, 154-157, 159, 160;
Mr J. Wynne Jones, 8, 110;

Extracts from Mavis Budd's book *Dust to Dust* reproduced in Chapter 10 appear by kind permission of the publisher, J. M. Dent & Sons;

The authors would like to record their appreciation to J. Roffey, General Secretary, The Evacuees Reunion Association, for reference to his original manuscript, *Big Boys Don't Cry*.

L. B. & S. C. R. Coy.

PUBLIC WARNING NOT TO TRESPASS

Persons trespassing upon any Railways belonging or leased to or worked by the London Brighton and South Coast Railway Company solely or in conjunction with any other Company or Companies are, under the "London Brighton and South Coast Railway (Various Powers) Act, 1899," section 15, liable on conviction to a Penalty of **FORTY SHILLINGS,** and in accordance with the provisions of the said Act public warning is hereby given to all persons not to trespass upon the said Railways.

LONDON BRIDGE TERMINUS. **J. J. BREWER,** Secretary.

PREFACE

Country railway branch lines have all but vanished. Today only the main railway routes connecting major centres of population exist. Yet there was a time when all the counties of England and Wales were criss-crossed with a network of railway lines. They provided the first tangible links of communication for rural communities previously isolated. The railway enabled ordinary people who for generations had been restricted to the boundaries of their small village to venture into the county towns or even the Metropolis to see the magnificent Crystal Palace. Similarly, branch lines enabled city dwellers to enjoy the sights and sounds of the countryside, savour the pastoral peace of the rural scene and take quiet refreshment in village inns and tea gardens.

West Sussex was such a county. Primarily agriculturally based, the rural lines also facilitated both the importation and exportation of goods. Coal was transported into the county in larger quantities than by the traditional horse and cart and could be sold at a lower cost. Agricultural produce could be sent speedily to markets, while the railway enabled the village shop to stock and sell a variety of goods which villages had never seen before but which were now in demand following shopping trips to the market towns.

Going off the Rails focuses on the branch lines to Midhurst and the Hundred of Manhood and Selsey Tramways. The Selsey Tramway was selected because this year celebrates the centenary of its opening, while the lines to Midhurst were chosen because many of the stations are still intact and the railway connection with local events are many and varied.

However, *Going off the Rails* is not a conventional railway enthusiast's book – essentially it is concerned with people. It does not seek to offer technical information on locomotives, rolling stock, or timetabling for example, for such material is already in print. Instead, it sets out to provide an insight into the operation of these local lines through personal memories, not only of railway workers but also of those who used the lines for travelling to work or school, for shopping in the nearest large town, or for the transportation of goods.

We are fortunate to have brought together as contributors to this book, two authors, Michael Harris and Tony Sullivan who have written extensively on the subject of railways. Michael's wide knowledge of both the railway press and book publication has been invaluable – indeed the theme of *Going off the Rails* was his idea.

The most pleasurable aspect of this book has been visiting people in their homes and recording their memories. They tell of the railway and its operation, as it was, and not according to inflexible rules and regulations. Without their stories this book would not have been written and our thanks are extended for their time and help.

Undoubtedly, there are many more anecdotes to be noted and we hope that this book will revive old memories so that they can be recorded before they are lost, just as the old lines are now images of history.

We have also drawn on the extensive resources of the West Sussex Record Office, the West Sussex Library Service, plus the specialist collections at the National Railway Museum and the Colonel Stephens Railway Museum in Kent, and our thanks are extended to their staffs.

The County Archivist, Richard Childs, has been unswerving in his support and without his help this book would not have been possible. We are also delighted that the world renowned astronomer and resident of Selsey, Dr Patrick Moore, has generously contributed the Foreword to the book. My own personal thanks also go to Alan Readman and Kim Leslie who throughout the project have always been available for advice and guidance.

Many people have helped by either providing information, or their own recollections and others have kindly allowed use to be made of their research, documents and photographs. They are referred to in the text but special thanks must be given here to Major J. Ainsworth, Mr B. Arnell, Mrs B. Aylwin, Mrs N. Boys, Commander D. G. F. Bird RN, Mr R. Blake, Mr D. Brough, Mr V. Clayton, Mr G. Collins, Mr R. Comber, Mr W. Crees, Mr M. Cruttenden, Mr G. Croughton, Mr L. Darbyshire, Lord Egremont, Mrs J. Gibbs, Mrs D. Ginman, Mrs S. Haynes, Mr P. Hounsham, Mr G. Howes, Mr H. Hunt, Mr C. Jago of Railtrack, Mr N. Langridge, Mr R. Lempriere, Mr L. Marshall, Mr K. Marx, Mr H. Merritt, Mr D. Millington, Mrs J. Nettles, Mr P. Norrell, Mr F. Osborne, Mr W. Ousley, Mrs N. Pike, Mr R. Pine, Mr J. Roffey, Mr E. Sadler, Miss W. Sayers, Mr G. Smith, Mr & Mrs J. Tupper, Mr G. White and Mr R. White.

Finally, we dedicate this book to the memory of all railway men and women and travellers of those West Sussex branch lines which are now just memories.

W. E. (Bill) Gage
West Sussex Record Office

Chapter 1: Cutting through the South Downs

2. *An early picture of West Dean Tunnel, on the Chichester-Midhurst line.*

Although the main lines of transport demand are north-south, the 'grain' of West Sussex is east-west. To cut through the South Downs calls for heavy earthworks and sharp gradients. The Romans had found that the case with Stane Street which ran from Chichester to London via Hardham, Pulborough, Dorking and Merton of the present-day. It is possible to avoid confronting the high chalk ridges and plateaux by taking to the valleys, or to use 'gaps' where the ridges are interrupted.

In the early years of the Railway Age, some towns were immediate choices for railways extending from London. At first, the goal was more important than intermediate settlements in the area traversed by the new line. Portsmouth was an obvious objective. At first through connection by rail with the capital involved the use of a ferry.

A branch was built from the London & Southampton Railway at Bishopstoke (now East-leigh) through Fareham to Gosport. The London & Southampton became the London & South Western Railway (LSWR) in 1839. Portsmouth was dissatisfied with the indirect rail service which was offered from early 1842 after an earlier halting start.

By 1845, three routes from London had been authorised, which aimed towards Portsmouth. One of these began as an extension from Woking on the LSWR main line to Guildford. This provided the starting-point for a proposed line named the Guildford, Chichester & Portsmouth, routed via Godalming, Haslemere and Midhurst. The Bill for this new railway did not pass through all stages in Parliament, and failed.[1]

Two other projects had the support of companies later forming the London Brighton & South Coast Railway (LBSCR). The LSWR made it clear that the Company regarded Portsmouth as being in its pocket and proclaimed that there was no real demand for a new and direct railway to London. This was during the prelude to what became known as the Railway Mania of 1846.

Railway politics became fast and furious. On one side was the LSWR, on the other the newly formed LBSCR. At one stage, a Direct Portsmouth line seemed the most likely new route, from Epsom by way of Dorking and Godalming. But the Railway Mania collapsed as a result of the financial problems affecting railways, and so did the Direct line. The LSWR and LBSCR did however agree to joint ownership of a single railway link into Portsmouth from Cosham.

A new line was approaching Portsmouth from the east. With the completion of this Brighton-Chichester-Portsmouth 'West Coast' line in 1847, the LBSCR could offer travellers a London-Portsmouth route, a circuitous 95¼ miles in length. This ceased to be competitive with the opening of the LSWR's Portsmouth Direct in 1859. That new-comer depended on using the LBSCR's line from Havant towards Portsmouth. The two railway companies fell out badly.

3. *Chichester station in the 1880s. The overall roof was replaced in 1894. The original station building was demolished to make way for the current station building in 1958.*

A court injunction forced them to work with each other but they continued their battles by means of a fares' war. Finally, they were forced to sink their differences, with agreement that they would stop poaching on each other's territory.

To the east of the Portsmouth Direct line was rural country, mainly in West Sussex but partly in Hampshire, which was to be clear of railways for a few years more as a result of the 'no poaching' agreement between the LSWR and LBSCR companies. True, there were towns in this area traversed by the River Rother and the South Downs. Each was the focus of its own locality, and communications were poor between the towns which as yet were some way from the existing railways bordering the area. The railhead to the east was at Horsham, located at the end of the LBSCR line from Three Bridges.

The LBSCR had come into the West Sussex Weald by means of an 8½-mile branch from its Brighton main line at Three Bridges to Horsham which was the principal market town of the area. The line opened early in 1848.

Horsham was to be the starting-point of the LBSCR's cut-off route to Portsmouth. This replaced the long trek via Brighton and Worthing. This new route was to become one side of a triangle of railway lines: popularly known as the Mid-Sussex line, this was the right-hand, and the Portsmouth Direct line of the LSWR was the left-hand side. The base of

the triangle was formed by the LBSCR's Brighton to Portsmouth line.

The Mid-Sussex was pieced together to form a main line. The motivation for its construction seems to have been on the basis that this region, West Sussex, was LBSCR Country, just as it was LSWR Country in Hampshire, beyond the boundary established by that company's Guildford-Petersfield-Havant line.

In the summer of 1857, the Mid-Sussex Railway was incorporated to build a line from Horsham to Coultershaw Mill, near Petworth, just over 17 miles in length. It opened to traffic in the autumn of 1859. For the Mid-Sussex route

4. **Top:** *Chichester's North Street.*

5. **Above:** *Horsham station in LBSCR days.*

London Brighton and South Coast Railway
Horsham Road to
Petworth

The West Sussex Gazette

CITY OF CHICHESTER CHRONICLE,

WORTHING, ARUNDEL, BOGNOR, BRIGHTON, &c.   PETWORTH, HORSHAM, STEYNING, MIDHURST,

...MPTON, SHOREHAM, HAVANT, EMSWORTH, SOUTHAMPTON, RYDE, GOSPORT,   PORTSMOUTH, PETERSFIELD, ALTON, STORRINGTON, PULBOROUGH, BILLINGSHURST,

HAYLING ISLAND, AND SOUTH COAST JOURNAL.   HASLEMERE, HORNDEAN, AND MID-SUSSEX HERALD.

SUSSEX, EAST HAMPSHIRE, AND SOUTH OF ENGLAND ADVERTISER.

is published every THURSDAY MORNING, and distributed by about EIGHTY officially appointed Local Agents throughout the whole of Western Sussex, also in Brighton, Portsmouth, and East Hampshire; and it has the LARGEST CIRCULATION OF ANY NEWSPAPER IN THE SOUTH OF ENGLAND.

No. 805.   REGISTERED FOR TRANSMISSION ABROAD.   **THURSDAY, OCTOBER 13th, 1859.**   WEEKLY CIRCULATION: } Between 11,000 and 12,000.

10   *Going off the rails*

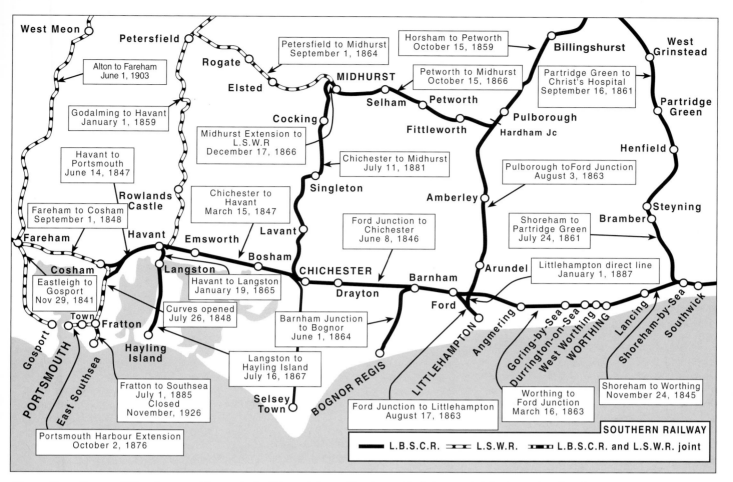

West Meon

Petersfield

Rogate

Alton to Fareham
June 1, 1903

Godalming to Havant
January 1, 1859

Havant to
Portsmouth
June 14, 1847

Rowlands
Castle

Fareham to Cosham
September 1, 1848

Fareham

Havant

Cosham

Eastleigh to
Gosport
Nov 29, 1841

Town

Gosport

Fratton

East Southsea

Hayling
Island

Fratton to Southsea
July 1, 1885
Closed
November, 1926

Portsmouth Harbour Extension
October 2, 1876

PORTSMOUTH

Petersfield to Midhurst
September 1, 1864

MIDHURST

Selham   Petworth

Cocking

Fittleworth

Midhurst Extension to
L.S.W.R
December 17, 1866

Chichester to Midhurst
July 11, 1881

Singleton

Chichester to
Havant
March 15, 1847

Lavant

Emsworth

Bosham

Langston

Havant to Langston
January 19, 1865

CHICHESTER

Drayton

Curves opened
July 26, 1848

Barnham Junction
to Bognor
June 1, 1864

Langston to
Hayling Island
July 16, 1867

Selsey
Town

BOGNOR REGIS

Horsham to Petworth
October 15, 1859

Petworth to Midhurst
October 15, 1866

Pulborough

Hardham Jc

Ford Junction to
Chichester
June 8, 1846

Barnham

Ford

Billingshurst

West
Grinstead

Partridge Green to
Christ's Hospital
September 16, 1861

Partridge
Green

Pulborough to Ford Junction
August 3, 1863

Henfield

Amberley

Shoreham to
Partridge Green
July 24, 1861

Bramber

Steyning

Arundel

Littlehampton direct line
January 1, 1887

LITTLEHAMPTON

Angmering

Goring-by-Sea

Durrington-on-Sea

West Worthing

WORTHING

Lancing

Shoreham-by-Sea

Southwick

Ford Junction to Littlehampton
August 17, 1863

Worthing to
Ford Junction
March 16, 1863

Shoreham to Worthing
November 24, 1845

SOUTHERN RAILWAY

L.B.S.C.R.   L.S.W.R.   L.B.S.C.R. and L.S.W.R. joint

Above: *The railways of West Sussex, with opening dates.*

6. Above left: *The West Sussex Gazette announces the introduction of the Horsham to Petworth service in 1859.*

7. Left: *Petworth Golden Square in 1912.*

to reach the coast the railway needed to be extended from what became Hardham Junction, near Pulborough – some miles short of Petworth – through Arundel and to Arundel Junction, east of Ford on the Brighton-Chichester-Portsmouth main line.

At first a single-line railway, the Mid-Sussex, opened from Horsham to Petworth in the autumn of 1859. A second track was laid to Hardham Junction for the opening through to Arundel junction section in 1863.

The Mid-Sussex line was hardly a fast route. It had not been planned as a through main line between major centres. It is no different today. Along its way between Horsham and Pulborough in particular, the line is curvaceous and features short, sharp gradients. By following

the River Adur valley it avoided the need to cross the South Downs and kept well clear of the High Weald.

So far the Mid-Sussex line made do with roundabout access from London via Croydon and Three Bridges. One of the companies forming the LBSCR reached Epsom Town in 1847. Then came the Epsom & Leatherhead line, which from 1859 was used by LSWR trains from Waterloo via Raynes Park and Epsom and LBSCR services. The Epsom & Leatherhead was jointly owned by both companies.

Then, in 1862, an independent company was set up to link Leatherhead and Horsham and also promised what was to be an unrealised junction with the South Eastern Railway's Redhill-Guildford-Reading line near Dorking. The LBSCR itself closed the gap from Leatherhead to Horsham, but not until 1877 was there a through route between London, Sutton, Horsham, Pulborough, Arundel, Chichester and Portsmouth.

Describing the completion of the through Mid-Sussex route means that we have jumped ahead of the story of other West Sussex railways. Before the LBSCR

had made the decision to push southwards to the coast, the original Mid-Sussex Company line terminated at Petworth.

In 1859, the same year that trains began serving Petworth, an independent company was set up, to extend the railway line from Petworth along the Rother Valley and on to Petersfield, almost following the escarpment of the South Downs. This company, the Mid-Sussex & Midhurst Junction, was sold to the LBSCR.

Remember that the LBSCR and LSWR had eventually agreed to keep out of each other's territory. In place of a through railway between Petworth and Petersfield there would be two separate sections. Having purchased the Mid-Sussex & Midhurst Junction the LBSCR was reminded of its agreement with the LSWR.[2] As a result, what became the Petersfield Railway went forward as an independent company. It was acquired by the South Western in 1863.

The Petworth-Midhurst section was opened in the autumn of 1866 and was worked by the LBSCR which opened its station at Midhurst. It was the second in the town. That was because the separate Petersfield Railway had opened two years earlier with its own terminus; the two stations were close.

This farcical situation had arisen because during the passage of the Bill for the Petersfield Railway through Parliament there were disagreements between the Mid-Sussex Company and the Petersfield Railway's promoters. These culminated in a clause being inserted in the Act of 1860 ordering that a deviation must be made at the Midhurst end,[3] and prohibiting a connection between the Petworth-Midhurst and Midhurst-Petersfield lines. A short connection between the two lines was made at the end of 1866, but for the interchange of goods traffic only.

So far, none of the railways of West Sussex had confronted the South Downs outright, perhaps wisely. North of Chichester and south of Midhurst, there is a gap which forms the watershed between the River Lavant running south, and a stream feeding the Rother towards Pulborough. The Chichester to Midhurst road used the gap, and it was an obvious conduit for a railway.

Proposals having been made for a railway from Chichester to Midhurst, an Act was obtained by a local company to build a line from immediately west of Chichester to Midhurst. The first Act was passed in 1864, another soon afterwards: the line would be joined to the Petersfield Railway and extended to Haslemere. The Haslemere extension was abandoned in 1868 and, before long, work had ceased on the rest of the route.

Some time later, in 1876, the LBSCR was stirred to take over the unfinished line and to complete it. The route was altered at the Chichester end, and more drastically at Midhurst. In the case of the latter, this was to enable trains to run through between the Petworth line and Chichester. The original company had after all planned to go northwards to Haslemere.

A new station was built at Midhurst just to the east of the junction of the Chichester and Petworth lines, and inconveniently located for the LSWR's Petersfield line station. The 12-mile Chichester-Midhurst single line through the Downs was opened in the summer of 1881. The folly of the enterprise showed in the fact

8. *The fisherman at East Beach, Selsey were among the local producers who benefited from the railway.*

that five brickworks were set up south of Midhurst to produce the millions of bricks required to line the tunnels and to build the bridges of this heavily engineered route. Even by taking the gap through the Downs, three tunnels were required.

Yet the Chichester-Midhurst line was not the last railway to be built in West Sussex. Still devoid of railways was the Hundred of Manhood, south of Chichester and with Selsey at the tip of the peninsula. The area's main activities were agriculture and fishing. In true Victorian style, a major initiative was taken by local people to propose both a Chichester-Selsey branch line, and a pier at Selsey. That was in 1887 but neither development materialised.

Then came a simpler scheme of 1895 for a standard gauge light railway only. Its proposals faced difficulties and the project was delayed. The timing is relevant because before Parliament was a Bill to make the promotion of light railways easier. Even so, rather than being built as a railway, the Selsey line was completed as a tramway.

At the beginning of 1897, the Hundred of Manhood and Selsey Tramways got under way, and opened late that summer. This impressive-sounding enterprise ran from its own terminus in Chichester to Selsey Town; a year later came a short extension used in summer only to Selsey Beach.

As the 20th century opened, West Sussex and the borders of Hampshire had its triangle of main lines: the coast line originating at Brighton and linking Chichester and Portsmouth, with the two sides of the triangle formed by the Portsmouth Direct line from Guildford-Petersfield-Havant, and the Mid-Sussex line from Horsham through Pulborough to join the coast line south of Arundel. The rural, secondary routes were in the form of a elongated letter 'T', from south of Pulborough through Petworth to Midhurst, then south to Chichester, and the 'semi-detached' Midhurst-Petersfield line pointing west. The last section of the downstroke of the 'T' took railway metals almost to Selsey Bill.

Going off the rails

Chapter 2: Rise and fall of the country branch lines

Having described the basic railway network in West Sussex west of the River Adur, what about the lines themselves and the places they served?

Horsham is a logical starting-point. At first sight, Horsham and Midhurst would have seemed to be natural centres to be linked by a railway line. As the history of the area's railways turned out, this was not to be. Even in the April 1910 timetable the service is firmly shown as between Pulborough, Midhurst and Chichester.[1] Midhurst was the most prominent town in that part of West Sussex which was 'Brighton Country'. The town had featured on the Guildford-Godalming-Haslemere-Midhurst-Chichester line proposed in 1845 but was fated not to be built, thanks to the collapse of the Railway Mania. In itself, this abortive line emphasised the fact that at first sight this was the most logical route for a main railway line through the borderlands of Hampshire and West Sussex.

Once the Portsmouth Direct and Mid-Sussex lines had been completed, the chances that Midhurst would be served by a main line were slim. The town was destined to be served by secondary, single-track branches, reaching out from competing railways' main lines, and denied the chance of being on a trunk route.

The strivings for influence in the region between the LSWR and LBSCR had been resolved by the previously mentioned agreement not to poach on each other's territory. One consequence was that the LBSCR had to forego support of a railway because it penetrated the territory of its rival. So Midhurst and Petersfield were to be linked by a different company, and this passed to the control of the LSWR. The loss, if it can be adjudged that, was borne by Petworth, Midhurst and Petersfield, destined not to enjoy a through railway route until after World War I. By then, it was too late for the railway to make much of the opportunity.

Another historical accident had ensured that Petworth was bypassed by a main line. The Mid-Sussex company had initially proposed that its line from Horsham would pass through Petworth, rather than by the branch actually built which diverged south of Pulborough.[2] The direct line to Petworth would have travelled on from where the line to Pulborough curved on its approach to Billingshurst, and a separate line would have served the area south of the Rother Valley. In the event, this second route was the one chosen for what became the Mid-Sussex line, and so the direct line from Billingshurst to Petworth was discarded. Throughout its life the Horsham to Arundel line tended to be referred to as the 'Mid-Sussex line'. More accurately, it was the Arun Valley line.

The late 1850s were a defining time for West Sussex railways. From Horsham, likely railway routes struck out south-west to the coast, making use of the valley of the River Arun, and south-east towards Shoreham, in due course to parallel the River Adur so as to make use of the Adur gap through the South Downs and to avoid heavy earthworks or indeed tunnelling. It is a reminder that West Sussex railways were primarily promoted as local concerns, although soon swallowed up by the large companies. With limited resources at their disposal, the promoters chose routes that would incur the least expense.

In the 1840s, a railway down the Adur Valley and via Shoreham might well have become the main line from London to Brighton instead of the one actually constructed by way of Redhill, Three Bridges,

9. The Mid-Sussex line: 'D' tank No 268 at Amberley in 1914.

10. *Midhurst town centre. North Street in the late 1870s.*

11. *The exterior of the old Horsham station.*

necting lines were mere branches from what since the 1920s was clearly regarded as a secondary route.

Away from Horsham, the alignment taken by the Mid-Sussex line meant that there are falling gradients to the future site of Christ's Hospital station. There is a short climb to the one-time divergence of the Shoreham line at Itchingfield. The Mid-Sussex line features a number of reverse curves on its route, both when running nearby and when remote from the River Arun which it encounters first soon after leaving Horsham. Saw-tooth gradients continue to Billingshurst as the railway descends into and then out of a valley whose stream feeds the Arun. Beyond Billingshurst, the Mid-Sussex line runs almost parallel to Stane Street, now the A29 road. The Arun lies to the west of railway and road. Along this stretch, 13 miles from Horsham and just over a mile short of Pulborough, the railway reaches to a summit followed by a sudden descent along which the line curves markedly.

Conveniently located for the town, the station at Pulborough comes before the railway's main crossing of the River Arun.

and Haywards Heath. By the mid-1850s, with some tacit support from the LSWR, there were thoughts of a railway along the Adur Valley. To outflank this potential threat, the LBSCR championed its own route between Horsham and Shoreham and the Bill for its construction received Royal Assent.[3] Before construction started, the route of this single-line railway, by no means a main line, was altered so that it commenced at Itchingfield on the Mid-Sussex line, not far from Horsham.

In three years, from 1857-59, the railway map of West Sussex was determined. Parliament approved the lines from Horsham to Pulborough and to Petworth, and west to Midhurst; and from Itchingfield and Steyning through the Adur gap to Shoreham. Work began on their construction in the same period. Petworth was reached in 1859, Shoreham in 1861, the Mid-Sussex extended beyond its junction with the branch to Petworth and on to Ford in 1863, and the railway entered Midhurst in 1866. The LBSCR had ensured that it would be the dominant company in the area, having excluded competitors.

Originally served only by the branch from Three Bridges, Horsham station was rebuilt to suit the route adopted for the line to Petworth and down the Arun Valley. The station was not greatly altered until electrification came in 1938. As memorably described by railway historian H. P. White, the new Southern Electric art deco station 'swept away a rambling, ramshackle warren full of bays, holes and corners into and out of which popped like

rabbits the ubiquitous "motor trains" .... propelled by diminutive tank engines.'[4]

The Mid-Sussex line is characterised by frequent changes of gradient and extensive curvature. There are numerous bridges, mostly taking the railway over streams, plenty of occupation and footpath crossings, and five level crossings. These features reflected on the line's origins as a local railway, lacking generous financial resources, and as a result restricting its value as a through route capable of permitting fast running. In turn, its con-

12. **Above right:** *Hardham Junction, divergence of the Mid-Sussex and Petworth lines. Note the signalbox on 'stilts'.*

13. **Right:** *Christ's Hospital station.*

Going off the rails

14. *A 1957 view from inside Midhurst Tunnel, with the station in the background.*

More curvature follows, and then the line comes to the site of Hardham Junction. The signalbox here was one of the LBSCR's 'Box on Stilts' type and it lasted until closure of the line to Petworth in 1966. From here, the branch to Petworth kept to the southern side of the River Rother which ensured a reasonably level run to the town. The only intermediate station was at Fittleworth, whose wooden building opened to traffic in September 1889.

There was method in the route adopted for the railway between Pulborough and Petworth. Despite the presence in the area of the two rivers – Arun

15. **Right:** *A small piece of history: the official Railtrack archives include a book of drawings of stations on the Petersfield-Midhurst line. The cover is marked 'Petersfield Railway', altered to 'Midhurst branch' to record the takeover by the LSWR before the line was opened.*

16. **Below:** *LBSCR plan showing the original and later station at Midhurst.*

and Rother – the Arun was crossed only once by the Mid-Sussex line, just after leaving Pulborough. The care taken to avoid bridging the Arun again meant that the Petworth branch was necessarily forced to the south side of that town, and east of the Petworth-Chichester road. The station was nearly 1½ miles distant from the town, but this location was better positioned for continuation of the railway to Midhurst.

To return to the Mid-Sussex 'main' line, another feature was – and remains – the widely-spaced stations, notably between Horsham and Billingshurst (the intermediate station of Christ's Hospital dated from 1902 when the school relocated), and Billingshurst and Pulborough. South of Hardham Junction, the line follows undulating gradients along the Arun valley to Amberley, after which at North Stoke there is the only tunnel on the line. Much of the continuation to Arundel Junction – with the Brighton-Portsmouth coast line – is almost level track.

From Petworth to Midhurst the railway's construction involved raising the Petworth-Chichester road so that the railway could pass beneath it. Along the section to Midhurst there was extensive cut and fill construction culminating in a tunnel (Midhurst Tunnel, 276 yards in length)

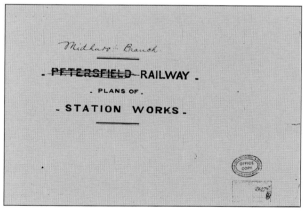

on the approach to the town. Despite these works the line featured gradients of 1 in 80 in its climb towards Midhurst, the steepness being made more exacting by track curvature.

Apart from Midhurst Tunnel, within a distance of just under six miles there were several underbridges, and almost as many overbridges. There was just one intermediate station, at Selham and it was not opened until July 1872, six years after the opening of the line. At Midhurst, the LBSCR station was on Bepton Road.

As mentioned earlier, the railway from Midhurst to Petersfield was the responsibility of the Petersfield Railway Company. This company was purchased by the LSWR which was responsible for completion of the line, and it opened in September 1864. The Petersfield line's terminus at Midhurst was on the opposite side of Bepton Road to the rival establishment. Once the Petworth line station had opened, the two branch lines were linked by a connecting line spanning Bepton Road, but the bridge was of light construction and could only be used for the exchange of goods wagons using horses as motive power. Passengers transferring between LBSCR and LSWR trains made use of a covered footway on this bridge.

The Midhurst-Petersfield line kept to the south of the Rother valley, and had two intermediate stations, at Elsted and at Rogate and Harting, both of which lay in West Sussex. Neither was handy for the village it apparently served. Rogate was later shown as 'Rogate, for Harting'. At Petersfield, the general theme of inconvenience for passengers persisted. The Midhurst passenger trains used a wooden platform devoid of shelter, and access

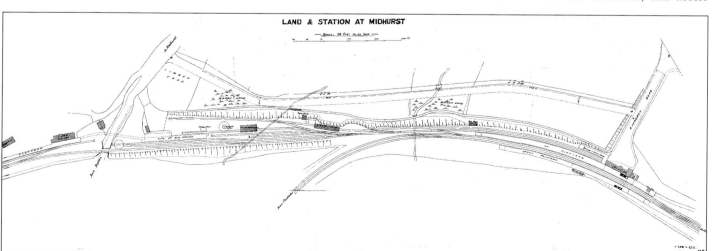

from the Portsmouth Direct line station involved crossing the main road.

The Chichester to Midhurst line was built after the local company fell by the wayside, and the LBSCR took over the project. Midhurst benefited by a new station but unhappily it was less conveniently located. The LBSCR facilities at Bepton Road dating from 1866 were abandoned for passenger traffic, but continued to be used by goods trains, and retained the exchange arrangements to and from the Petersfield line.

The first station on the Chichester-Midhurst line was Lavant, three miles from its junction with the Brighton-Portsmouth coast line at Fishbourne Crossing, and with an imposing three-storey station building. The subsequent climb towards the gap in the South Downs involved heavy gradients, and the railway made its approach by extensive curvature.

Before reaching Singleton station, a gra-

17. Above: *Satirical comment on the directors of the LBSCR, at the time of the first promotion of a Chichester-Midhurst line, as printed in* **Fun** *magazine, June 1867.*

18. Right: *The line to Midhurst diverging from the Brighton-Portsmouth line at Fishbourne.*

19. Bottom: *The 1886 washout at Selham, on the Petworth-Midhurst section.*

dient of 1 in 75 began which eased through the station, and briefly resumed at this severity. The first tunnel (West Dean, 443 yards in length) was just on the Chichester side of Singleton station and was curved throughout its length as the line came to the gap in the South Downs. Singleton Tunnel (744 yards in length) was the second of the tunnels, and the bore was straight; by the time a train passed under its north portal it had come to the summit of its climb. Excavation through the chalk of the South Downs brought problems. Traffic was stopped for a time by a chalk-fall at West Dean in December 1886. At the same time, a culvert had been washed out near Selham on the Petworth-Midhurst line, and the debris from West Dean was transported to reinstate the embankment near Selham.

From the summit the line had a steep

Going off the rails

descent towards Midhurst, some of it at a gradient of 1 in 60. Halfway or so down the bank was the third tunnel on the line – Cocking, at 740 yards in length. Its north portal was just south of Cocking station. The sharp curve taking trains into Midhurst station imposed a speed restriction of 20mph. Apart from its three tunnels with their combined length of over a mile, there were some 35 bridges on the Chichester-Midhurst line. The LBSCR treated the Chichester and Midhurst line as an extension of the line from Hardham Junction on the Mid-Sussex line by way of Petworth. The new line opened on 11 July 1881.[5]

Singleton station revealed the main reason for the LBSCR's keenness to build this heavily graded railway. It boasted facilities above and beyond those to be expected at a country station on the Downs to fulfil its function of handling passenger and horsebox traffic to Goodwood Races. Previously this had been dealt with either at Drayton or Chichester stations.

Singleton boasted two island platforms, each with a main and bay platform. A turntable was installed close-by so that locomotives of special trains could be turned. Accompanying these facilities were extensive sidings, designed to hold up to 14 20-coach trains. All this required the provision of two signalboxes.

Curiously, operation of this single-track line was not helped by the fact that passenger trains were not allowed to cross at either Lavant or Cocking stations. All stations on the line were of the ornate 'half-timbered' appearance adopted by the LBSCR in the 1880s and also used in East Sussex on what is nowadays called the Bluebell line, but Singleton was positively exuberant. The down platform included a refreshment room and there was a separate gents' lavatory block to cater for needs during Goodwood Races.

The Hundred of Manhood and Selsey Tramways was built cheaply and lightly and, because it did not possess established rights of way, at times skirted fields and ran through farmyards. To tap as much passenger traffic as possible it had no less than 11 stations or halts in its full eight-mile length from Chichester to Selsey Beach. 'Stations' are perhaps too grand a descrip-

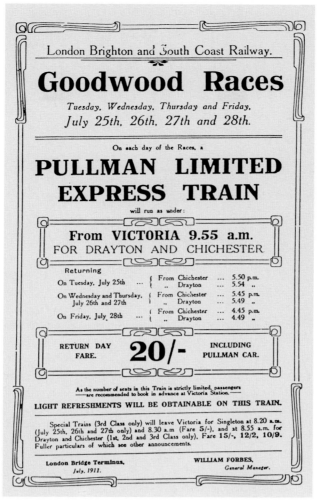

20. *A 1911 poster for a Pullman car excursion from Victoria to Drayton and Chichester.*

tion of the Tramway's facilities for passengers. They were glorified shelters fashioned from timber and corrugated-iron. Traffic was exchanged with the LBSCR by means of a siding at Chichester, where the town's gasworks nearby helped to generate the tramway station's ambience.[6]

These then were some of the characteristics of the West Sussex railways. How

were they operated? The first point to make is that with the exceptions of the Midhurst-Petersfield line and the Selsey Tramway they all came under the control of one company. The LBSCR was therefore unchallenged by another company, and for most of its existence it took life philosophically – some would say complacently. After all, it did not need to match competing services locally. But what of the competing routes between London and Portsmouth – the LSWR's Direct Portsmouth line, and the LBSCR's Mid-Sussex line?

Describing the LBSCR's passenger services, railway writer, E. L. Ahrons quoted an editorial from *The Times* of 1895.[7] This contended that, compared with the main lines north of the Thames, instead of competing in terms of speed the LBSCR and South Eastern Railway 'have chosen frankly a very different form of distinction, and the struggle between them now is which of them can claim to have established the slowest, the most unpunctual, and the most inconvenient service of trains'. Perhaps such criticism was exaggerated, but demonstrates that the LBSCR was not universally held in high esteem, except perhaps when it came to its 'showpiece' services between London and Brighton.

Competition between the LBSCR and LSWR for London to Portsmouth traffic might have been expected to result in attractive schedules, but at the turn of the

21. *Locomotive* **Sidlesham** *at Selsey Town station, c 1908.*

THE LAST TRAIN
from Selsey

22. **Left:** *A frequent theme for local postcards!*

23. **Bottom:** *The main line railways of West Sussex.*

the longest non-stop run in the south-east. This summer train ran until early Southern Railway days. From Portsmouth Harbour, the 9.40 and 11.35am to Victoria each had a journey time of 130min.[8]

Much had changed on the LBSCR by 1910 with the recent appointment of a new Superintendent of the Line, Finlay Scott. He remodelled the timetable, but not however to the advantage of the Mid-Sussex line whose fastest trains now took 1¾-2½hr to Chichester, just 69 miles distant from London. Even at their best, the line's trains were semi-fasts.

If that was what was offered on the main line, what about the branches serving West Sussex? The routine of the country branches seldom changed. After all, there was no road competition. The locomotives and coaches employed had seen better days elsewhere. Passenger trains

century the best times made over the 74 miles of the LSWR's routes were a few minutes over two hours. The LBSCR's route between London and Portsmouth was longer by 13 miles. At that time, all Portsmouth expresses ran via Mitcham Junction, Sutton and Dorking, a route hampered by several speed restrictions and steady climbs in both directions through the North Downs. An overall time of 125min was booked for the LBSCR's two crack trains of 1898, the 8.45am Portsmouth Harbour-London Bridge and 4.55pm return, each of which made three intermediate stops. Victoria was the terminus for the off-peak trains, one of which was the 3.37pm down, running to Fratton in 128 minutes for 84¼ miles, at the time

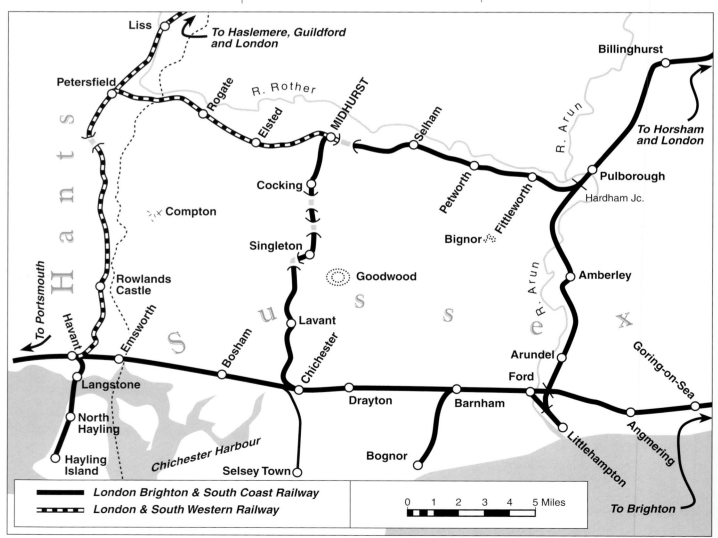

London Brighton & South Coast Railway
London & South Western Railway

0 1 2 3 4 5 Miles

Going off the rails

probably did more business with parcels and milk traffic at local stations.

In April 1910, on weekdays there were five down and six up through passenger trains running between Pulborough and Chichester. Journey time for the 23 miles lasted just over an hour. In addition, there were two or three trains in each direction between Pulborough and Midhurst only. One special working was a Monday mornings only 7am from Midhurst to Pulborough and Three Bridges, described in a Midhurst guide book of the time as 'for the benefit of week-enders'. Even before the onset of the motor age Sunday trains were restricted to two trains each way between Pulborough and Midhurst.[9]

The through journey from Victoria or London Bridge to Midhurst usually occupied 2¼-2½ hours for the 65 miles. The exception was a fast 2hour 7minute service by virtue of catching the weekday 3.55pm from Victoria to Portsmouth which made limited stops only to Pulborough where the connecting train awaited. Of course, Midhurst was also served by the LSWR, and in the fateful summer 1914 timetable a traveller using the 9.10am Waterloo to Portsmouth Harbour could expect to arrive in Midhurst at 11.3am – in under 2 hours for the 64 miles. The LSWR's Midhurst branch featured 11 trains out to Midhurst, and 10 back; there were four trains each way on summer Sundays in 1914.[10]

The relationship at Midhurst between the LSWR and LBSCR stations and their staffs was tellingly evoked by railway writer and historian Hamilton Ellis: 'in 1919, a South Western porter at Midhurst "didn't know" the way to the Brighton station down the road, and his opposite number on the Brighton, learning we had come in by the South Western from Petersfield, prevaricated about the time of the next train to Petworth.'[11] While amusing to recount, unhelpful attitudes of this sort lost business once the bus services had developed.

Between Chichester and Selsey Town the 'Selsey Tramway' – as it tended to be referred to in the *Bradshaw* timetable – advertised a service of eight or so trains each way on weekdays, taking half an hour for their 7¾mile journey. This reflected the fact that speeds seldom exceeded 15-20mph. Confidence in the service was hardly bolstered by the Company's 'small print' in the timetable which warned that 'The Company does not undertake that the Trams shall start or

24. *The rivals alongside - a scene at Fratton station showing an LSWR train hauled by a Drummond 4-4-0 (left) with an LBSCR 'B1' 0-4-2 (right).*

arrive at the times specified in the Table'! In summer before World War I there were 11 trains each way on the line.

Services between the capital and stations on the Mid-Sussex line had improved by the summer of 1922 [12] although comparison with April 1910 is misleading as summer services were always expanded in the days before World War II, and April still counted as 'winter'.

There had been a move towards routing the principal Mid-Sussex line trains via Three Bridges instead of via Sutton and Dorking. One of the best trains of July 1922 was the 8.55am from Victoria to Portsmouth Harbour, blessed with '3rd class Pullman Breakfast Car' but it ran non-stop between Horsham and Arundel. Chichester was reached at 10.45. The return Pullman express from Portsmouth by this route even missed out Chichester and Arundel. One innovation was a through train between Midhurst and Victoria, leaving at 9.17am, but its 2½hr journey suggested that the working was more to suit the railway's operations than its users.

Between Chichester and Pulborough there were by now five down and seven up trains – an obvious enquiry was, why the difference? As in 1910, between Pulborough and Midhurst there were two or three additional trains. In the summer 1922 timetable, the LSWR continued to offer Midhurst more or less the same level of service as in 1910, but one seasonal feature of these years was the operation of Sunday trains between Midhurst, Petersfield and Portsmouth and Southsea.

Notable seasonal trains offered by the LBSCR naturally included the excursions from London for racegoers attending the Goodwood Races in late July. A 9.55am 'Pullman Limited Express Train' from Victoria was run 'on each day of the races' in 1911. Significantly though it operated to Drayton and Chichester, as did another train from Victoria. Just the third-class only excursion worked to Singleton's spacious station. The Selsey Tramway anticipated an increase in seasonal traffic by providing seven trains each way at the height of the summer; four each way ran on Sundays.

When the LBSCR and LSWR combined with other constituent companies to form the Southern Railway in 1923, an early decision was made by the new organisation to concentrate the London-Portsmouth service on the former South Western route. In the summer 1924 timetable of the new company the service over the Mid-Sussex line was slowed down considerably, and even reduced. Complaints were many and included some from the diocesan offices at Chichester.[13] The Southern took note and improved services for the winter 1924/5 timetable but the impression had been given that West Sussex was not seen as particularly rewarding territory for the Railway; users were confirmed in their feeling that the Mid-Sussex route was second-best. By the time electrification came in 1938 it was probably too late to woo traffic back to the trains.

Certainly, the Southern Railway made economies in operating West Sussex services, some not before time. The nonsense of two stations at Midhurst was tackled by strengthening the Bepton Road bridge to take locomotives and coaches. From July 1925, trains from Petersfield ran into the

Key dates for West Sussex lines

1845	Proposed 'Guildford Extension & Portsmouth & Fareham Railway Company's' Guildford-Godalming-Haslemere-Midhurst-Chichester line. Powers granted only for Guildford-Godalming Goods, and Fareham-Portsmouth
1846	Coast line opened in stages from Shoreham-Ford Junction, and on to Chichester opened by London & Brighton company
1847	Chichester-Havant, and Havant-Portsmouth lines opened
1853	Direct Portsmouth Railway Co obtained authority for Godalming-Havant line
1857	Mid-Sussex company authorised to build Horsham-Pulborough-Petworth line
1859	24 January – First train arrives at Portsmouth via the Portsmouth Direct line
	10 October – Horsham-Pulborough-Petworth line brought into use
	Mid-Sussex & Midhurst Junction authorised to build Petworth-Midhurst line
	Acquired by London Brighton & South Coast Railway in 1862
1860	Petersfield Railway authorised to build Petersfield-Midhurst line
1863	3 August – LBSCR opens the Mid-Sussex Junction line from Hardham Junction-Ford
1864	1 September – LSWR opens Petersfield-Midhurst line
	Chichester & Midhurst Railway authorised to build line, extension to Haslemere approved 1865. Abandoned 1868
1866	15 October – Petersfield-Midhurst line opened by LBSCR
1876	LBSCR revives proposed Chichester-Midhurst line
1881	11 July – LBSCR opens Chichester-Midhurst line
1897	15 January – The Hundred of Manhood and Selsey Tramways decides to proceed with construction of line from Chichester-Selsey line
	27 August – Opening of the Chichester-Selsey line
1923	1 January – Grouping of the railways under Railways Act, 1921
	Southern Railway commences business
1925	Rationalisation of stations at Midhurst. Former LSWR station closes
1935	as from 19 January – All services suspended on West Sussex Railway – Chichester-Selsey
	as from 6 July – Chichester-Midhurst closed to passenger traffic
	Petersfield-Midhurst passenger service extended to Pulborough
1938	as from 3 July – electrified services commence Dorking North-Bognor/Littlehampton and Portsmouth
1951	Chichester-Midhurst closed to through traffic
1955	as from 7 February – Petersfield-Pulborough passenger service withdrawn and all service ceased Petersfield-Midhurst
1966	20 May – last goods train ran Petworth-Hardham Junction-Pulborough
	Hardham Junction-Petworth closes to all traffic
1970	1 January – official date of Lavant-Fishbourne Crossing used for sugar beet traffic
1991	Fishbourne Crossing-Lavant officially declared as out of use

former LBSCR station at Midhurst, and the LSWR station closed to passenger traffic.

The next move was to convert most of the local workings to what the Southern Railway termed 'motor-trains'. This meant that the locomotive was coupled to one or a pair of coaches and remained with this set throughout the day, and did not have to run round its train when working it in the opposite direction. When propelling its train the engine was controlled by the driver who sat at controls in a cab in the leading coach. The fireman remained on the footplate to keep the engine at work. The motive for bringing in such working was not so much tidymindness but to reduce staffing, notably guards and porters.

'Motor-trains' were used by the LBSCR, but before World War I they did not generally feature on West Sussex branch trains, with the exception of the Monday morning service from Midhurst. From 1926, motor-train working was introduced, and included the use of Stroudley's 'D1' 0-4-2 tank engines. Some of this class were based at Fratton depot, near Portsmouth. In earlier days a trio of 'D1s' had worked from

Midhurst but then the town's locomotive shed lost its allocation and engines worked instead from Horsham or Fratton depots.[14] More economies were possible following closure of the Chichester-Midhurst line in 1935. The two engine sheds at Midhurst closed completely in 1937; thereafter the engines working the Petersfield trains were supplied from Guildford or Horsham, and in any case trains worked through to Pulborough. Throughout their history the Mid-Sussex branches were worked by smallish steam tank engines, and six-coupled goods tender or tank engines handled the branch goods trains.

To study the official records over the years of passenger and goods traffic handled at British railway stations reveals a similar pattern on the majority of lines. From the late 1920s an alarming drop in tickets sold at rural stations is all too clear, and local goods traffic similarly declines, often offset by still flourishing business at bigger stations or from customers' sidings. The onset of the Depression brought reduced business activity and less traffic, of course, but by the early 1930s road services, passenger and freight alike, were often more convenient and cheaper. The traffic was lost to road.

The lines serving West Sussex were no different. Probably the Chichester-Midhurst line had never really paid its way, but by the mid-1930s the Southern Railway decided that for the passenger service enough was enough. It ceased on and from 6 July 1935 when Cocking, Lavant and Singleton closed to passengers. The line's goods traffic continued much longer. Not that it was heavy. Based on the Railway's traffic records for 1938, one estimate is that the two regular goods trains that operated every week between Chichester and Midhurst each brought no more than six loaded wagons to the line's stations and collected five that had been loaded at Cocking, Singleton and Lavant.[15]

With the ending of the passenger service between Midhurst and Chichester the through trains from Pulborough were at last diverted to run to Petersfield. Other economies implemented by this time included the removal of passing loops at stations which also experienced staff reductions. Even so, in 1938 even at Midhurst only 5,618 tickets were issued and 10,660 collected. This suggests that on average each train collected just one passenger at the station and brought two people.[16]

Principal goods traffic from local stations comprised agricultural produce, household coal to local stations, the output from Nyewood brickworks at Rogate, sand from a quarry at Midhurst, sugar beet from stations including Fittleworth, and milk despatched by passenger train from several of the stations.

By the late 1930s, the Mid-Sussex line and its branches could be fairly described as a preserve of elderly locomotives, those that had been built before the Grouping of 1923 and the majority of which had entered service before the death of Queen Victoria. One reason was that the Southern Railway's latest types were banned from using the drawbridge at Ford over the River Arun; it was simply too weak to take heavy engines. The little ex-LBSCR 'D1' tank engines worked extensively on Mid-Sussex line stopping services operated by motor-trains, and these also ran to and from Midhurst. The engines were based on Horsham, and also worked from Littlehampton and Bognor. The branch goods trains were handled by larger ex-LBSCR tank engines such as class 'E5X'. To take an example, one of these set out from its home shed of Horsham at 3.35am with a goods for Midhurst, and during that day also visited Bognor and Brighton.[17]

Government financial assistance offered to the railway companies with the aim of reducing unemployment provided a spur to the scheme approved by the Southern Railway Board in July 1936 for third-rail direct current electrification of the Mid-Sussex lines: from Dorking North and Three Bridges to Horsham, and on to Arundel and Littlehampton, and from West Worthing to Havant, as well as the Bognor Regis branch. Electric trains began regular services as from 3 July 1938.

Apart from electrification, colour-light signalling was introduced on the Mid-Sussex line, platforms were lengthened at principal stations and Ford's drawbridge was replaced by a fixed span. The train service in the new timetable featured appreciably reduced journey times and was roughly doubled in volume as compared with steam operations. There were hourly fast trains between Victoria and Portsmouth Harbour and Bognor, supplemented by semi-fast and stopping trains along the length of the Mid-Sussex line.

Immediately before electrification, the branch passenger services in summer comprised six or seven through trains each way between Pulborough and Petersfield, taking at best 1¾ hours for the 20 miles; some had a layover at Midhurst. In addition, there were a couple of trains each way between Midhurst and Petersfield only. There were four or so Sunday trains each way between Petersfield and Pulborough.[18] With electrification of the Portsmouth Direct line in 1937 many through journeys between Waterloo and Midhurst now took a shade under 2 hours; much the same times were also possible to and from Victoria after the Mid-Sussex or, as it was known to the Southern Railway, the Portsmouth No 2 electrification.

The level of passenger service between Petersfield and Pulborough was adequate for a rural line, but clearly the ageing motor-trains were no longer attractive to the general traveller with their usual motive power of an ex-LSWR tank engine matched by contemporary coaches. They could not compare with recently-built electric trains. It was no real surprise when in late 1954 British Railways announced that the regular passenger service on the line would be withdrawn as from 7 February 1955; from this date all traffic ceased west of Midhurst.

Another rural line, the former LSWR Meon Valley line between Alton, Droxford and Fareham also lost its passenger service at the same time as the Petersfield-Pulborough line. To mark the end of both passenger services, an enthusiasts' train originating at London Waterloo worked the length of both on 6 February 1955. An occasional special passenger train appeared at Midhurst bringing ramblers or railway enthusiasts, but the final 'special' left on 18 October 1964.

Goods services continued to be offered on the Hardham Junction to Midhurst, Petersfield to Midhurst, and Midhurst and Chichester lines until after World War II. During the war services over the last-named line were disrupted because the tunnels on the line were used for the storage of naval

An account of the opening of the Mid-Sussex Railway from the *West Sussex Gazette* of 13 October 1859

The railway from Horsham to Pulborough and on to Petworth was opened on October 10, the first train carrying railway officials as well as porters, gatekeepers, and others who were deposited at their various posts with their wives, families, furniture and tools. Our reporter also travelled on this train and the following are extracts from his account.

The tract from Horsham to Pulborough is singularly wild, running through woods and barren land. We do not recollect seeing more than one or two houses above the common run of laborers' cottages on our way. The people, when they were seen, looked scared at the appearance of a steam engine, as also did the horses, beasts, turkeys, and other things which ran from us in great terror........

At Barn's Green the line crosses the highway on a level, and a gatekeeper and his wife and chattels were left here..... The gatekeeper was supplied with hammers axes, flags, fog signals, and a book of the rules.

The natives came out of their cottages as soon as they heard 'Puffing Billy' but they all seemed to keep a distance of 50 yards from the train, fearing that it might go off. It's always best to be on the safe side; for there's no knowing what may happen.

At Cray's Lane level crossing near Pulborough another gatekeeper and his wife and three or four children, with beds and bedsteads, and tables and chairs were taken out of the train. A neat cottage is built for their reception. It is the duty of the women to signal the trains, and the man usually works as a ganger on the line.

If the situation of the station at Petworth is not a very convenient one for the town, it certainly has the merit of being one of the most picturesque that we know on the Brighton line. The little station, which is built of polished deal, lies nestling under the hill in all pride of perfect security. Opposite the station and high on the hill is the house of the station master. From the town of Petworth to the station is a gradual slope of about two miles, close to the station is Coultershaw watermill.... Near to the station is building a new inn.... Mr Dempster's omnibus will run to meet all trains at, we suppose, the usual sixpenny fare. The station might, perhaps, have been in a more convenient spot for the inhabitants but this is no fault of the railway company.

25. *Electrification in progress at Pulborough in 1938. The live-rail is already in place. A former LBSCR 'I3' class 4-4-2T, No 2091, takes water during the station stop with its Bognor-Victoria train. Note the characteristic LBSCR running-in board with its serif lettering.*

ammunition trains. The first line to lose its goods trains did so by default. Through traffic between Midhurst and Chichester came to a premature end on 19 November 1951. Torrential rain had resulted in a swollen stream undermining a bridge north of Cocking. The bridge collapsed, leaving the rails to sag over an abyss. The crew of the approaching 9.30am daily goods train from Chichester saw the danger in time to jump clear, but their engine and some of the wagons went into the gap. They were recovered but the incident spelt the end for the line between Cocking and Singleton stations, both of which closed completely on 28 August 1953.

The remaining stub of the Chichester line lasted longer. Lavant station was chosen to be a railhead for all the sugar beet in West Sussex passing to rail and, to handle this traffic, in 1953 the north end of the platform was adapted as a loading area. A loop was put in so that engines could run round the wagons awaiting loading. The station continued to deal with general goods traffic until 1968; sugar beet movements ceased after the 1969 season.

There remained the goods service to Midhurst which travelled over the line from Hardham Junction. The signalling on this line was reduced to one only, this being Hardham Junction's fixed distant signal. Goods traffic was no longer handled at Fittleworth and at Selham stations after May 1963, but Petworth survived until 20 May 1966 when the last pieces of station furniture were loaded on to the final goods train to depart. Detonators were placed on the track and were set off to commemorate the end of railway services to the town.

One more development remained for the West Sussex rural lines. In 1972, gravel extraction was begun to the south-west of Lavant, planning consent having been given by the local authority on the condition that rail was used for conveyance of the gravel in block trains of modern high-capacity wagons to a washing and screening plant at Drayton. The rumble of the gravel trains through Chichester ceased in 1991, and the track between Fishbourne Crossing and Lavant was removed in 1993. There was still another hope for a reprieve. A railway preservation society was formed with the aim of reopening the line once more to Singleton but their project foundered in the face of local opposition. During 1994, West Sussex County Council purchased the trackbed between Chichester and Lavant and, with substantial funding from English Partnerships, a cycle/pedestrian path known as 'Centurion Way' has been created using the trackbed to provide a popular and delightful country walk.

What else? There was of course the Selsey Tramway which in later days was known as the West Sussex Railway. It had been able to retain traffic until the late 1920s when buses and lorries proved more attractive. By 1931, passenger receipts were down to an average of less than £1 daily;[19] even the introduction of petrol-engined railbuses using Ford and other petrol-engined road chassis adapted for rail use could not reduce costs to this level.

The company went into receivership later in 1931, and by November 1934 the service was reduced to a single, pitiful train daily. As always, there were glimmers of a rescue, particularly when the Southern Railway showed a brief interest in 1934. There were thoughts of using the right of way for an electrified branch line. The Southern was offered, but declined, the freehold of the line.[20] Before long, notices were posted at the line's stations that on 19 January 1935 all services would be suspended 'until further notice'. Five days later one of the locomotives was in steam for the last time, and then the line's assets and land were put up for sale. The equipment was auctioned but an order for abandonment of the line was never made.

Going off the rails

Chapter 3: Quiet days at Midhurst

26. *The road approach to the second LBSCR station at Midhurst.*

Philip Hounsham lived in Petworth and attended the Grammar School in Midhurst. For five years he travelled daily during term time on the railway from Petworth to Midhurst. This journey involved a cycle ride of nearly two miles from his home to the station at Petworth, a train journey lasting approximately 15 minutes and a walk of nearly a mile to the school. The whole journey was reversed in the afternoon when returning home.

After leaving school in 1941 Philip initially applied for a job with the Post Office, but heard nothing and so decided that he would try his luck with the railway. He was encouraged to do so by the thought of cheap and free travel facilities.

After acceptance for railway service, Philip was sent to Croydon for about eight weeks to attend the training school. But first he had to undergo a medical examination and most importantly an eye-test to ensure that he was not colour-blind. Anyone who suffered from colour-blindness would not be employed by a railway company.

Philip's stay at Croydon was more prolonged than originally envisaged. He caught chicken-pox and was away for four weeks. Philip seemed to get lost in the system until higher authority one day asked about his whereabouts and he was sent to Midhurst! In 1941 there was still work to be done at the station but Philip felt that the existing staff were not really pushed and he felt that he was something of a supernumerary.

Philip spent the mornings in the passenger station, and the afternoons in the goods shed. Things were so slow that he used to go home for lunch – all the way to Petworth. So two hours for lunch became the norm! He felt that the station master at Midhurst really did not know what to do with him. Nevertheless, he gained a sound basic training in railway accounting. Over the years this training stood him in good stead when it came to his employment in the railway industry.

The other staff at Midhurst allowed Philip to issue tickets, at first under supervision, but soon without someone looking over his shoulder. It wasn't very long before be learnt about a common fiddle practised by those booking clerks about to leave the railway, or to be moved away.

Older readers will probably remember the card tickets that were issued to passengers. Known as Edmondson card tickets, these were kept in vertical racks, with the lowest number at the bottom of the rack, and the highest number at the top. An opportunity was taken when a passenger wanted two tickets – probably first-class returns to a station some way away – and the booking clerk took the tickets from the top of the rack where their use would not be discovered for some time. The miscreant pocketed the money for the tickets sold.

After a few months Philip left Midhurst to work at his home station at Petworth, but later returned to Midhurst. Passenger traffic was fairly light, as indeed it was even in the 1930s. The exigencies of war had ensured that the freight traffic became heavy, especially when ammunition was stored in the area.

The Midhurst to Chichester line passed through three tunnels and during World War II they were used for storing wagons containing shells, land-mines and other items of ammunition, as described in Chapter 11. Every so often, these wagons had to be shunted out and sent off to the war zones. As far as Philip can recollect, Cocking Tunnel held about 100 wagons and was worked from the Midhurst end of the line. Control of the stored wagons was centred on Midhurst and in the morning the station received telephone-calls detailing the wagons to be moved out. Of course, new wagons would also be coming

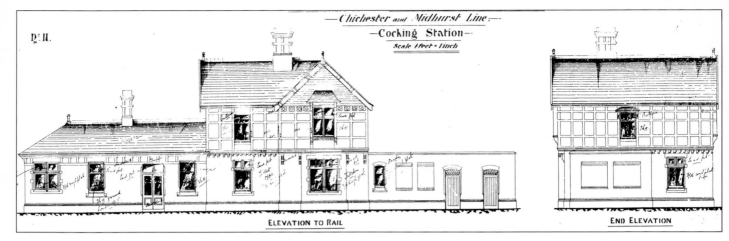

ELEVATION TO RAIL

END ELEVATION

for storage. There were three telephones at Midhurst station: two on the railway omnibus system, using a bell-code to contact the relevant location, and the third was linked to the national system.

Cocking goods yard was small and on most occasions all the wagons had to be brought down to Midhurst to be sorted. An additional problem was that when the wind blew it swept across both ends of the tunnel and smoke from the engine remained in the bore. Then working conditions became extremely unpleasant. The shunters hated the task and swore volubly. Completion of the shunt frequently lasted a long time and often the men who had started early in the morning did not finish until 8pm. The engine crews

worked down from Horsham and greatly disliked the long turns of duty.

Singleton Tunnel was worked from the Chichester end of the line with the engine coming from Fratton. The yard at Singleton was much larger – a legacy from the days when special trains used to arrive for the racing at Goodwood – so all the shunting could be done 'on site' without taking wagons to Midhurst.

Philip recalls that when he worked at Midhurst he was only able to start after the arrival of the first train in the morning, which left Petworth at 8.10am. His leaving time was 5pm. The early and late duties were covered by the two porters.

In February 1943, Philip received his call-up papers. He told the station master

27. Above: *The LBSCR Chief Engineer's drawings of the railway side elevation and end elevation of Cocking station - an imposing structure for so small a station.*

28. Right: *The old Post Office and omnibus and town bus office adjacent to the Omnibus & Horses public-house in Midhurst. The photograph is dated 1910.*

29. Below right: *A two-coach motor-train waiting at Midhurst in the 1950s.*

30. Below: *Extract from the Ordnance Survey map of 1913 illustrating well the isolation of the second LBSCR station, and the scarcely more convenient LSWR station.*

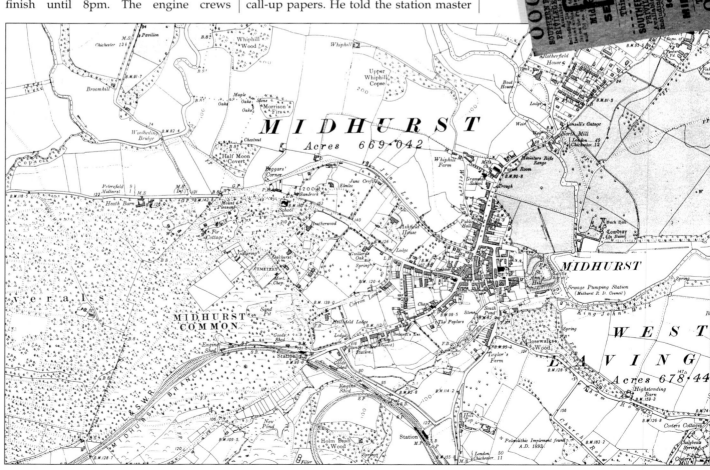

31. *In BR days, a former LBSCR 'D3' 0-4-4T No 32364 heads out of Elsted, bound for Midhurst and Pulborough.*

that he would be leaving in ten days' time. The response was 'that Philip couldn't do that'. On telephoning the area office at Redhill, he soon learnt that Philip 'could' and had to go for war service.

I well remember my one and only trip over the line in 1955. The date was 3 February, shortly before the closure of the passenger service between Pulborough and Petersfield. At that time living in Rottingdean, near Brighton, I commenced the journey by good old Southern Electric, first to Littlehampton and then on via the Mid-Sussex line to Pulborough. The train to Petersfield was hauled by former London & South Western Railway 'M7' 0-4-4T No 30028 and the intention was to travel through to Rogate – even though I knew that the service was so limited that there might not be a return train.

The station nameboard at Rogate announced that this was 'Rogate for Harting'. It was somewhat of a culture-shock to an impressionable teenager to catch the voice of the porter announcing the station's name in stentorian tones in full. Try it for yourself to appreciate what I thought had been said!

To continue with the story of my trip, the gods must have been smiling as a pick-up goods was running from Petersfield to Midhurst shortly after the departure of the service train. The kindly porter/booking clerk made arrangements for me to travel in the brake van of the freight back to Midhurst, which was hauled by former London Brighton & South Coast Railway 'E4' 0-6-2T No 32469.

The trip back to Pulborough was completed in a passenger train hauled by another 'M7' tank engine, No 30049, and the day's travelling concluded with journeys by electric train, to Littlehampton and then to Brighton.

At the time steam engines were still being constructed at Brighton Works and many of the services on the secondary lines from Brighton and Horsham were worked by these magnificent beasts. On every journey that I made to and from Brighton, I was certain to be rewarded with sightings of numerous steam engines.

The depot at Brighton then housed around 50 locomotives at this time and there were smaller sheds at Horsham, Three Bridges, Littlehampton and Bognor Regis. The importance of the last two named had declined with the late 1930s' electrification of the lines along the South Coast. Ironically, the shed building at Littlehampton is the only one still in existence, although not in railway use.

32. *'E4' 0-6-2T No 32520 nears Petworth with the daily branch goods on 5 February 1955.*

Going off the rails

Chapter 4: Wartime wagons at Petworth

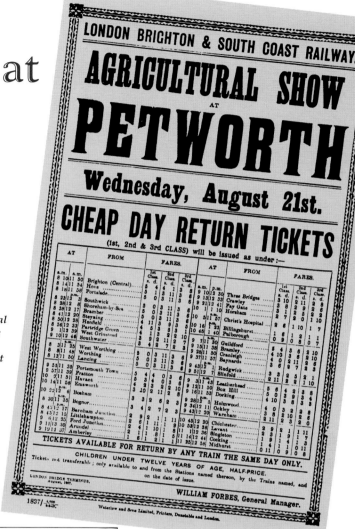

The opening of the line from Pulborough through Amberley and Arundel, for many years referred to as the 'Mid-Sussex Line' but more recently named the 'Arun Valley line', probably instigated the decline of the original line through the sleepy Rother Valley villages and towns. In any case, partly as a consequence of the influence of Lord Leconfield whose estate was centred on Petworth, the railway line was constructed out of sight of the stately home, and almost two miles south of the town itself.

33. Cheap Day Return tickets were issued in connection with special events, in this case the agricultural show at Petworth on 21 August 1907.

34. Left: The first station at Petworth which served until c 1890. This view dates from 1889.

35. Below left: The LBSCR named locomotives after the towns and villages served by the Company. This is the 2-2-2 express locomotive No 334 Petworth, built in 1881 and taken out of service in 1908.

In 1871 the population of Petworth numbered 3,368, while Fittleworth boasted 695 inhabitants. The figures for 1951 are not directly comparable as the districts listed in the census returns differ from those of the 19th century. However, the population of Petworth Rural District in 1951 was recorded as 9,190. Bearing in mind that a larger area was included to that of the earlier census, this was hardly a dramatic increase in numbers.[1]

In expectation of expanding traffic, Petworth was provided not only with a spacious station building but a goods yard and goods shed, as well as a signalbox and initially a small locomotive shed. No photographs appear to have been taken of the locomotive shed and few records refer to

36./37. *Two views of the second Petworth station, photographed in 1892 by Walter Kervis:*

36. **Top:** *The road approach.*

37. **Above:** *Track gangers at work, watched by some of the station staff.*

38. **Left:** *Porter White of Petworth, in August 1895.*

the line and again at the top of the cutting. At the far end of the yard there was another wooden-built cottage which could only be reached by walking along the line. It is thought that this cottage was for the use of the locomotive department.

Although the line was closed to all traffic as long ago as 20 May 1966, somewhat surprisingly the station building and most of the railway houses survive to this day. The terrace of three wooden cottages collapsed in 1943 as a consequence of the blast from a bomb exploding nearby. Fortunately, none of the occupiers was at home at the time.

It is not known when the other wooden cottage was demolished. It was certainly

occupied during World War II, by a lady known as 'Granny' Smith, presumably the widow of a railway employee. Philip Hounsham, who worked at Petworth, says that he inspected the property after the war and found the rooms to be relatively spacious with large windows similar to those in the station building. In common with the other railway houses, the cottage lacked an electricity supply and mains drainage. Apparently, the wooden cottages had a water supply.

One of the earliest recollections of life at Petworth concerns the engine shed. On the evening of 21 October 1879, LBSCR engine No 79 – a Sharp Brothers Single, built in 1847 – was left in the shed. At about 3am next morning its fire was lit. A couple of hours later, while being polished-up by a cleaner, the engine suddenly moved away out of the yard and on to the line towards Horsham. For nearly 17½ miles it ran on its own, crashing through three sets of level crossing gates, and only being stopped by an engine cleaner going on duty at Horsham shed. He had realised that something was wrong on noticing debris from level crossing gates adorning the engine's front buffer beam. Fortunately, the runaway was slowed on a rising gradient and the cleaner was able to climb on to the footplate and bring No 79 to a halt. He was deservedly rewarded by immediate promotion to fireman, and a gratuity of £3.[2]

Born in Petworth, from 1937 Philip Hounsham regularly travelled by train to Midhurst to attend the town's Grammar School. He usually cycled the two miles to the station, left his bike at the *Railway Inn*

it. In addition, the area around the station was blessed with a detached house located at the top of the cutting above the station and originally intended for the station master, two pairs of brick-built cottages on the other side of the drive leading to the station, and three small wooden-built terraced cottages set almost at right-angles to

– nowadays called *The Racehorse* – and caught the 8.28am train to Midhurst. In winter the train was often delayed by the late running of electric trains serving Pulborough, as the service to Midhurst was an advertised connection.

Philip's journeys to and from Midhurst continued during term-time until the middle of 1941. At that time, pupils came to the school from as far away as Billingshurst, and changing trains at Pulborough in wintertime was most unpleasant when cold winds swept across the platforms.

In 1941 Philip left school and joined the railway. After initial training, and a spell at Midhurst related in Chapter 3, he returned to Petworth to work as the junior. At that time, the staff consisted of a clerk, two signalmen and a porter/signalman. All of these employees lived in one or other of the railway cottages dotted around the station. As at that time there were nine different houses, five of these must have been occupied by retired railway employees.

Apparently, one of the clerks at Petworth was suffering from ill-health and it

39. *Until the 1960s the railways contracted to move the stock and equipment of farms from one part of the country to another. This picture of Petworth dated 1932 shows one such farm removal train that has arrived from a station served by the Great Western Railway.*

was decided that Philip would be better employed there than at Midhurst, particularly as he lived in the town. The booking office had a mahogany counter and, unusually for a station of that size, two ticket windows, with the ticket cabinet – minus doors – set in-between. There was the usual ticket date-punch and the date had to be changed at the beginning of each day. This could be a messy job: ink from the tape easily transferred to fingers and was sticky. The tickets issued at Petworth were of the standard Edmondson card type, pre-printed to a limited number of destinations. Tickets issued for destinations away from the local stations used a blank pre-printed with Petworth, and the clerk filled-in the destination in ink. Most of the older generation of clerks had excellent handwriting – an essential skill, as day-books had to be kept to record ticket sales. In addition, the dockets for the goods wagons, the entries in the parcels book and virtually every other record of the day's work had to be handwritten meticulously.

A virtue of those days, regrettably no longer available, was the ability to issue tickets to any railway destination in the country. That was possible because each station had a fares directory which quoted the fares to every station in the land.

The booking office contained a selection of stools – for use at the ticket windows – a massive table and some chairs to match. The mahogany counter was set atop a selection of cupboards – some with drawers – all useful for storing the multitude of forms necessary for the day to day running of the station. Returns had to be

Goods traffic in Petworth station goods yard:

40. **Above left:** *Loading sugar beet.*

41. **Left:** *Unloading coal from a railway wagon into one of Sadler's lorries. Note the goods shed in the background.*

made to the central office of the railway of all transactions carried out at the station. The weekly returns – 'Yellow' forms – were made out in Indian ink and copied into a tissue book with the aid of a press.

In the yard was a small goods shed with a crane and another hand crane was provided in the yard. There was also a weighbridge for wagons, and a loading dock for horseboxes. For many years the regular goods traffic to Petworth included wagons of coal for the gasworks, the laundry and *The Swan* public-house. Coal usually arrived in three 10-ton wagons every seven to ten days and was transported to its final destinations by a small fleet of lorries operated by Sadler & Sons. Eric Sadler recalls arriving at the station at 4am in the morning, to work solidly until lunchtime emptying the coal from the three railway wagons on to the lorry. Using a No 8 shovel it was shovelled loose and never bagged! Eric always took three five-gallon drums brimful of water to lay the dust as the lumps of coal easily broke-up.

The 10-ton rail wagons suffered both heavy usage and rough treatment. Their bodies were built mainly of timber, and the planks forming the bottom of the wagon were often damaged. They should have been repaired by taking out the broken planks but, more often than not, and partly a result of wartime shortages, another piece of timber was simply nailed across the broken section. The jarring shock received from pushing the shovel-blade was not easily forgotten! Eric's remedy was to have a heavy sledgehammer with him. On finding a wagon 'repaired' in this way, he would knock out the offending piece of wood and have the wagon taken out of use until it was properly repaired.

Another regular traffic flow into the goods yard was that of wagons loaded with wheat for the nearby mill. Before the war, the miller had ordered what he wanted when he wanted it, but wartime rationing meant that sometimes the wheat ration arrived loaded in eight or as many as ten wagons. They could not be cleared readily and in any case the miller did not have sufficient storage space.

Petworth's goods yard was only able to hold about 20 wagons. The problem was compounded when the yard was full because its layout meant that not every wagon could be reached for unloading. Then there was the carriage of horses, which meant that the dock had to be kept

clear. Brood mares from the various stables in the area were conveyed in horseboxes – another traffic no longer carried on rail.

During the early part of 1942, the problem was made worse by the arrival at Petworth of wagons full of rubble which had been cleared from bomb-sites in the London area. It was consigned to Petworth for use in the construction of army camps in Petworth Park, to provide hardcore for the camp road foundations, and for the solid floors of some of the camp buildings. The wagons' contents were emptied into army lorries by a sapper platoon. It was reckoned to be hard work and sometimes it was said that the rubble was not exactly clean. The reader must deduce what that meant!

Not long after his transfer to Petworth, Philip Hounsham recounts that the clerk went sick for a lengthy period and the authorities decided that the station should not be left in charge of a 17-year old. A more senior clerk was sent along but he had to travel every day and soon realised that 'he wasn't that necessary'. Before long, he used whatever train suited him and left the running of the station once more to Philip who didn't mind. Indeed he revelled in his task, doing everything and knowing how to do everything.

One of the wooden cottages at Petworth station was occupied by Harry Greenfield, whose wife May was Dick Millington's aunt. Today Dick draws a cartoon which appears every day in the

Daily Mail. But in the dark years of the war Dick was a young lad who lived in Dagenham – not one of the safest places to be. After a somewhat disastrous stay in another part of the country, he was evacuated to his aunt and uncle in the station cottage which he had visited in the years before the war.

The cottage had no electricity, illumination being that provided by oil-lamps. Dick has no difficulty recalling the distinctive and all-pervading smell of oil burning on the lamp wicks. He is adamant that the long winter nights with very little to occupy a young lad's mind started him on his career as he spent much of his time drawing by the light of an oil-lamp.

Dick also recalls the Home Guard exercising in the station yard. Many of the railway staff, including Dick's Uncle Harry, were in the Home Guard. Just as depicted in *Dad's Army* on television there were no rifles and the platoon paraded with broomsticks or odd pieces of wood. Dick himself used to march up and down behind the men carrying a wooden toy rifle and wearing an imitation tin-helmet.

After the wagonloads of rubble ceased to arrive at Petworth with completion of the camps, the troops started to arrive. Their trains were much longer than those usually seen on the branch and had to draw up three or four times at the short platforms to discharge the soldiers, who lined-up in the station yard before marching off the two or so miles to the camps. To

42. *Dick Millington portrays himself as a small boy marching behind a Home Guard platoon in Petworth station yard.*

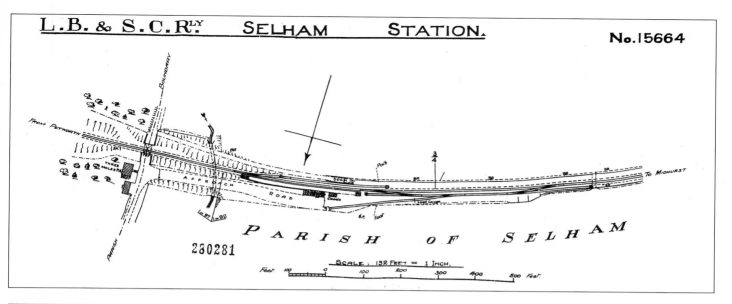

someone of Dick's young age the engines hauling these troop trains appeared massive and he says that they might even have been 'Merchant Navy' class locomotives. Wishful thinking perhaps!

Dick doesn't remember the army camps themselves but, on his many walks through the woods to the south of the line, recalls seeing tanks, army lorries and guns stored there, all camouflaged with sacking and branches. His impression was that the whole area was a target for the German bombers, a feeling strengthened by the earlier related collapse of the wooden cottages – in one of which Dick's uncle and aunt lived – following blast from a bomb dropped nearby.

Some of Dick's other memories of those dark times concern the town of Petworth rather than the railway. He recalls the time he went into the town centre one day and saw a sign which read 'No Ice Creams for the duration'. On another visit

he saw a smashed-up pub. This was when French Canadian soldiers were billeted in the area. Henceforth they were banned from visiting any pub in the locality.

Another of Dick's memories concerning the town centre was a Messerschmitt fighter plane – presumably one that had been shot down – on display outside the cinema, with posters urging everybody to give to the war effort. Although it was not the case this time, apparently it was the practice to buy savings stamps and stick them on bombs and planes and thus the money raised would help to purchase more ammunition and planes.

Dick lived with Uncle and Aunt at the railway cottage for about a year. As the Greenfield family grew up the cottage became crowded and so Dick moved out to live in Barlavington Manor. During his sojourn in Petworth he attended Duncton School and his first day there was somewhat of a surprise for the first lesson was

43. Top: *The LBSCR track plan for Selham.*

44. Above: *A Petersfield-Pulborough train hauled by an 'M7' 0-4-4T leaving Selham.*

knitting – which to a boy from Dagenham was something of a culture-shock!

However, he still came down regularly to the railway station and helped his aunt with some of the day-to-day tasks. One of these was to keep the family chickens off the railway lines when a train approached. Actually, the sound of the engine coming down the line usually did a better job than Dick could; they scattered in all directions! When the family took a trip to Midhurst or Pulborough, Aunty May would invariably still be doing the washing-up when the train arrived. She used to call out 'hold on Charlie, the washing-up is still to be done'.

Philip Hounsham remembers that one of the gangers, Bert Cole, lived in one of the wooden cottages. The third one was

empty for a while until one of the staff from the Surveyor's office in London evacuated himself to Petworth and lived there until the cottages collapsed.

The next station up the line towards Midhurst – Selham – was much used by Richard Comber in the period from 1926 until just after the war. Richard farmed Moorland Farm at Ambersham. He well remembers driving sheep and cattle along the roads for about two miles to the station – not something that could be done with safety today. In those days virtually every station had a loading dock with two or three pens on it for keeping the cattle or sheep secure before loading into cattle wagons. Again the carriage of livestock is no longer catered for on today's railway.

Grain was also taken out by rail and in the early days it was moved to Selham station by horse-drawn trailer, and later on by tractor and trailer. One of the slogans commonly seen on posters during those dark times was 'Dig for Victory'. During World War II sugar beet was an important commodity to be moved by rail as imports of sugar cane were extremely restricted. The Sugar Beet Corporation sent huge consignments of sugar beet grown in West Sussex to processing plants in East Anglia. Richard Comber does not recall paying for the wagons and thinks that they were provided by the Sugar Corporation, and paid for at the destination. He clearly remembers that he was paid by weight – so much per ton – so obviously the wagons had to be weighed once they had been loaded.

Another of Richard's memories is that of hard-pressed engine crews passing along the section of line that ran close to Ambersham Common, throwing out hot clinker and regularly setting light to surrounding vegetation.

After a period of disuse and dereliction, the station buildings at Petworth have been lovingly restored and, as well as being the private residence of owners Mike and Mary Rapley, provide bed and breakfast accommodation. It is still possible to gain some impression of the little community that once served the railway. The station master's house stands sentinel on the bank above the station and the two pairs of brick-built cottages on the other side of the station drive are private residences. All the buildings have electric light and running water, luxuries unavailable when Dick Millington spent his schooldays in wartime Petworth.

45. Petworth station today, converted for residential use.

Going off the rails

LONDON BRIGHTON AND SOUTH COAST RAILWAY.
PULBOROUGH, MIDHURST & CHICHESTER LINE.
OPENING OF FITTLEWORTH STATION.

On and from Monday, September 2nd, 1889,
A
NEW STATION at FITTLEWORTH

MIDWAY BETWEEN PULBOROUGH AND PETWORTH,
WILL BE OPENED FOR
PASSENGER TRAFFIC

And Trains will call there as shown below :—

To CHICHESTER.			WEEK DAYS.							SUNDAYS.		
	A.M.	A.M.	A.M.	P.M.	P.M.	P.M.	P.M.	P.M.		A.M.	P.M.	P.M.
PULBOROUGH .... dep.	...	8 15	10 28	12 20	1 35	3 50	5 35	6 56	...	9 6	9 27	8 43
Fittleworth .... ,,	...	8 21	10 34	12 26	1 41	3 56	5 41	7 2	...	9 12	9 33	8 49
Petworth .... ,,	...	8 26	10 39	12 31	1 46	4 1	5 46	7 7	...	9 17	9 38	8 54
Selham .... ,,	...	8 33	10 46	12 38	1 54	4 9	5 54	7 15	...	9 25	9 44	9 2
Midhurst .... arr.	...	8 41	10 54	12 46	2 2	4 18	6 3	7 24	...	9 34	9 55	9 11
,, ... dep.	7 5	8 48	10 55	1 10		4 32	6 25		7 42	...	9 57	3 30	9 13
Cocking .... ,,	7 11	8 54	11 1	1 16		4 36	6 31		7 48	...	10 3	3 36	9 19
Singleton .... ,,	7 19	9 2	11 9	1 24		4 46	6 39		7 56	...	10 11	3 44	9 27
Lavant .... ,,	7 27	9 10	11 16	1 32		4 54	6 47		8 4	...	10 19	3 52	9 35
CHICHESTER .... arr.	7 36	9 19	11 25	1 41		5 3	6 56		8 13	...	10 28	4 1	9 41

From CHICHESTER.			WEEK DAYS.							SUNDAYS.		
	A.M.	A.M.	A.M.	P.M.	P.M.	P.M.	P.M.	P.M.		A.M.	P.M.	P.M.
CHICHESTER .... dep.	...	8 16	10 10	12 20	2 10	4 0	...	5 25	7 10	8 25	...	11 15	4 55	10 15
Lavant .... ,,	...	8 24	10 18	12 28	2 18	4 8	...	5 33	7 18	8 33	...	11 23	5 3	10 23
Singleton .... ,,	...	8 32	10 28	12 36	2 26	4 16	...	5 41	7 26	8 41	...	11 31	5 11	10 31
Cocking .... ,,	...	8 40	10 34	12 44	2 34	4 24	...	5 49	7 34	8 49	...	11 39	5 19	10 39
Midhurst .... arr.	...	8 47	10 41	12 51	2 41	4 31	...	5 56	7 41	8 56	...	11 46	5 26	10 46
,, ... dep.	7 35	9 15	11 30	12 58	2 50			4 45	6 12	7 52	...	7 0	5 30	...
Selham .... ,,	7 43	9 23	11 37	1 6	2 58			4 53	6 20	8 0	...	7 8	5 38	...
Petworth .... ,,	7 52	9 32	11 46	1 15	3 7			5 2	6 29	8 9	...	7 17	5 47	...
Fittleworth .... ,,	7 57	9 36	11 51	1 20	3 12			5 7	6 34	8 14	...	7 22	5 52	...
PULBOROUGH .... arr.	8 4	9 43	11 58	1 27	3 19			5 14	6 41	8 21	...	7 29	5 59	...

ALL TRAINS FIRST, SECOND AND THIRD CLASS.

Fares between Fittleworth and the undermentioned places.

	SINGLE TICKETS. ORDINARY.			RETURN TICKETS. ORDINARY.		
	1st	2nd	3rd	1st	2nd	3rd
	s. d.	s. d.	s. [d.	s. d.	s. d.	s. d.
Pulborough	0 6	0 4	0 2½	0 10	0 7	0 5
Petworth	0 6	0 4	0 2½	0 10	0 7	0 5
Selham	1 0	0 8	0 5	1 8	1 3	0 10
Midhurst	1 5	1 2	0 8½	2 10	2 2	1 6
Cocking	2 1	1 6	0 11	3 3	2 6	1 9
Singleton	2 8	1 11	1 2	4 3	3 6	2 3
Lavant	3 3	2 4	1 5	5 8	4 3	2 9
Chichester	3 11	2 10	1 7½	6 10	5 2	3 3

POSTAL TELEGRAPHS.—By appointment of the Postmaster-General, Fittleworth will be appointed a Postal Telegraph Station for the receipt and despatch of Telegrams to and from all parts.

London Bridge Terminus, August, 1889.   (By Order)   A. SARLE, Secretary and General Manager.

2,000—30-8-89.   Waterlow and Sons Limited, Printers, London Wall, London.

46. LBSCR notice announcing the opening of Fittleworth station for passenger traffic.

Back down the line at Fittleworth, the little country station which was in a dilapidated condition for a good number of years has been rebuilt as a private residence and although not original looks very much as it did in former years – without the canopy. This station was rather nearer the village it served than most on the line – ½mile, in fact.

Internally, the building is now arranged in keeping with present-day domestic requirements. Interestingly, the design of the buildings is the same as that used by the LBSCR for the station at Willingdon, near Eastbourne. Indeed, the original architect's drawings – beautifully coloured – were captioned Willingdon and Fittleworth. In sharp contrast, Willingdon remains open to this day and since 1903 has been known as Hampden Park, the first station outside of Eastbourne.

When the railway reached Petworth in 1859, Fittleworth was ignored and villagers had to join the railway at Pulborough on the Mid-Sussex line. However, with the extension of the railway from Petworth to Midhurst where passengers could transfer to the LSWR for the journey to Petersfield, demands began to be made for a 'Fittleworth' station.

A deputation of traders and residents, represented by Sir John Walter Barttelot, MP, was in 1888 successful in persuading the directors of the LBSCR to obtain an estimate of the cost of a station both for passengers and goods. In due course, a tender of £1,067 was accepted from a Richard Cook and work was commenced.[1]

The station buildings were constructed entirely of timber and there was a small wooden goods shed with a sliding door. The goods was also equipped with a horse and carriage dock. Living accommodation was eventually provided with the erection of two cottages by the LBSCR on the approach road to the station.[2]

On 30 August 1889, an inspection of the new station was carried out by General Hutchinson of the Board of Trade. His report read:

I have inspected the new station at Fittleworth between Pulborough and Petworth stations on the Pulborough and Midhurst (single-line) Branch of the London, Brighton and South Coast Railway, This new station has been provided with the necessary accommodation. The points and signals are worked from a new raised cabin containing 15 levers of which three are not in use. Clocks are not yet put up either on the platform or in the signal cabin but this is to be done before the station is brought into use.

Subject to this being done I can, as the arrangements are otherwise satisfactory, recommend the Board of Trade to sanction the use of this new station.[3]

47. Fittleworth village, photographed from Lea Hill, 1908.

The station opened for passenger traffic on Sunday, 1 September 1889, but 14 months were to pass before the Fittleworth was officially open on Monday, 3 November for goods and mineral traffic.

During the early years the train services remained unchanged. Holiday times saw augmented services bringing flurries of trains to this 'anglers' paradise'. 'Such was its reputation that the LBSCR saw fit to bestow upon Fittleworth its very own 'Anglers' Special' which ran on Sunday only, for which cheap tickets were made available. Goods traffic was mainly local agricultural produce while nearby was Maxey's fruit farm renowned for producing the best English Cox apples'. [4]

The beauty of the area with leafy winding lanes, picture postcard cottages and wooded hillsides, together with its remoteness and solitude provided the ideal refuge for one of this country's most brilliant composers, Sir Edward Elgar.

Edward Elgar was born in 1857. His father owned a music shop in Worcester and yet before taking up a musical career he was employed in a lawyer's office. However, the call of music became irresistible and he went to London to study the violin. On completion of his studies he initially earned his living as a violin teacher while composing such works as *The Serenade for Strings*. However, the turning-point in his musical career as a composer came with *The Enigma Variations* which were an immense success when the piece was performed in London in 1899. There was immediate musical recognition of his talents, including those earlier works which had hitherto been disregarded. Other famous compositions followed including the famous *Pomp and Circumstance* marches, the *Violin Concerto*, *Second Symphony*, *Coronation Ode* and many more. In 1904 he received a knighthood.

In 1917, now aged 60, Elgar was living in London with his wife, Caroline Alice, who was some eight years older. He was weary and troubled by ill-health. In low spirits and depressed at the suffering of his fellow men during the Great War, he had written very little music while in London and was in need of the stimulus of the English countryside which would also provide the seclusion he desperately craved.

Elgar's devoted wife provided the solution – 'Brinkwells', an isolated thatched cottage, situated two miles north of Fittleworth, deep in wooded bluebell

48. *Sir Edward Elgar, c 1920.*

country. On an early visit with her daughter the area had a profound effect upon her as shown by the entry in her diary.

'Carice and I had a lovely walk from Fittleworth station through woods and by primroses. It was a hot, hot day and we sat in the wood and heard a nightingale, turtle doves, saw lizards and heard the cuckoo. I was much perplexed as the cottage is so primitive, but there is a large detached studio surrounded by woods and a lovely view to Chanctonbury Ring'. [5]

Elgar was enchanted with 'Brinkwells' which was so isolated that he had to draw a map to guide his close friends to find the cottage. He exclaimed 'It's too lovely for words.' [6] 'From the cottage garden the view extended uninterrupted towards the graceful line of the South Downs, with not another dwelling in sight. In fact, the only probable evidence of humanity, looking across the carpet of treetops in the valley, would be the white wisps of steam as the branch trains drifted in and out of Fittleworth station'. [7] In May 1918, Elgar took up residence at 'Brinkwells'.

The Sussex countryside provided Elgar with that vital change. He loved the countryside and found immense pleasure in country walks.

Of his pattern of life while in Sussex he wrote 'I rise about seven – work till 8.15 – then dress. Breakfast – pipe (I smoke all day!) work till 12.30: lunch (pipe) – rest an hour – work till tea (pipe) – then work till 7.30 – change – dinner at 8. bed at 10 – every day practically goes thus – of course instead of work, which means carpenting of the roughest kind, sawing wood, repairing furniture etc. and weeding, we go on lovely walks.....' [8]

At 'Brinkwells' Elgar led the rural life. The family travelled locally by pony and trap or horse, much loaned by a neighbouring farmer, Mr Aylwin, for whom Elgar had high regard. Mr Aylwin collected most of the visitors to 'Brinkwells' from Fittleworth station, otherwise they would not have found this idyllic hideaway. 'The end of July found Elgar cleaning out the studio, whitewashing it, building steps to its door and clearing out its view through the wild garden to see over the Downs to Chanctonbury Ring. [9]

In August, the piano arrived via the railway on Mr Aylwin's wagon. Refreshed by the country air and sounds, Elgar resumed his music. His wife recorded 'He has been playing some lovely tunes – such a joy to hear again.' [10] New compositions followed, with his wife recording in her diary. 'E. writing wonderful new music, different from anything else of his. A. calls it wood magic, So elusive & delicate.' [11]

It *was* 'wood magic' and became a *Sonata for Piano and Violin in E minor*. This was followed by a piano quintet and part of his outstanding *Cello Concerto*. But this period was destined to be shortlived for

49. *Fittleworth station, looking east in the days before World War I.*

Going off the rails

50. *Soon after the opening of Fittleworth station, the station staff including station master pose for the cameraman.*

Lady Elgar passed away in April 1920. Waves of despair overcame him as he wrote 'Music I loathe....The old life is over & everything seems blotted out.' [12] Nevertheless, he was still enchanted with the cottage and stayed frequently during 1920 and the following year.

Elgar endeavoured to stay at 'Brinkwells' but the artist Rex Vicant Cole and his wife, the owners of the lease, wished to return there. [13] Before he left he wrote 'I feel like these woods all aglow. A spark would start a flame – but no human spark comes.' [14] After a final fortnight at the cottage during August 1921, Elgar caught the train from Fittleworth station for the very last time.

We have some idea of the routine of a country station such as Fittleworth at the time Elgar was living nearby. Some years ago, two railwayman, Jack Tulett and F. Osborne, reminisced about their time at the station.

Mr Osborne worked at Fittleworth during World War I.

On 9 November 1917, I was given a pass and sent to the Stores Dept at New Cross, to be fitted out with my new uniform, and the following day I started work as a porter at Fittleworth station, taking the place of the porter who had been called up for National Service.

There were two of us, the other one who was to knock me into shape was a retired policeman, and he did his best to do so, as if I did not do things correctly he had to get it right. We worked alternate shifts, 6.15am to 5.15pm and 2pm to 10pm but each time I was on the late turn each Wednesday I did not get away until

after midnight, as the goods train from Midhurst to Horsham had been retimed. Apart from working in the goods yard, we cleaned lamps and windows in the station building, and scrubbed floors.

We also had to deliver parcels within an area of one mile of the station. This was done by the late turn man, but it was suggested that I should do it each day, and on my way call in at home and have my lunch before getting back to work in the goods yard. The woods around were being cleared of the big trees whose timber was used for duck boards and shoring-up the trenches or for sleepers for use on the Army railways in France. These were brought to the station. We had to secure these loads with ropes and ensure that the loaded wagons were within the railway loading gauge.[15]

Mr Osborne also had to attend to signal-lamps. 'We had to go out to the signals at Fittleworth and bring in the signal-lamps (to the station), clean them and take them out again. They were supposed to burn for an hour in the lamp-room before being replaced in the signals in order to avoid failures. One one occasion I was replacing a lamp, and there was a strong wind. I had to remove my jacket and wrap it around the lamp to keep it alight. I had almost reached the top of the post when a fierce gust blew me off. The signal was on top of a bank and I fell 30ft.....I lay gasping for breath for at least 10 minutes before I could move......I took the lamp back to the lamp-room, refilled it and replaced the broken glass, went out and put it in the signal.' [16]

Mr Tulett was also employed at Fittleworth during World War I, but had much to say of interest regarding station work in later days.

When the eight-hour day came in – in 1919 – the numbers employed at the station went up to six, with an additional porter and clerk. The station was busy in those early days before the internal combustion engine had really made its mark. What always seemed to me a turning-point was the General Strike of 1926. Fittleworth station was moving 1,000 gallons of milk a day, with 18 different milk carts coming in night and morning. The strike forced the farmers to look for alternative methods of transport and with motorised transport becoming more efficient they found they could take the milk direct to the big depots, cutting out the railway as an unnecessary middleman.

Loading the milk churns would take six minutes. There wasn't a special milk train and passengers just had to be patient. Selham loaded even more than we did and the churns of course made a rare old din. You had to work hard on the loading – if six minutes was the time allotted for it and it took seven, then this would go into the guard's notebook. Delays, however small, at each station could make a big difference by the end of the journey.

All sorts of goods came in and out of Fittleworth goods yard: two coun-

51. *Fittleworth station taken from the overbridge of the B2138 road from Fittleworth. Calling at the station is a Petersfield-Pulborough train of the 1950s, for which just a single coach is sufficient.*

cil traction engines would draw road-stone from the pits at Flexham or by the Cottage Hospital and bring it out to the railway. My job in the goods yard wasn't basically to load, more to ensure that the loads were correct for travelling. I did however usually help with the wheat sacks, each one weighing 2 cwt 1 qtr 4 lbs. Hay and straw were packed already bundled; animals also were conveyed by train in a special kind of truck, and somewhat later apples from the Little Bognor orchards.

Fertiliser and sugar beet were important items for us and there was a lot of parcel traffic then. There was no delivery from Fittleworth station but people came and collected them. They were usually marked, 'To be called for by Mr..... 's milk-cart'. It was a useful sideline for the farmers who would otherwise be returning home with an empty cart. When Gray and Rowsell began dealing in motorcycles and cycles their stock would come down to Fittleworth by rail. Even if you were working in the goods yard you had to attend every passenger train, dealing with luggage and railway parcels. You might have to run a hundred yards to attend a train if one caught you unawares.

There was no signalbox as such at Fittleworth but only a 'shunting cabin'. The cabin could give signals but it could not control trains. It was really only a safeguard for the goods yard. If a train was coming from Pet-worth to Pulborough the box could work the points so that the train would not go straight into the goods yard. The shunting box was replaced in 1931 with a ground frame which was unlocked by the single line token carried between Hardham Junction and Petworth. Before a train could leave Hardham Junction, Petworth signalbox had to hold down an electric lever to release the 'staff' at Hardham.

In the aftermath of the General Strike and the switch to road transport the station staff began to dwindle..... by 1933 the staff was reduced to myself only. Probably if all the different jobs had been put on to me at once I would have given up in despair, but after all I had got used to most of the jobs over the years. I had had to be clerk, porter and general cleaner (the station's oil-lamps had to be kept clean and filled).

There was a lot of paper-work too – for instance, you had to calculate the oil so that the lamps burned no more in the current month than they had burned in the corresponding month the previous year. Or you might have to work out and write down the precise shunting time for each wagon. I now did all the monthly returns, for goods, excess fares and parcels among other things. When I had a holiday a relief man came up.

In the early days there had been three goods trains a day; one early in the morning, one at midday and one in the later afternoon. There were 18 passenger trains, nine each way. I remember the hikers' special train that used to run between the wars. Hikers could get off at Fittleworth and walk over to Amberley or alight at Amberley and catch the train back at Fittleworth. I went on at Fittleworth until it closed in 1963. It was part of the Beeching rationalisation but the closure came as no surprise. The station had been put forward for closure long before Beeching.[17]

52. *Fittleworth's station building today, converted for residential use.*

Chapter 6: Aristocracy at Arundel Station

53. *Ford station in Victorian days.*

Arundel was originally served by the station at Ford – which upon its opening had been named Arundel. This point was reached on 16 March 1846, the line being extended westwards to Chichester on 8 June 1846. The station at Ford lies about 1¾ miles south of Arundel town centre, and the road connecting them was constructed by the railway company, and a toll was charged for its use. Eventually, on 31 December 1938, the road was transferred to West Sussex County Council and the toll charge ceased. Nevertheless, the LBSCR and its successor the Southern Railway must have collected a goodly sum of money over the intervening 92 years.

Almost from the opening of the railway there was a signalbox at Ford, so it was not too costly to provide staff to collect the tolls. Just to the east of the station the line crosses the River Arun and for many years the bridge carried only a single line of rails. In addition, the river was navigable as far as Arundel and so the railway company had to provide a drawbridge to allow the sailing vessels of the time access upstream to wharves adjacent to the town. Although the bridge was reconstructed to take double track in 1862 it was not rebuilt as a fixed link until 1938.

The line through the Arun gap was completed on 3 August 1863, and, although the new station at Arundel was nearer to the town, it was still over ½mile from the town centre. Indeed, being set to the east of the river it was actually in the parish of Lyminster, rather than Arundel.

The land used for the construction of the railway was sold by the Duke of Norfolk on condition that all London trains stopped at the station. An opulent private waiting-room was provided for use by the family but is no longer used. As well as the up and down platforms, a bay platform was provided on the down side. This was used principally by a shuttle service which connected Littlehampton with the fast trains to and from London but ceased to be used as recently as 1972.

A goods shed and a reasonably commodious goods yard were provided at Arundel, a facility which contributed to the decline of the town as a port. Early photographs show a large variety of wagons and vans in the yard – not all owned by the railway companies – several being private owners' wagons. The goods yard eventually closed in September 1963 and its site taken over by the station car park. The goods shed still stands and is used by a builder's merchant.

Because of its association with the Dukes of Norfolk, Arundel station was the scene of many a notable occasion in earlier

54. *Paying the toll at Ford station to use the private road to Arundel. The road was transferred to the West Sussex County Council on the last day of 1938.*

55. Above: *Henry, 15th Duke of Norfolk, about to leave Arundel station with his bride, Gwendoline Mary on 2 February 1904.*

56. Below: *Arundel Castle dominates the background in a picture primarily showing Arundel's goods yard in late Victorian days.*

years. One of the most glittering took place on 2 February 1904 when Henry, the 15th Duke of Norfolk, brought home his bride, Gwendoline Mary, eldest daughter of Marmaduke 11th Baron Herries of Terregles, following their marriage at Brompton Oratory in London. Since 1897 the castle grounds have regularly hosted cricket matches. Before the onset of private motoring, such gatherings brought many a distinguished personage to the station, en route to and from the castle.

The line through Arundel was electrified in 1938 and at that time the Southern Railway replaced the original LBSCR signalbox with a modern brick-built structure. These signalboxes with flat roofs came to be known as 'Odeon' style.

Now living in retirement at Ferring, Robert White worked for long periods in the signalboxes both at Ford and Arundel.[1] He joined the railway as a junior porter at Norbury on 16 October 1928 at the age of 15½. After holding a number of positions elsewhere, Bob moved in 1939 to Arundel where he was put in charge of livestock on foot. In those days cattle were regularly moved on foot to and from stations, each of which had a cattle loading dock with pens.

Going off the rails

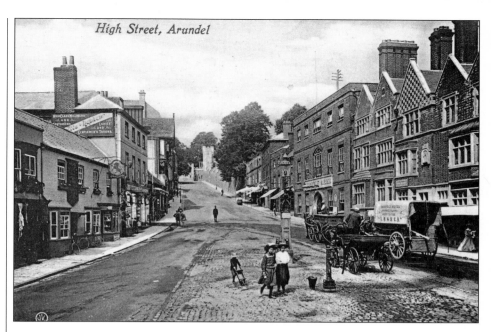

He was soon on the move again, and in 1948 took charge of his first signalbox – Goring-by-Sea. Eventually, Bob transferred to Ford as signalman in August 1954 and stayed there until August 1970. Ford had, and indeed retains, a level crossing, which in earlier days was protected by gates rather than the barriers which are common today. He recalls that the gate wheel required 22 turns of the wheel either to open or close the gates. On an average eight-hour shift Bob calculated that the wheel usually turned through 3,000 revolutions. The gates at Ford were very heavy!

Signalmen usually worked one of three eight-hour shifts: from 6am to 2pm, 2pm to 10pm, and 10pm to 6am. If the box was open for 24 hours continuously at weekends it was normal to work a 12-hour shift, so that the turns of duty could be rotated.

As far as Bob can recollect, the mechanical lever-frame in Ford signalbox had 52 levers, including the locking levers for the crossing gates and the wickets – the small gates to allow the passage of people. In addition to the usual block instruments there were 11 or so repeaters, these being the dials that indicate the display of signals.

Incidents that stand out in Bob's memories of his stay at Ford include the occasion when he looked out of the signalbox windows only to see that at the far end of the station a small boy was dragging a tricycle across the lines – including the live-rails! Bob can only think that the boy avoided electrocution because he was wearing rubber boots and the trike had rubber tyres.

In January 1955, the embankment adjacent to the abutments of the bridge over the River Arun caught fire and Bob had all trains stopped so that the fire brigade could extinguish the flames. He was subsequently ordered to attend an enquiry and reprimanded for causing delays to the train service. But what would it have cost British Railways had the fire got out of control and severely damaged the bridge?

One freezing winter a seal swam up the river and stayed for some time in the vicinity of the bridge. One day a group of fisherman went down to the river to have a day's

60. *Arundel station in LBSCR days showing an 'I3' 4-4-2T working a London Bridge-Portsmouth train.*

fishing. Soon two of the men came back and Bob heard one say to the other that he was going to fetch a gun and shoot the seal. The fisherman felt that the presence of the seal meant that they would not make a catch. Fortunately, the seal disappeared and fishing proceeded without hindrance.

In April 1971, Bob moved to Arundel signalbox. He remembers getting into trouble with authority when the 6.55am up service from Bognor Regis was running 20 minutes late and Control ordered him to tell the driver to miss all stops to Horsham to recover the lost time. Bob felt that the regular passengers who travelled to such destinations as Pulborough and Billingshurst to get to work would be even further delayed and omitted to pass Control's instructions to the driver.

During Bob's stint at Arundel, the box had a 48-lever frame with Tyer's block instruments. The bay platform remained in use on the down side of the station, and a crossover from down to up line south of the station. This box is still there although no longer with a lever-frame; nowadays a panel controls the signals.

Bob has one other recollection of his time

at Arundel. After closure of the airfield at Ford – formerly used by the Royal Navy – the open prison was constructed on part of the site. Visitors to the prison frequently travelled by train to Arundel on their way to the prison. On one occasion, a group of ladies returning to London and other points north crowded out the platform and booking hall of the station. At this point, the then Duke of Norfolk, Bernard, and his Duchess, Lavinia, arrived at Ford station to travel to London. The special waiting-room for use of the Duke had long since closed. Observing the crowded platform and booking hall, His Grace decided that he and the Duchess would adjourn to the ladies waiting-room. Shortly afterwards, one of the other travellers decided to make use of the amenities next to the ladies waiting room. Very soon she shot out of the waiting room, exclaiming to the effect that 'there was a b........strange gent in the ladies!'

The South Down Hunt used to meet at Arundel station, the horses, hounds and

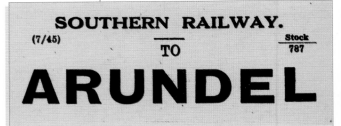

huntsmen congregating in the station drive before setting out for a day's hunting. Those were the days when road traffic was light enough for the hunt to trot safely along the main roads. It wouldn't be possible today!

As mentioned in Chapter 1, the gateway to the Mid-Sussex Line was and remains Horsham. The original part of the line reached Petworth, and the route down through the Arun Gap to Arundel and Ford followed four years later. Two other lines – one to Guildford and the other to Brighton through Steyning and Shoreham – branched off the Mid-Sussex line at the picturesquely named Itchingfield Junction, south of Christ's Hospital. It was at Christ's Hospital that a large station was opened on 28 April 1902.

Once boasting five platforms – one of which was an island – the station was built in an otherwise rural location two or so miles south-west of Horsham in order to serve the relocated Christ's Hospital School. Founded by King Edward VI the school dates back to 1554 and was established on the site of the former Grey Friars in Newgate Street, London.

Rollo Denys Lempriere started school at Christ's Hospital in January 1916, and recalls that at the beginning and the end of each term the LBSCR put on a special train to convey the boys to and from Clapham Junction and Victoria. Rollo recalls that the fare was 2/6. He lived in Chichester, so his journeys to and from school were in the other direction. During his time at the school steam still ruled the railways, and in their spare time many of the boys watched the passing trains with their magnificent locomotives and some of the best services sported Pullman cars.[2]

61. *Pupils joining a train at Christ's Hospital station.*

Chapter 7: Racehorses, sugar-beet and rifle-butts –
memories of the Chichester-Midhurst line

On 27 April 1865 the *West Sussex Gazette* reported: 'Until lately Midhurst has always been supposed to be ten miles from everywhere. It is pretty much so now, as persons residing on the coast of Sussex know. But this state of things is no longer to exist. The hitherto benighted town.... is to have its railway running to all points of the compass. It has already a line running to Petersfield on the west; it has a line in progress..... running on the east to Petworth; it has now commenced a line to the north and south' when on Saturday last the first sod was turned by Lord Henry Lennox, MP for Chichester.

So began the works of the Chichester to Midhurst Railway Company, but misfortunes overtook the project and it was not until the LBSCR revived the scheme under an Act of 13 July 1876 that the works which had come to a standstill in the early 1870s were recommenced. In early years, the LBSCR had not been very enthusiastic about the project.

62. Cutting of first sod of the Chichester-Midhurst line.

Twelve miles in length and single throughout, the line was opened on 11 July 1881 and served the villages of Lavant, Singleton and Cocking. Before opening it had been announced that the stations would be at Lavant, West Dean and Cocking, but West Dean was named Singleton; to this day that remains a mystery to the people of the village of Singleton who remember the long walk to West Dean to collect goods from the station. It is interesting that all the station plaques had been carved with the date, 1880, so it seems that the opening date was delayed.

The *West Sussex Gazette* of 14 July 1881 stated 'Mr Ellcombe's omnibus which has for many years plied between Midhurst and Chichester ran for the last time on Saturday. It has been a good public servant, but it has now given way – as many buses and stage-coaches have previously – before the onward march of King Steam. On Monday, the new railway, which has for several years been in the course of construction between the two towns was opened for traffic, and the journey by rail, which formerly occupied nearly three hours when travellers had to go either via Pulborough, or Petersfield, can now be accomplished in forty minutes.'

The first train was drawn by a Craven

*63. The locomotive **Fred**, a Manning Wardle 0-4-0ST used by T. Oliver of Horsham, the contractor building the line. The location is Singleton, c 1880.*

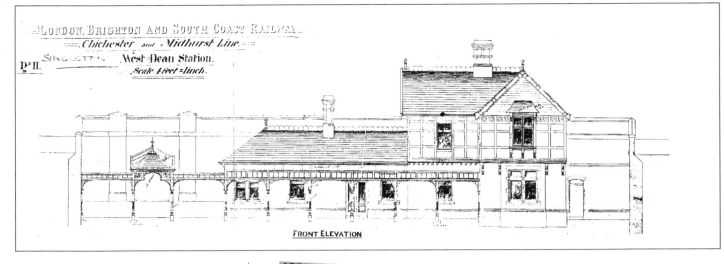

London, Brighton and South Coast Railway
Chichester and Midhurst Line.
Singleton. **West Dean Station.**
Pl. II. *Scale 1 foot = 1 inch.*

FRONT ELEVATION

64. Above: *The LBSCR engineer's drawing for the front - road - elevation of Singleton station building, dated April 1880. Note that the station was originally referred to as West Dean, but on opening it was known as Singleton.*

65. Right: *The official LBSCR opening notice for the line.*

2-2-2 engine by the name of *Egmont* and was decorated with a wreath of flowers. There were 57 passengers for the first train but this number was exceeded on subsequent trains throughout the day. It was a great relief to the directors that the line had been opened, as it had become the most expensive branch line the Brighton Company was to own.

In his book *The Country Railway* David St John Thomas gave the average building costs for a branch line ten miles in length to be between £12-15,000 a mile provided there were no major engineering works[1]. The £25,000 a mile costs of the Chichester to Midhurst line were probably due to the three tunnels on the line, namely West Dean, Singleton and Cocking. The grandeur of the mock timber-framed country stations with moulded stucco panels also contributed to the high cost of the line. No wonder Samuel Laing said at a Special General Meeting of the LBSCR on 30 May 1881: 'I am sure as far as I and my brother directors are concerned we heartily hope that we never may have a new line again.'[2]

When opened, there were seven trains each way on weekdays, some running through to and from Pulborough. On Sundays the line was closed. Just six months later, 'the working timetable for January 1882 indicated four trains each way with goods traffic for Singleton from Midhurst, Selham or Petworth

---

London Brighton and South Coast Railway.

OPENING OF THE Chichester & Midhurst LINE

ON MONDAY, 11th JULY, 1881.

The above New Line will be opened for Passenger Traffic on and from Monday, 11th July, 1881, and Trains will run as under between

Pulborough and Chichester.

TO CHICHESTER.

	WEEK DAYS										SUNDAYS					
	a.m.	a.m.	a.m.	p.m.	p.m.	p.m.	p.m.	p.m.	p.m.	p.m.	a.m.	a.m.	a.m.	p.m.	p.m.	p.m.
PULBOROUGH dep.	...	8 22	10 25	...	1 50	3 50	5 35	7 1	9 7		...	9 15	10 15	...	...	8 43
PETWORTH "	...	8 32	10 35	...	2 0	4 0	5 45	7 11	9 17		...	9 25	10 25	...	...	8 53
SELHAM "	...	8 41	10 44	...	2 9	4 9	5 54	7 20	9 26		...	9 34	10 34	...	...	9 2
MIDHURST "	7 0	8 50	10 53	1 42	2 18	4 18	6 3	7 29	9 35		6 5	9 43	10 43	3 30	6 50	9 11
COCKING "	7 10	9 2	11 4	1 52		4 30		8 1			6 13	9 55		3 38	6 58	9 21
SINGLETON "	7 21	9 13	11 15	2 3		4 41		8 12			6 24	10 6		3 49	7 9	9 32
LAVANT "	7 30	9 22	11 24	2 12		4 50		8 21			6 35	10 17		4 0	7 20	9 43
CHICHESTER arr.	7 41	9 33	11 35	2 23		5 1		8 32			6 46	10 31		4 11	7 31	9 55

FROM CHICHESTER.

	WEEK DAYS										SUNDAYS					
	a.m.	a.m.	a.m.	p.m.	p.m.	p.m.	p.m.	p.m.	p.m.	p.m.	a.m.	a.m.	a.m.	p.m.	p.m.	p.m.
CHICHESTER dep.	...	8 10	10 53	12 55	...	2 45	...	7 9	8 40		...	7 40	11 5	4 47	7 45	10 25
LAVANT "	...	8 20	11 3	1 5	...	2 55	...	7 19	8 50		...	7 50	11 15	4 55	7 55	10 35
SINGLETON "	...	8 31	11 14	1 16	...	3 6	...	7 30	9 1		...	8 1	11 26	5 8	8 8	10 46
COCKING "	...	8 42	11 27	1 27	...	3 17	...	7 41	9 12		...	8 12	11 37	5 19	8 19	10 57
MIDHURST "	6 52	8 51	11 36	1 36	2 42	3 26	4 47	6 12	7 50	9 21	7 0	8 21	11 46	5 28	8 26	11 6
SELHAM "	7 0	9 3	11 44		2 50		4 55	6 20	8 0			5 38				
PETWORTH "	7 9	9 14	11 55		2 59		5 46	6 28	8 0		7 8	8 31		5 45		
PULBOROUGH arr.	7 20	9 27	12 6		3 10		5 15	6 40	8 20		7 28	8 51		5 57		

ALL TRAINS FIRST, SECOND AND THIRD CLASS.

London Bridge Terminus,
8th July, 1881.

(By Order)

J. P. KNIGHT,
General Manager.

(5,000-8-7-81.)

Waterlow and Sons Limited, Printers, London Wall, London.

66. *This photograph of the cutting leading to the southern portal of Singleton Tunnel was taken on completion of the line.*

and vice versa worked by passenger trains up to a maximum of ten trucks per train.' [3]

One notable train service using the line was the London train. It left Brighton at 6.25am and arrived in Chichester at 7.40am. Departing from there at 8.40 am, it then called at Lavant, Cocking, Singleton, Midhurst and went round on to the Petworth line to stop at virtually every station, via Dorking and Mitcham Junction until it reached Victoria at 11.36am – a journey of 101 miles. The same train then departed at 12.40pm for the return to Brighton over the same 37 mile route to Horsham, but then took the line via Steyning to Brighton – a total of 165 miles for the crew.[4] A through London service continued until 1928.

Although it fulfilled the aims as contained in the prospectus allowing 'Chichester and Midhurst to sustain their important agricultural and mercantile connection and....develop a large trade in timber chalk, lime, bricks, tiles',[5] the line never attracted the numbers of passengers expected of it. As with many country railways it seemed not to be built for the convenience of its passengers.

On many country branches railway companies attempted to save money by building lines over the most accessible route rather than taking the line nearer to the larger villages. Sometimes two villages were served by a joint station convenient for neither. Although the stations on the Chichester-Midhurst line were better located than most, it still possessed its oddities, of which one was Midhurst station.

Before the line was completed from Petworth there were problems with the route from a highly influential section of society. The *West Sussex Gazette* reported on 24 March 1859 of 'objections having been raised by six landlords, led by the Earl of Egmont, of Cowdray Park, who complained that the line would be visible from his dining-room, drawing-room and bedrooms....... Whatever may be the conclusion – and it seems pretty certain that a railway will now be made – one cannot grieve at the result of opposition to the line. To meet the whim of one or two individuals, the line is to make a deviation of some two and a half miles, thus imposing on the present inhabitants of Midhurst and posterity an inconvenience and tax, of which they can never be relieved..... In three instances we have seen this narrow policy pursued in West Sussex. At Arundel the station is pushed three miles from the town (at Lyminster); at Petworth, a similar inconvenience will be felt; and now Midhurst is to be visited with a like infliction. And all this simply to gratify the peculiar prejudices of one or two great land owners of the old school, who have not yet learnt to adopt modern improvements.'[6] Undeterred by bad publicity, the land owners had their way and the railway was removed out of their sight.

Coming in from Petersfield in the west, the London & South Western Railway reached Midhurst in 1864. 'The two antiquated towns have at length shaken hands and connected themselves with a link of their own, and have thus opened up a communication by steam with the south and south west of England'.[7]

Two years later the Petworth to Midhurst line reached the town. Reported in the *West Sussex Gazette* as 'Wonders will never cease – The Petworth and Midhurst Railway, alias "Death's Line", was opened on Monday last. This project has been so long in hand that we began to despair of seeing it fully carried out during the present generation.'[8] It had taken seven years to complete the railway, 5¾ miles long from Petworth to Midhurst.

However, this meant that the small market town of Midhurst had two railway stations. A weak bridge in the rail connection which had been built between the two stations in 1866 ensured that through trains were not possible. A passenger wishing to travel throughout the Mid-Sussex line had to disembark with all his or her luggage, have it reloaded on to the train at the next station and find a seat. This was probably quite acceptable on a warm sunny day, but in the depths of winter it was hardly an entertaining prospect for the passengers.

While the distance between the two original Midhurst stations was an irritating inconvenience, when the line was opened from Chichester the LBSCR relo-

67. *A 1920s' view looking west of the 1880 LBSCR station at Midhurst, taken from near the tunnel-mouth. The wagons seen are in the siding serving Hall & Co's sand-pit.*

cated its station ¼mile east of its predecessor. This was the last straw and passengers complained bitterly to West Sussex County Council. At its quarterly meeting in July 1890 the Council agreed to form a Committee to report on the matter.[9]

Accordingly, the Midhurst Railway Committee decided that passengers were entitled to have use of the two railways at Midhurst as a continuous route and recommended that the sum of £400 would be sufficient for the cost of any legal proceedings before the Railway Commissioners.

Before a hearing was arranged, the Railway Committee endeavoured to find an amicable solution to the problem. February 1891 saw the Committee reporting to the County Council that the traffic managers of the respective companies had expressed a desire to remedy the inconvenience.[10] Subsequent negotiations moved apace with the Railway Committee nearly obtaining the agreement of the railways that the LSWR would have running powers over the LBSCR with entry into Brighton station, thereby creating the need for only one station at Midhurst, accordingly providing a through service.[11]

Unfortunately, the two railway companies could not agree and proposed an alternative that they should construct a footpath between the two stations. This fell short of the County Council's condi-

tions and a hearing was obtained before the Railway Commissioners who decided that a covered way should be provided between the two stations. Even though the County Council did not achieve its objectives, at a meeting on 24 November 1893 it approved the conversion of the footpath into a carriage road 25ft wide and that arrangements be made by the companies 'that passengers from either station to the other should, if they desired, be carried at a charge not exceeding 3d each and that passengers luggage should be carried free of charge.'

This ridiculous state of affairs was not addressed until the two companies were absorbed into the Southern Railway which in 1925 replaced the Bepton Road bridge and closed the former LSWR station. The LBSCR locomotive shed at Midhurst was also closed soon after the railway Grouping in 1923, when Horsham

shed assumed working for the Pulborough to Petersfield section of the line. Before closure, Stroudley 'Terriers' No 41 *Tulsehill* and No 77 *Wonersh* were familiar engines at Midhurst shed. They were in turn replaced by 'D1' class 0-4-2 tanks.

Many railway companies would also build country stations to a grander standard and scale than their customers justified. This is perhaps true of Singleton although royal patronage of this station and the anticipated lucrative traffic on Goodwood race days probably influenced the plans for this station. However, even during race meetings, the traffic never reached the anticipated numbers.

Nevertheless, Goodwood Races required special arrangements which Frederick Osborne, now aged 95, well remembers. At 15 years of age he was working at Fittleworth station as a porter towards the end of World War I.

68. Right: *LBSCR 'A' 0-6-0T No 77* Wonersh, *an engine once allocated to Midhurst shed.*

69. Below: *The road approach to Singleton station, at the time of opening.*

Going off the rails

70. **Above:** *Looking north at Singleton station, soon after opening. The goods shed appears in the distance. The station building appears to the right of the picture.*

71. **Right:** *The royal box in Goodwood's grandstand, showing Edward VII in 1903.*

Frederick Osborne recalls:

Each week a special notice booklet was sent out to all concerned, giving notice of speed restrictions, engineers' work, invalid passengers requiring special attention and parties needing special reservations.

When we received the weekly notice I saw my name posted to Singleton for Goodwood Races from Monday to Saturday. A passenger coach was to be stabled in a siding to provide sleeping accommodation for all the extra staff, but as I had a cousin living at Charlton I stayed overnight with him.

On the Monday morning all appointed staff arrived and it was decided that Percy Drew, a relief signalman, being senior in grade should act as foreman. Horseboxes began to arrive which were shunted into the loading bays. The grooms and stable boys travelled with the horses and the boxes had a separate compartment from which they could feed the horses, up to three in each horsebox. Each horse was separated from the other by a padded partition and many of these horseboxes were privately owned and carried the owner's name.

In the bay the doors were opened and the horses led out. The railwaymen then had to clean out the vehicles ready for the return journey. On arrival of the train, one stable-lad had slipped over to the buffet for a drink of lemonade. The trainer subsequently arrived only

to observe his absence and in time to see the stable-lad returning with his bottle of lemonade. The trainer's language was terrible! Although the special horsebox train had come from Newmarket and the lad was incredibly thirsty there was no excuse for leaving his horse unattended.

My duties were in the station washroom and lavatories on the lower level by the road. There were three or four washbasins in the middle with a long row of toilets on either side. There were also clothes-brushes for a quick brush-down if required, and I had to give each person a clean towel and charge them 2d. I stood clear of the basins with the towels.

When the racegoers returned you could hardly move. I tried to give each person a towel but they were packed like sardines and passed the towels on from one to the other, and handed me the money with the comment 'OK, son, keep the change'. After the rush a railway detective came in and I explained the situation. 'That's OK, lad', he said. 'Pay in 2d

for every dirty towel and have the remainder.'

On another occasion, when a special train had arrived full to capacity there was the usual rush to leave the station. The railway detectives stood at the top of the platform steps which led down to the subway to the station exit when they saw a gang of people pressing close to the racegoers, reaching over their shoulders, and taking their wallets from their inside jacket pockets. With the mass of people the detectives could not stop the pickpockets' activities for there was a quarter of a mile to get to the front of the station via the platform and the goods yard.

There were a lot of travellers with vehicles of all kinds, including flat tops with orange boxes for seats, waiting outside the station for the passengers to emerge from the subway. Fares started at £1 right up to the course, then another would say 15/- whereupon the price would drop to 5/-. Right up to the course in fact meant as far as the Lodge Gates.

A number of the railway staff

72. **Above:** *Goodwood racecourse in 1904.*

73. **Left:** *Road traffic including charabancs at the Railway Inn, Petworth during Goodwood Week, 1925.*

liked to bet and when unloading the horses wanted to know their names. There was always a slack time when the races were being run, provided the horseboxes had been cleaned out, and it was agreed that one of the porters should go up to the course and place all the bets.

On this particular occasion the porter collected the money and slips of the bets and went off to the racecourse. Upon his return he was a very rejected man – and without any winnings.

While crowding round the bookies a man pressed against him holding a rather large banknote and asked him if he would be kind enough to change it for him so he would be able to place a small bet. The porter obliged and held out his hand for the note, whereupon the man denied he had received any change. A heated argument ensued, as a result of which the con-man won and the porter came away dejected. Fortunately, we had agreed early on that any tips received would be shared by all and that Percy Drew would take charge of the money. I

became the hero for without the money from the towels there would have been very little money to share.

Mr Osborne also recollected that towards the end of race week there would be a special train of horseboxes to Newmarket. Having loaded the horses the train was ready to leave behind one of the LBSCR's 'Vulcan' 0-6-0 goods engines. The climb out of Singleton into the tunnel towards Midhurst was steep and everyone watched the train, wondering whether it would make the grade. Gradually, it picked up speed and they returned to their normal duties.

Going off the rails

Vic Clayton of Chichester was born at Singleton in a now demolished cottage next to the *Horse and Groom* public house. As a young lad during Goodwood Week he used to sit on the bridge at Singleton taking the car numbers: they amounted only to a dozen each day. The races brought in much business to the small surrounding villages. His mother boarded a couple of gentlemen racegoers with the result that he was turned out of his own bedroom. Upon their return from the races his mother gave them dinner which they would eat in the front room after which one would sing while the other would accompany him on the piano.

Vic also remembered the delivery of horses which were walked from the station up the road to Singleton and then via Summersdean Bottom to the stables. On one occasion when the horses were being loaded for the return journey a horse slipped between the horsebox and the 'four-foot' (the railway track) and everyone including the police had to be called to help to extract the stricken creature.

Mike Cruttenden of The Brighton Circle records that as early as World War I passenger traffic on the Chichester-Midhurst line was declining. On short-haul journeys especially it was being challenged by the newfangled motorbuses. These demonstrated their superior flexi-

bility as compared with the train, and an ability to undertake longer journeys inland including cross-country runs.

The railway company fought back by introducing a railmotor train which was successful, both in reducing operating costs and at least for a time by regaining some of the passengers lost to road. Following their success along the coast lines, railmotor trains were introduced on inland and cross-country services. Unfortunately, they could not compete on fares as the buses were generally cheaper, a major factor for country people whose wages were usually lower than those of townfolk. The buses offered comfort with good springing and pneumatic tyres, making journeys more pleasurable; moreover they went from where people lived to where they wanted to go.[12]

In 1925, the Government hardly helped to maintain railway passenger traffic with the announcement that, as part of a package of measures to relieve rising unemployment, it would agree to fund the sealing of all country roads. For a couple of years the railway benefited from increased mineral traffic as supplies were brought in to carry out the work. But the improved roads enabled the buses to provide an even speedier service and a smoother ride. They proceeded to take from the railway whatever short-distance passenger traffic still remained.[13]

74. A record of the mishap that occurred just beyond Park Lane underbridge near Cocking on 9 September 1904. LBSCR 'D' class 0-4-2T No 239 **Patcham** *derailed when working a Midhurst to Singleton goods. Here breakdown cranes are being used to lift the engine. To the left of the picture is the damaged brake van from* **Patcham's** *train.*

Even after World War I when the Goodwood Races were revived, the more affluent now came by car and others arrived by motorbus or charabanc. Passenger traffic dwindled on the Chichester-Midhurst line, eventually to such an extent that passenger services were withdrawn on 6 July 1935.

No formal public announcement was made and the *West Sussex Gazette* on 23 May 1935 conveyed the news: 'After our official denial of any local official knowledge of the closing of the passenger line from Midhurst to Chichester ... came "the bomb" (from HQ on Thursday) in the shape of the official summer timetable, which shows that no passenger trains will run to Chichester after July 6. The Chichester service has never been very good, but to close the line entirely is a serious decision, especially in view of the fact that there are about 40 season ticket-holders including pupils of Chichester High School and Midhurst Grammar School. Their tickets do not expire until near the end of July.'

75. *The penultimate train of the Pulborough-Midhurst-Chichester passenger service arrives at Midhurst on 5 July 1935. One coach only, hauled by an ex-LBSCR 'D1' 0-4-2T.*

There was little public reaction to the cessation of the five trains each way daily excluding Sundays, save from a letter addressed by 'A Shareholder' to the Editor of the *West Sussex Gazette* who complained about the lack of effort of the Southern Railway to increase traffic[14]. It seemed fitting that the then retired George Batchelor, fireman of the first train in 1881, was also on its last train 54 years later on the Saturday the line closed to passenger traffic.[15]

One minor fear – or pleasure – was lost with the ending of the passenger service. Former passengers vividly recall the passage of Cocking Tunnel. John Ainsworth lived at Midhurst and visited his grandmother in Chichester. For him the return journey was associated with anxiety as the train gathered speed downhill through the tunnel, accompanied by a whistling sound that affected his ears. Yet for Mildred Duncton the passage through all three tunnels on the line was the highlight and the most thrilling part of the journey!

Without passenger traffic there was little need for staff at the stations along the line. By the late 1930s only a junior porter was employed at each of the line's stations, even at Singleton which saw considerable timber and sugar beet traffic.

Phil Norrell of Singleton joined the railway in September 1938. He took over from Vic Clayton's brother-in-law as junior porter at Singleton under the control of the station master at Midhurst, a Mr Chave. By this time the activities of the station had changed considerably. The horsebox specials had long gone and the station was a shadow of its former grandeur.

There was just one goods train a day which arrived at 10am and shunted off and attached the return empty wagons. There was a limited amount of box traffic and articles under 5 cwt were unloaded on to the platform and put into store until collected. Phil Norrell then helped the guard shunt the train, afterwards carrying out the limited office work. His 8am to 5pm working day with an hour for lunch could hardly be called hectic.

Household coal was one of the staple traffics handled at the station, and was consigned to the two main coal merchants, E. Whitney & Sons from Charlton, and T. W. Kennet & Sons from East Dean. At this time in the late 1930s the main traffic was timber, delivered from the Charlton sawmill of J. H. & F. W. Green which had been established a few years earlier and had purchased all the beech trees in the forest. The firm would despatch planks by the wagonload and a considerable quantity of round timber was also loaded at Singleton.

Located on the Midhurst side, the station crane was used for loading small round

76. *Cocking station, looking north in the days when the signalbox was in use. Economies introduced in the early 1930s included closure of the signalbox and subsequent downgrading of the station to an unstaffed halt.*

Going off the rails

timber while on the Chichester side a long length of line was used by a mobile crane for loading long timber of larch and fir trees. A gang of railwaymen from Brighton would come to load the round timber, and Phil Norrell would help them with calculations as to cubic capacity for completion of the invoicing and booking. To transport large timber, arrangements would have to be made for bogie bolster wagons to be made available. Sometimes they had to be requested by a telephoned stock return to Chichester, two days in advance.

Singleton was busy with seasonal sugar beet traffic. By the late 1930s milk traffic had ceased to be transported by rail although there were numerous diary herds in the area.

The station's two signalboxes, North and South, had gone by this time and train working was carried out using staffs. Lavant and Singleton had pillars into which a staff could be inserted. The staff was a release key for the token. Once this had been engaged a train would be allowed access to the sidings and this prevented any other train from entering the line as it did not possess the signalling release staff.

The onset of World War II considerably changed the use being made of the line. Let Vic Clayton once more take up the story. He took over at Singleton in 1942 when Phil Norrell joined the RAF. Vic had known the station from an early age as his brother-in-law had worked there and taken him on unofficial shoots along the cutting towards Singleton Tunnel. His brother-in-law liked driving the locomotives. He would shoot a couple of pheasants to give to the driver the next day in return for driving his engine. Not only would he drive the train but would carry out shunting that particular morning.

Even though the Singleton and Cocking Tunnels were blocked by the ammunition trains during World War II, a daily goods train continued to run. Timber traffic increased as Green's sawmills was producing rifle-butts from beech, steam-dried at the mill and coated in wax. Three or four times a day Bill Treagust would come to the station with a tractor and trailer loaded with rifle-butts. Four wagons were loaded and tarpaulined-up, ready for despatch the next day.

With the demise of the passenger service, parcel traffic was handled at Chichester and parcels for Singleton were sent on the goods train. Once a week the little

77. Above: *Vic Clayton and Phil Norrell today, at Singleton station building.*

78. Right: *Dereliction at Singleton, looking north.*

shop called 'The Forge' at West Dean had a delivery by the goods train marked 'Carriage Paid Home'. Whoever delivered such goods received a fee for delivery. Vic Clayton used to look forward to the train bringing the box of cakes destined for 'The Forge' because, during his lunch-hour, upon their arrival by the daily goods he would take the cakes down to the shop, and at the end of the month make out a form for the delivery of the cakes. He also supplemented his income by deliveries to the grocers at Singleton, and by taking other items to 'The Forge'. The only other way was to wire the shop to request collection or to persuade the milkman or postman to take the item down.

So Vic's typical day at Singleton was to arrive at 7.30am, light the fire in the office, and get ready for the 10 o'clock goods. This required writing out the labels for the wagons loaded the previous day, with goods such as pit-props, rifle butts and charcoal.

Because of the considerable tonnage of sugar beet handled at Singleton, special trains of up to 60 wagons were organised and despatched. As soon as the goods train arrived, the number of wagons would be entered in a log and this information would be phoned to head office with a request for any wagons needed.

Such was the routine, Mondays to Fridays, the official hours being 8 – 5 with no work on Saturdays.

Once a week, the relief clerk, Percy Whale, would travel from Lavant to check the books and there was the occasional visit from the station master at Midhurst to check that all was well.

There was also a weekly visit from a man who came from Chichester to attend to the pumping of water into the tank for the locomotives. On one occasion, Vic helped to water the engine. The water crane had been swung across and the bag placed in the tank. He then turned the wheel to release water into the engine's tanks. On being given a signal to turn off the supply, he tried, but to no avail: hundreds of gallons of water flowed over the engine and on to the track. Water was everywhere and the supply could not be turned off until the large water tank had been drained completely of thousands of gallons. This required an urgent call to Chichester to summon the man to restore the supply to the tank.

To while away the time other semi-official duties were undertaken. Coal was brought into Singleton for the local merchant, Fred Whitney. Vic Clayton notified

79. **Above:** *Graham White and George Howes today, photographed on Centurion Way.*

80. **Left:** *A view of Bognor engine shed: Graham White and George Howes worked from this depot with goods trains to Midhurst during World War II.*

him of the wagons' arrival, either by popping up to his house when going home to lunch or sending him a card. Fred Whitney was getting on in years, and could only clear half a wagon of coal, and that with the help of his relatives. So he offered Vic Clayton the job of filling 20 cwt sacks at 1/- a time. As Vic says, 'I was only a young lad. The bags were heavy to lift, but Fred paid up regularly.' In 1940, the best house coal was sold at about 2/- a cwt.

Both Vic Clayton and Phil Norrell joined the RAF, and after being demobbed came back to railway service.

What of the enginemen who worked the trains over the Chichester-Midhurst line? We have been unable to trace any drivers. Sadly, few are likely to be alive because through journeys to Midhurst stopped somewhat dramatically in 1951. Of the firemen we have been able to talk to, Graham White and George Howes were formerly of Bognor shed.

They joined the railway within months of each other. At this time in the early 1940s there was a sizable engine shed at Bognor Regis under the rule of the Running Loco Foreman, a Mr Jack Tribe, whose characteristics included a large moustache and a penchant for smoking a vile herbal tobacco. Twenty-two sets of men (each set comprising driver and fireman) worked from Bognor shed which provided motive power for goods trains, including the Chichester to Midhurst goods turn.

Both men started as engine cleaners but a shortage of manpower meant that spare fireman were allocated to a firing duty as required, and the following day reverted to engine-cleaning duties. The cleaning shifts were 6am to 2pm and 2pm to 10pm. Even though Graham and George had fired engines on the line they were not allowed into the Driver and Firemens' Lobby. To gain admittance, a cleaner had to become a Passed Fireman. That was achieved once he had completed the requisite number of 313 firing duties. In the meantime, to emphasise their exclusion, a detonator was dropped down the chimney of the Lobby and a loud explosion ensued!

The requirement for a Passed Cleaner to complete 313 firing turns to qualify as a Passed Fireman had remained the same since the days of the LBSCR. Before 1923 it could take several years to notch up the required turns. There was no shortage of

manpower and young men remained cleaners for years before firing an engine on the line.

Enginemen working from Bognor looked forward to the 'Midhurst Turn', not least because the booking-on time was 8.30am rather than the usual 3.30am! The duty was looked upon as a week's holiday. It started each day by taking a light engine – frequently a 'Vulcan', one of the old LBSCR's 0-6-0 tender engines of class 'C2x' – to Chichester, where it waited for 15 minutes.

During World War II Chichester had an extensive marshalling yard at which additional sidings had been installed for wartime traffic. Also there was a triangle for turning engines. The site is occupied now by the Westgate Leisure Centre. After a quick sip of tea the crew would back the engine on to the goods train for Midhurst which usually comprised box vans with supplies for the village shops, and wagons – some full, others empty – for the coal yards at Lavant and Singleton.

On obtaining the right of way from the yard the train set out, and the signalman in Fishbourne Crossing signalbox would be ready, holding out the staff for the fireman to grab as they passed, whereupon the train had a clear path up the line. The climb out of Chichester to the first station of Lavant was on a gradient of 1 in 75 and on the return journey care had to be taken, especially with heavy sugar beet trains. In the days when goods trains did not have continuous brakes there were always fears that the wagons might overpower an engine on down grades. George Howes recalled how one driver misjudged his approach and smashed into the Fishbourne Crossing gates which had only been repaired the previous day. The driver had such a fright as he thought he might hit a bus on the crossing: he lost all his hair after the accident and it never grew back.

Henry Hunt was a junior porter at Chichester station and remembers this section of the line and the extra sidings put in on the down side of the coast main line for marshalling trains; the site is now the city's industrial estate. A number of American wagons arrived for storage before going over to France after the D-Day landings. These had air-operated brakes. British railway wagons were vacuum-braked, if they had through brakes at all. The majority had a hand-brake only.

Wagons were also worked up the

Chichester to Midhurst line for storage but the crew had a particular method of moving them.

Henry Hunt describes what happened.

A small tank engine was always used at the front and as usual a goods brake van was at the rear of the train which would pause in the Midhurst bay at Chichester station while the engine got up as much steam as possible. When ready, the West signal-box at Chichester would tell the Fishbourne signalman to stand by. The signalman would then close the gates of the Fishbourne Level Crossing to road traffic, obtain a tablet (signalling staff) from the machine in the box which controlled access to the single line, and then go out of the signalbox with the staff in his hand.

He poised ready to give the staff to the engine crew who were now going 'hell for leather' so that the train could get a good run up the bank to Lavant. As the engine passed, the signalman would hold the staff for the fireman to grab as the engine rushed by. If the driver missed, the guard had to catch the staff. If the guard missed, the signalman would throw it into the rear of the brake van which was why the guard stood at the front of his van ready to take the staff.

The signalman would then open the gates for the road traffic. He went next to the other end of the signalbox, opened the window, and sat there listening to the train chugging up the bank towards Lavant. The exhaust beats became slower as the train approached the summit and he would wait for the puffing to quicken. If they did not, he could expect a whistle from the driver which meant that the train had failed to climb the bank and would be coming back. If the driver signalled, the gates of the level crossing would be opened to the train which would return to the Midhurst bay to get up steam for its second attempt to reach Lavant.

Two views at Chichester showing ex-LBSCR 'E4' 0-6-2Ts, of the type of engine featuring in the account of rushing the bank towards Lavant.

81. Above right: *In Chichester yard. Westgate Fields are on the right of the picture.*

82. Right: *The crew water their 'E4' at the column at Chichester station platform.*

In wartime Canadian troops were billeted under canvas on land by the railway at the point where the Chichester to Midhurst branch curved away from the main line. Graham White used to get Freddie Gun, the coalman at Bognor shed, to throw up some extra coal when he was refuelling the engine. As they proceeded past the troops he used to throw out large lumps of coal which the soldiers would retrieve for use in the stoves of their field kitchens. In return, they threw all sorts of items into empty wagons in the train, such as chocolate, tins of corned beef, tinned soup, dried egg and Canadian cigarettes called Sweet Capreol. Such goodies were in short supply to civilians subjected to wartime rationing. At Lavant the spoils were retrieved from the wagons and shared out between enginemen and guard.

The American armed forces had a large mess-tent on Singleton station and likewise gave the train crew food such as cheese, butter and bacon which was in far from plentiful supply in local shops. The

platelayer would also present the crew with a rabbit when he had one. That goes some way to explain why work on Midhurst the line was so popular: nobody wanted to miss their turn!

George Howes also found this turn of duty quite profitable for shooting game. In the locality of Singleton station pheasants were always to be found and the landlord at *The Terminus* at Bognor would give him 30/- a brace which would boost his earnings quite considerably. The *modus operandi* was that if George bagged two pheasants with his pistol the driver would slow-up. George would then jump off the engine and try to get back: if unable to do so he would clamber aboard the guard's brake van. According to George, 'I really wanted to get back on the engine as my mate would load the gun. One day I came away with 18 pheasants.'

This pastime wasn't a preserve of the footplate crew as Graham White knew of a guard from Littlehampton who fired a shotgun from his brake van. Graham and the

83. *Petworth station with No 32441, one of the faithful ex-LBSCR 'C2x' 0-6-0 goods engines. This was the end of the turn for Bognor enginemen working the 'Midhurst Turn'.*

driver used to keep an eye on him, and if he found his target they wound on the brakes.

Once allied forces had invaded Europe the line was no longer used for the storage of wagons of ammunition and once more trains went through to Midhurst. But the line's attraction for the footplate crews remained. At Christmas-time holly and mistletoe would be collected from the lineside for use at home and Christmas trees were readily available at Cocking.

On arrival at Midhurst at about noon, the train would pull up to the tunnel near the station. The fireman would jump off the locomotive and go straight into the porter's hut where a kettle was always on the boil. Billycans were filled and, as the engine chugged back into the goods yard, the fireman would climb aboard the engine. Driver and fireman would have their meal before shunting the yard. If not much shunting was indicated, the crew would stroll down the town, leaving the engine to simmer on its own.

Midhurst's goods yard was extensive and coal was always an important commodity, as indeed it was at most wayside stations. Mr Merritt lived at Easebourne and recalls that during school holidays he would help the local coalman, Gillham's of Easebourne Street, to deliver coal. As soon as the coal arrived in the yard, the coal merchant wanted the wagon to be emptied as soon as possible as otherwise he had to pay demurrage, a rate payable to the railway for failure to clear the railway wagons within a specified time.

Bricks were brought in from Midhurst

Whites to be shipped out. The bricks were white in colour – hence their name, for they were baked from material extracted from the chalk-pit which could be seen from Cocking Causeway. In springtime railway banks were full of primroses and cowslips which people would walk out from the town to pick. The embankment had been built of chalk and in the 1920s most peoples' doorsteps had to be white. Mr Merritt's mother would often ask him to bring back some chalk to use as whitening. When mixed with water, it made an ideal substitute for the expensive whitener available in the shops.

Milk was also sent to Chichester Diaries. Even though there were a number of dairy farms in the area, on occasions Whiphill Farm Dairy on the Cowdray Estate would telephone to Chichester for milk to provide for the round. In a matter of hours the milk would be waiting at the station. During early autumn there were also the sugar beet special trains which went all the way to Midhurst, dropping-off empties at stations and bringing back loaded wagons.

On a normal rostered turn the train would make its way to Petworth. Out of Petworth was uphill and the crew would have an unpleasant time when the engine was working hard with steam and smoke filling the cab. In winter, the crew wouldn't risk putting their heads out of the cab as icicles might be hanging down from the roof of Midhurst Tunnel. Quite thick at the top, the icicles tapered down, and frequently almost touched the ground.

While passing through Midhurst Tunnel, driver and fireman would hold their breath hoping that the engine would give them little trouble so that their ordeal would be over as soon as possible. It would help if the locomotive was being

fired properly and emitting the minimum of smoke. Just after the war George Howes recalled that 'smoke-jacks' were out and about, intent on keeping their eye on engines coming up the line, and ready to file a report if they thought that too much smoke was being emitted.

On to Selham where the normal routine would take place of trucks being delivered and coupled up. From here loads of chestnut fencing were sent out, then to Petworth. With a passenger service still in operation strict timekeeping had to be observed on this part of the line.

Petworth was the end of the turn for the Bognor crew. They would go to the signal-box situated on the bank to make a cup of tea, or on very hot days the local pub would be visited. First the yard had to be shunted, the train marshalled, and the locomotive made ready for the relief crew. Coal was moved forward in the tender, and the engine oiled round for the Horsham men who worked the train from Pulborough to Petersfield. Then the Bognor crew travelled home 'passenger', first on the motor-train to Pulborough and then by electric service to Bognor Regis. For railwaymen, a journey home by passenger train in this way was said to be 'on the cushions'.

The Chichester to Midhurst turn ceased quite abruptly for the Bognor men in 1951. Chapter 11 explains why and tells of the day the engine of the Midhurst goods train met with disaster but lived to fight another day.

The stretch of railway between Singleton and Midhurst was abandoned. The decision was taken that it was uneconomic to restore, and thereafter the Chichester to Midhurst goods service ceased. As explained in Chapter 2, goods trains continued to serve Lavant, Singleton and Cocking stations.

Chapter 8: Sunny, happy days on the Selsey Tram

It is a Sunday at 12.15 pm. As the signature tune of *Desert Island Discs* floats across the room from the radio, thoughts of a sun-soaked island with crystal-clear water lapping on a golden-yellow palm beach may enter your mind. But for others a distant image dominates their thoughts of an antiquated steam engine pulling a single coach and a string of wagons and puffing its way through the countryside to the seaside.

No, dear reader, the writer isn't mad, although I've been dotty about steam trains since I was three years old. There is a connection, for Eric Coates who wrote the introductory music, travelled down the Selsey peninsula in West Sussex on the antiquated train. Moreover, it is known that the view from Selsey across the bay to Bognor inspired Eric Coates to compose *By the Sleepy Lagoon* which has long been the signature tune of this ever popular programme of a celebrity's eight favourite discs.

Eric Coates, whose other compositions included the famous *Dam Busters' March*, and the theme tune from *Workers' Playtime*, fell in love with Selsey in the 1920s; his 'Sussex by the Sea' as he called it where he had a house in the main street. Here he could live without being thought eccentric, and spend lovely summer days walking to the beach to swim 'in waters as clear and almost as warm as you would find in any South Sea lagoon.'[1]

Although his wife frequently used the slow, local omnibus to go shopping in Chichester, Eric Coates remembered the even slower Selsey Tram which he described as an 'antiquated one-track railway which twisted its eccentric way over dykes through meadows, across land habitually waterlogged during the spring tides; the little tank-engine and its strange conglomeration of coaches frequently leaving the metals in favour of the inviting meadowland beside the track. The one and only guard the railway company pos-

sessed was even more obliging than the omnibus service, for he made it his business to call at the Station Hotel to arouse from their slumbers any intending passengers for the early morning train, the engine driver and his mate not daring to start before his flock was safely on board.'[2] Could there *really* be a railway which fitted such a description?

The answer is yes: 'The Selsey Tram' officially known at its opening on 27 August 1897 as The Hundred of Manhood and Selsey Tramways, and described in

84. **Top:** *The railway's seal.*

85. **Below:** *A commercial postcard of pre-1914 days entitled 'How we arrived at Selsey'. The engine is the Railway's first* **Chichester** *which lasted until 1913. A second* **Chichester** *was acquired in 1919.*

People in the picture include Edward G. Arnell, magistrate (by lamppost), lady with bike, Mrs H. A. Smith, the lady behind is Mildred Phipps (Mrs J. Tupper's mother), gentleman with arms folded, Walter Smith, proprietor of Fisherman's Joy Inn.

86. Above: *Commercial postcard of Selsey High Street.*

87. Left: *The route of the Selsey Tram, also showing the proposed extensions to the line.*

Seven miles long, the Selsey line was built and worked as a tramway to avoid the expense of protected level crossings which were numerous on this line. Constructed without any formal parliamentary order it had no compulsory powers of purchase, hence some inconvenient detours at times to skirt fields and, in at least one place, running through a farmyard to maintain its right of way. The line was entirely unsignalled and the ungated level crossings protected only by warning signs. It was not until 1924 that any measure of legal formality was sought when the line was renamed 'The West Sussex Railway'.

The promoters of the tramway, as quoted in the *West Sussex Gazette* on 23 March 1896, said that 'it was not intended to run trains at express speeds, nor was that intended'. This was never possible for the engineer of the line was Mr (later Lieut-Colonel) Holman Fred Stephens of Tonbridge who operated a number of similar light railways across the country; the revived Kent and East Sussex Railway is a notable survivor.

In true Stephens' tradition no frivolous expenses were incurred. The cost of the whole line, including 11

stations or halts, amounted to £21,000 with the track wherever possible being laid directly on to bare ground. The ride that resulted from following the undulations of the ground earn the line another nickname of 'The Bumpity Bump'.[4] The bends were often so tight, and the track poorly laid, that speeds greater than 15mph were impossible.

As the journey along the line was more of an amble, it was a source of fun for local children. For instance, Mr Tadd of Chichester recalled jumping off the train when it was moving, picking flowers at the side of the track and then jumping back on again. Another favourite game of older children, according to Mr Pine of Fishbourne, was to clamber outside the coaches, Wild West-style, from one end to another as the train was travelling between stations. Obviously, the strict conductor, Mr Walker, could not have been on duty that day because Sally Haynes of Selsey who used to travel on the Tram to Chichester High School with Barbara Aylwin of Hunston said he would not brook any tomfoolery; it would soon have been stopped with a thick ear. No one knows to this day how the Ellis boys managed to uncouple the engine from the train at Hunston.

Sally Haynes' family had moved to Selsey in 1918 because of the Zeppelin air-raids on London, while Barbara Aylwin was born and bred in Hunston where her father owned the mill from which he flew a flag on the opening day of the railway.

The quality of the stations was reflected in the overall cost of the line: they were constructed of corrugated iron and resembled small sheds. Gas-lamps were confined to the stations of Chichester and Selsey and, to save further operating costs, only Chichester, Hunston and Selsey stations were staffed. The conductor of the train acted as guard and also issued tickets for passengers joining the train at other points along the line.

The only other major expenses were incurred by the construction of a road bridge over the line at Selsey, a bridge over the Ferry Ponds Rife, and for crossing the canal between Hunston and Donnington, a rather extraordinary bridge. The latter resembled the drawbridge of an early feudal castle and to allow vessels to pass had to be raised upright by means of two hand-operated winches.

Dolly Ginman's (née Withall) father

the local newspaper as the noisiest and most rickety railway in England[3].

It was built to provide an alternative form of transport for the Selsey peninsula which hitherto had been dependent upon horse-drawn transport. The railway contributed to the development of Selsey on the West Sussex coast with the promotion of agriculture in this fertile region, not to mention the importance of rail transport of coal, fish, building materials and the famous Pullinger Mousetraps which were exported all over the world.

Going off the rails

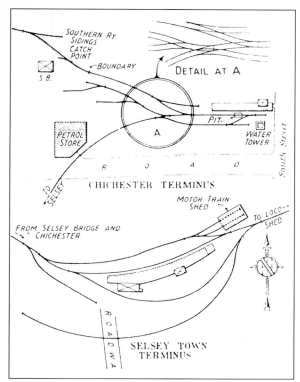

railway, but with the seaside as its destination. The Mayor of Chichester insisted upon driving the first train, even though he was not professionally qualified, and this departed an hour behind schedule.[5]

Thereafter trains ran according to the local circumstances and while a timetable was issued, nobody could be sure when a train would arrive at the other end of the line. If the driver was in need of a tasty meal he would stop the train and go shooting in the nearby fields with the shotgun he carried on the footplate. Then again he would bring the train to a halt to pick any greens for his rabbits and in the autumn another favourite diversion was blackberrying. It seemed that punctuality was not a concern of the staff. Winnie Sayers lived in Selsey for six months of the year and travelled to school in Chichester with Uncle Walter in the guard's van, and she remembered that if a businessman had to catch a main line connection to London he would have to bribe the driver to get a move-on.

The line's rolling stock was extraordinary. Only one locomotive, *Selsey*, was constructed specially for the line. A 2-4-2 side tank, it was purchased from Peckett & Co of Bristol in 1897. Together with a rake of bogie carriages built by Falcon of Loughborough, the engine was the only new rolling stock purchased by the line. The remainder, as Mrs Haynes remem-

bers of her schooldays, was antediluvian and consisted of secondhand relics from the 19th century. Frederick Hull of Chichester was a locomotive enthusiast fascinated by the dilapidated state of the Tram, compared with the smart and efficient operations of the adjacent LBSCR.

Most of the coaches used by the Selsey Tramway comprised discards from other railways which the Company never bothered to repaint following purchase. Individual compartments were full of litter and stank of stale tobacco. Frederick Hull vividly remembers how clouds of dust could be raised by a child just by hitting the seats. In addition, an unprotected heating pipe ran the length of certain coaches and led to the occasional scald if passengers were careless.

Apart from *Selsey* the other locomotives were veteran machines which had long seen better days. Three of them were Manning Wardle saddle tanks – *Sidlesham*, *Ringing Rock* and *Morous* – built in 1861, 1883 and 1866 respectively. The line had been opened by *Chichester* built in 1847 as an 0-6-0 but subsequently converted to an 0-4-2 to allow easier running over the tight curves. Officially named *Hesperus*, another 0-4-2 tank built in 1872 by Neilson was affectionately and appropriately dubbed *The Wreck*.

The Wreck had been obtained following attempts to purchase another brand-new locomotive, a 'Triana Type' from locomotive builder, Kerr, Stuart & Co of Stoke on Trent. The cost of the new locomotive was £1,098, plus an advance of 6%. At the request of the Tramway it was to be supplied with a copper firebox and brass tubes.[6] Another engine was needed in 1912 because the railway required to run

was employed by the line from the start of World War I to operate the bridge and to undertake some track maintenance. The whole family lived in a railway cottage situated on the south side of the bridge. However, when her father wasn't there, especially during the evenings, Dolly would have to raise the bridge with the help of her brother. She recalls: 'We would have to walk over the bridge on boards to get to the winches on the other side and raise the bridge – it wasn't too heavy once it got started. Curley and Friday Coombes from Dell Quay were frequent users with their coal-boats and they would give us sweets, and other bargemen would stop and give my mother jars of dripping. The railwaymen were also good to us and they dropped off huge lumps of coal from the engine which we would have to break up and take in the house.'

This escapade of walking the bridge had to be carried out for every Tram – it had to be given the 'all clear' that it was safe to pass over the bridge. Dolly still lives in Hunston and remembers vividly the evenings when a lamp would be used to light the Tram over the bridge. To report any difficulties should the bridge be found unsafe or become stuck the little railway cottage was also equipped with a telephone.

From the date of opening in August 1897 the Selsey Tram was destined to be an eccentric and typically English country

89. *The remarkable lifting span of the bridge crossing the Chichester Canal, near Hunston.*

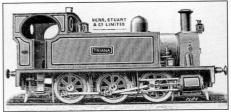

92. *Diagram of a 'Triana Type' locomotive – the locomotive that never was as far as the Selsey Tramway was concerned.*

90. **Above:** *For tracklaying on the southern part of the line, the locomotive* Chichester *was towed on road by a traction engine, and is seen in 1897 at the* Anchor *public-house, the nearest inn to Chalder station. Such movements of engines on road were not unusual in Victorian times.*

91. **Right:** *In winter only one engine was in steam, but in summer two-train operation required the issue of train-staff tickets to protect against both trains being in the same section at once.*

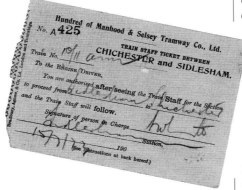

two trains from 15 July to 14 September and it was essential to have a reliable third engine for the augmented service.[7] By this time the valiant engine *Chichester* was derelict.

According to Kerr, Stuart the engine would haul approximately 260 tons 'depending to a great extent upon the type and condition of the trucks and the state of the Railway Track.'[8] F. Sanden Street, a Director of the Tramway Company, was convinced of the need for a new locomotive. To Henry Phillips, Secretary and Manager, he wrote on 23 May 1912 that 'it is no use buying second-hand trash but much better to have a new and reliable engine.'[9]

Even though arrangements went so far

as to instruct Kerr, Stuart to paint the name *Chichester* on the new engine, Mr Stephens, the engineer, was not convinced. He thought that a another second-hand locomotive 'a little Kent and East Sussex or Plymouth & Devonport engine would no doubt serve your purpose'[10].

A stipulation had been made by the Tramway that the engine should not exceed 20 tons in weight, otherwise the Company would have to strengthen the permanent way. However, when informed by Kerr, Stuart that the new engine would weigh 25 tons 5 cwt, Stephens asked Kerr, Stuart to send him a draughtsman, but the firm refused and accused him of dictatorial behaviour.[11]

Thereafter relations between the Company and Kerr, Stuart deteriorated almost daily. Street wrote on 13 June 1912 'I am heartily sick of the whole business about the locomotive.....I suppose that the result will be that we shall have no engine.'[12]

He was correct. After further exchanges, a meeting of the directors on 20 June 1912 authorised a despatch of a letter informing Kerr, Stuart that the company were prepared to go no further with the order.[13]

Despite this, Kerr, Stuart claimed to be working night and day to meet the delivery date of 15 July.[14] Finally, a letter from the Company's solicitors, Messrs Raper & Co of Chichester, stated that no order had been placed and the Company threatened to refuse acceptance of the locomotive if the builder attempted to deliver it.[15]

The line still required a third engine and Stephens persuaded the Company to acquire a little 'Plymouth and Devonport' engine. Hence *Hesperus* was delivered to the railway in 1912, and the 'Triana' was really 'The engine that never was'.

For the people of Selsey, the Tramway was an asset. Mrs Aylwin remembers that

93. *Winnie Sayers today, recalling her memories of the Tram.*

Going off the rails

94. **Above:** *The 'Wreck', officially named Hesperus.*

95. **Right: Selsey,** *the one locomotive built for the line and which was used until just before closure. Photographed in 1905, by then it had been rebuilt with shortened side-tanks. The patterning on the tank-side was produced using tallow. Seen at Chichester.*

her husband's family, who were farmers, used to have coal sent down on the Tram to Sidlesham station for the traction engines when threshing was taking place. Sugar beet and cattle were also sent up the line. Farmers had a good relationship with the line for they were able to stop the Tram anywhere on route rather than having to start from a recognised place of departure – this was a stipulation if the farmer had allowed the Tramway over their land.

Brickworks along the line at Hunston and Selsey were also well served by the Tram. Coal frequently went right down the line to Selsey station where Jim Prior and Edward Arnell had coal dumps, and as a young lad, Mr Pine of Lavant used to dirty his white plimsolls. This spoilt his day out as his mother complained about the blackened footwear.

The fishermen found the line vital for the transportation of their catches. They would always be waiting at Selsey for the five o'clock Tram to arrive so that they could load their crabs and lobsters for the return journey to Chichester, and then on to the main line for shipment to Brighton, or to Billingsgate fish market. 'Honest' Bill Arnell is from a long line of Selsey fisher-

96. *The flooding of the line near Sidlesham in December 1910. The sea broke through the shingle bank and two miles of track between Chalder and Ferry were flooded to depths of 8-12ft. Fortunately, the Railway had its stock divided between Chichester and Selsey and so was able to maintain a service with the aid of a horse-drawn coach and a wagon which met the trains at the flooded points.*

men and well remembers taking the day's catch to Selsey Town station. 'We used only to put prawns, crabs and lobsters on the Tram: nearly a ton of prawns a day from all the boats would be loaded. Wet fish we'd sell up in the village, or send it to Chichester by horse and cart. In those days there was a lot of mackerel round here and Fidler, the carrier, would take and hawk the fish in Chichester.

'Honest' Bill thought the Tram had been essential not only to the fishermen but also the ordinary people before there was a bus service to Chichester. He recalled 'You didn't know if you were going to get there – it was always breaking down but you didn't take any notice. The Tram always went by the old time as they never changed the time of the village clock!' How passengers managed to make their main line connections remains a mystery!

The railway also offered a personal service to its regulars. Winnie Sayers' uncle lived at 'Northlands' a house situated near Selsey station. Always having a liking for tea, he used to call out if there was time for a second cup at breakfast; if there was, he'd leave his cup at the station and collect it on his return. The driver would frequently wait for regular passengers to arrive. The Tram staff would even go and knock on their doors if they failed to turn up as expected. On one occasion at Selsey, the driver went to knock-up John Sayers, Winnie's cousin, who regularly used the line to go to school. The drivers also made stops at remote farmhouses to deliver post and parcels and naturally exchange all the local news with total disregard for the timetable.

Many children travelled on the line to school and travelled to Selsey Town station on bikes. Outside the station office where Mr Pennycord worked, there was a space where bikes could be left during the day. If stern Mr Walker was in a good mood that day he would keep an eye out for the youngsters coming up the road and would hold the 'School Tram' (the 8 am service) until they arrived – on other days he would keep to time. Even so, the children were frequently late for school thanks to breakdowns of the locomotives. Nancy Boys and her sister Barbara Aylwin didn't mind being late but didn't rel-

SELSEY TRAMWAYS.

NOTICE IS HEREBY GIVEN, that on account of the flooding of the line between Ferry and Sidlesham Stations, the Company cannot undertake to book passengers from Chichester further than Sidlesham, or from Selsey further than Ferry. The line between Sidlesham and Ferry Stations will be closed for Passenger Traffic until re-construction works are complete. Meanwhile a 'Bus Service has been arranged between Sidlesham and Ferry for passengers wishing to proceed from Chichester to Selsey, and vice versa. No extra charge will be made for this service, but the same cannot be guaranteed.

All Cheap Bookings are suspended.

Also, the Company cannot guarantee the delivery of Goods or Parcels without delay between Chichester and Selsey, until further notice. Every effort will be made, however, to give prompt delivery.

The line will be re-opened for through Passenger Traffic on or before June 1st, 1911.

H. G. PHILLIPS,
Manager.

Selsey, February, 1911.

P. F. ACFORD, Ltd. PRINTERS 67 SOUTH STREET, CHICHESTER.

Cheap Excursion Tickets,

CHICHESTER
TO
. . SELSEY,

Return 9d. Fare.

Will be issued by the 2.15 p.m tram

EVERY SUNDAY,

and by the 2.20 p.m. tram

EVERY THURSDAY,

Available to return by any tram on day of issue only.

Restall's Excursions

EVERY THURSDAY

During July, August & September,
except August 1st.

~ RESTALL'S CHEAP TRAINS ~
RUN FROM

London Bridge ...	11.50 a.m.
New Cross	11.55 a.m,
Victoria	11.50 a.m.
Clapham Junction...	11.55 a.m.
Balham	12.0 noon
West Croydon ...	12.15 p.m.

TO
SELSEY-ON-SEA.

Return Fare 3s. if taken before the day
Return Fare 3s. 6d. if taken on the day.
Return Train Leaves Selsey 7.5 p.m.
See Restall's Bills for Conditions, &c.

99. **Above:** *Lobster-pots and the lifeboat at Selsey.*

100. **Left:** *Selsey Beach.*

The single fare from Chichester to Selsey was 7½d or 1/3 return with a cheap excursion ticket available on certain Sunday trains, and all day on Thursdays. [16] The

ish the journey home. Sally Haynes, who travelled the length of the line, recalls how the 35-minute journey often took an hour to complete, and remembered the frustration of being in the Tram while all she wanted to do was to get home from school and play with her friends.

In its heyday, before World War I, the line was carrying 80,000 people a year, all eager to enjoy the air and sea bathing of this Sussex heaven. By the summer of 1913, there was an augmented service of 11 trains a day each way, with an additional train on Mondays and Thursdays.

98. **Left:** *For the first half of the 20th century Restall's chartered regular trains on main line railways to take city-dwellers to the coast, as seen in this advertisement in the Selsey Tramway's timetable.*

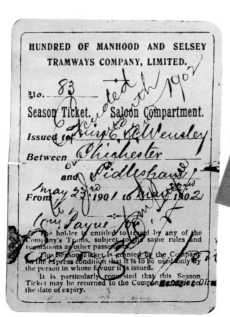

101. **Above:** *A Bell Punch Co ticket.*

102. **Left:** *Chichester-Sidlesham season ticket.*

London Brighton & South Coast Railway. 167 (34G)

TO SELSEY

hot journey to Selsey could be made more bearable by the purchase of a delicious ice-cream (2d a wafer) from Guarnacchio of North Street, Chichester, on his way to sell his wares to the hordes on Selsey beach. Should there be a prolonged delay, the journey could be made even more unbearable by the impromptu sing-songs led by Tram staff such as Charlie Fullick who was nicknamed 'Constantinople' because he was forever singing that song.

There were plans before World War I to extend the line with two branches, one to East Wittering, the other to West Itchenor. Although surveyed, and powers granted for their construction, the onset of war placed the scheme in abeyance and it was not resumed. [17] At this time came closure of the extension to Selsey Beach which had opened in August 1898 to serve the increasing number of visitors during the summer months. The East Beach station had also been the destination of the select visitors from London to Beacon House which was connected by road to the station. With lifting of this stretch of the line, the conductor's call of 'Keep your seats for Selsey Beach' was lost.

By the 1920s the railway had become a joke: cyclists raced the train and occasion-

ally won. Rollo Lempriere of Bognor remembers one such occasion during his school holidays from Christ's Hospital. Near Hunston station he saw the Tram about to leave for Chichester. 'I raced along and reached the Chichester terminus at the same time as the train. Admittedly, the railway was about half a mile longer than the road, and where the line crossed Stockbridge Road the Tram had to slow down and the engine sound its whistle as there were no gates.'

The steam locomotives found it increasingly difficult to climb Kipson's bank on the southern side of Hunston even though the passengers would frequently get out and ease the load while the engine would back up and have another run at the incline. Breakdowns were becoming numerous and as this was a single line it meant that every time serious incidents occurred the service would be finished for the day. The Company therefore introduced an efficient warning system in the form of a lad who was sent along the line to warn intending passengers that trains would not be running that day.

In an attempt to alleviate the frequent breakdowns among the ailing fleet of locomotives, Colonel Stephens, who had become a director of the line, introduced petrol-driven railcars. Two types were used, Ford and Shefflex, and initially they were quite successful, proving cheaper to operate than steam locomotives. However, when working, their interiors

103. *Lt-Col Holman Fred Stephens. Born 1868, the son of Frederick George Stephens, a member of the pre-Raphaelite group of painters. In addition to railway service Holman Fred Stephens was engaged in part-time military service and attained the rank of Lieut-Colonel in 1916. He died in 1931.*

became filled with exhaust fumes and, although fitted with exhaust-operated whistles, it hardly mattered for the roar of the railcar engines could be heard for miles. Jack Tupper of Selsey recalls the introduction of the railcars. He says that the line started off badly by converting Ford Model T one-ton lorries which had a propensity for overheating and caused a lot of trouble. They were replaced by Shefflex railcars. These were much heavier and by that time the track was in a bad state of repair. Compared with the main line railways where the line was held in place by cast-iron chairs, the rail on the Tramway was simply spiked down on to the sleepers.

In 1927, William Crees, of Portsmouth, aged 14 years, joined the West Sussex Railway as an apprentice. By this time the majority of the Tram's passengers were conveyed by the railcars which were popular with young mothers as the small low-sided truck they towed enabled prams to be conveyed without any difficulty. William was employed as an assistant to Mr Smith, the station master at Selsey, where initially his duties were to cover and remove tarpaulins from the goods wagons. Then he progressed to riding on the Tram, trains and railcars alike, to issue tickets for which he was paid 10/- a week,

104. *The one fatal accident on the line occurred on 3 September 1923 when the locomotive* **Wembley,** *later the second* **Chichester,** *derailed on poor track near the Golf Club, Selsey. The fireman of* **Wembley** *was crushed against the boiler backhead.*

Going off the rails

Railcars on the Selsey Tramway:

105. **Left:** *The Ford railcars worked with a wagon in-between, as remembered by Mr Pine.*

106. **Below:** *The Shefflex set has come to grief on one of the road crossings.*

107. **Bottom:** *The Shefflex set in its prime.*

working from 7.30am till 6pm. Overtime was paid on days called 'Restall Trips' when chartered rail excursions from London to Chichester brought daytrippers to Selsey who were provided with a 9pm connecting return to the 'Smoke'. He was never issued with a uniform and, to the best of his recollection, nobody wore one. To this day, Mr Crees remembers the misery arising from the absence of toilet facilities at Selsey station.

Steam locomotives continued to be used for mixed trains – 'mixed' because they conveyed passenger coaches and goods wagons – and William remembers one summer's day when a large throng of holidaymakers was packed on to the small platform at Selsey Town. They waited impatiently for the decrepit *Hesperus* to raise steam to take them to Chichester. Leaking steam from every conceivable place the aged tank engine heaved and wheezed itself out of the engine shed to loud cheers from the passengers on the platform. Their joy was short-lived. To the accompaniment of a loud bang, the engine derailed itself between the platform and the shed, effectively curtailing services for the rest of the day.

The railcars were not universally popular with passengers who remember them as being too hot in the summer, and too cold in the winter. William Crees also believed them to be less stable than their steam counterparts, rocking alarmingly as they passed over an open girder bridge near Ferry Ponds with the sea rolling underneath. As a young lad of eight, Mr

Pine of Lavant liked the small truck in-between the two cars which he negotiated as he worked his way from one end of the moving Tram to the other.

Maintenance of the 'motor buses' was not an easy task. They were serviced and driven by H. J. Blake of Manor Road, Selsey, whose son Roy still lives in the village. He used to take his father's lunch down to Selsey Town station and recalled that he only heard his father swearing when working underneath the railcars in his attempts to carry out running repairs. With instructions to keep down costs it was a thankless task trying to keep the railcars in operation. Two years later Roy's father left the railway and set up his own taxi business in competition to the Tram.

Reputedly, Colonel Stephens, who had visited the Blakes' family home on a number of occasions, never forgave Roy's father for this act which was considered to akin to betrayal. On one occasion, his father's taxi was jacked up off its wheels in 'divine retribution'.

108. Above: *Steam and petrol railcars were used in traffic together, as seen in this view at Selsey Town with* **Ringing Rock** *in the background and the Ford railcars in the foreground.*

109. Right and below right: *Nearing the end - the winter 1933/4 timetable.*

Accidents at the ungated level crossings caused by cars hitting trains were common. This was hardly surprising as the engine would merely blow its whistle on its approach. Fortunately, nobody was seriously hurt. Eventually though all trains had to stop at crossings, the fireman halting traffic with a red flag by day and a red lamp at night before the train could proceed.

Mrs Nina Pike of Portsmouth remembers journeys on the railcars when Charlie Fullick would stop the traffic, but his face was so red with embarrassment when performing this task that he didn't need a red flag.

In spite of all these adversities the Tram still functioned: that it did so at all was a tribute to its overworked staff. A typical example of 'all hands to the wheel' is illustrated by the story of Nina Pike. It happened in 1922 when her family, who had been staying at Hillfield Road, Selsey, were due to return to South Africa. All the family possessions had been packed up, including a large tin-bath which accompanied the family in the 'steam tram' to Chichester. All went well until the Tram came to a grinding halt, just in sight of Terminus Road station to the west of the present Chichester High School for Girls.

The prospect of missing the main line connection to Southampton Docks and also their booked passage on the Union Castle RMS *Arundel Castle* was too appalling for words. But customer care is not an invention of the 1990s. To the rescue came the driver, fireman and guard who carried all the Pikes's possessions, including the tin-bath, along the track to

the Chichester station of the LBSCR where the family caught their train and subsequently caught the boat to South Africa.

On another occasion, Nina's brother's new grey felt hat blew off when they were travelling in the open truck which was frequently coupled between the two Shefflex railcars. The hat landed in a field next to the line but there was great consternation at the thought of her mother's reaction. The driver was advised of the loss and there was great relief when he stopped the Tram on the return journey. The area was scoured by staff and passengers alike until the hat was eventually discovered – another happy ending!

By the late 1920s the fortunes of the company began to decline steadily. The railway was hit badly by the local bus service which had started after the war, combined with the increasing use of private cars and lorries. As locals have remarked, the Tram went anywhere but where the people lived. Its unpredictability resulted in schoolchildren opting for the bus which got them to school on time, and at night set them down close to their homes.

The Tram could hardly compete. Bill Ousley of Selsey remembered a family trip on the line in the 1930s when the journey to Chichester should have started

Pullinger mousetraps made from beech wood were self-setting, caught more than a dozen mice alive and did not harm them. Invented by Colin Pullinger who was born in Ivy Cottage, Selsey in 1815, they were first exhibited at the Great Exhibition in 1851. They were an enormous success, with Pullinger's factory in the High Street employing 40 people and producing 960 traps a week. Pullinger died in 1920 and is buried at Selsey.

110. *One of the Pullinger mouse-traps, a regular traffic for the Tram.*

Going off the rails

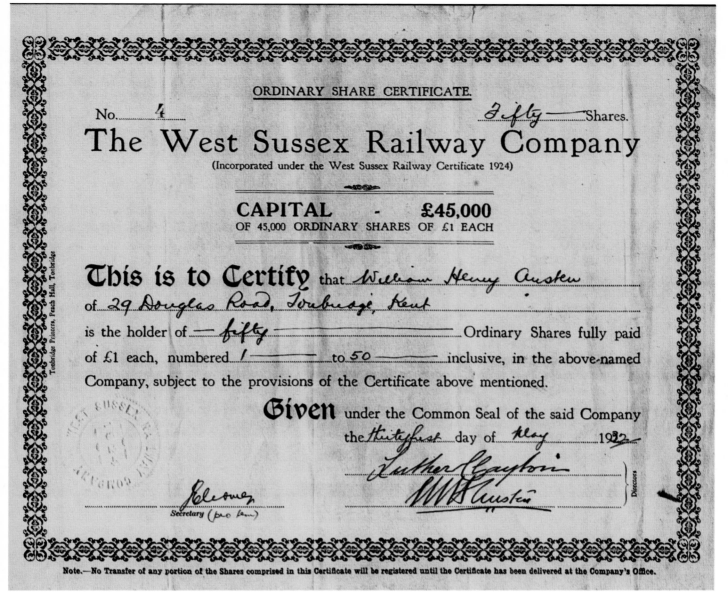

ORDINARY SHARE CERTIFICATE.

No. *4*   *Fifty* Shares.

The West Sussex Railway Company

(Incorporated under the West Sussex Railway Certificate 1924)

CAPITAL - £45,000
OF 45,000 ORDINARY SHARES OF £1 EACH

This is to Certify that *William Henry Austen*

of *29 Douglas Road, Tonbridge, Kent*

is the holder of ———*fifty*——————— Ordinary Shares fully paid

of £1 each, numbered *1* to *50* inclusive, in the above-named

Company, subject to the provisions of the Certificate above mentioned.

Given under the Common Seal of the said Company

the *thirty-first* day of *May* 19*32*

Luther Clayton

W. H. Austen

Directors

Secretary (pro tem)

Tonbridge Printers, Peach Hall, Tonbridge

Note.—No Transfer of any portion of the Shares comprised in this Certificate will be registered until the Certificate has been delivered at the Company's Office.

---

111. How it ended - notice of the auction of some of the line's effects.

around 10am, after arrival of the train from Chichester. The Tram didn't appear until 10.45am, whereupon the locomotive disappeared inside the shed for repairs and didn't emerge until 11.20am; by that time six Southdown buses had passed by. Chichester was finally reached at 1pm – 2½ hours behind time.

Without proper maintenance the track deteriorated severely. This had already caused a fatal accident in 1923 when the steam locomotive *Wembley* jumped the track on its way to Chichester, having just passed Golf Links Halt. The engine ploughed down the bank and the Fireman – 'Dirg' Barnes – was crushed against the firebox of the locomotive. The subsequent enquiry laid the blame on the railway for neglect of its permanent way.

Eventually, on 19 January 1935 the insolvent railway was closed by the Official Receiver.[18] All railway equipment and stock was sold for scrap, although nameplates

112. Ordinary Share Certificate issued to W. H. Austen, successor to Lt-Col Stephens as manager of the group of light railways run from an office at Tonbridge.

from *Selsey* and *Ringing Rock* have survived, as have some coaches which are now holiday homes on East Beach at Selsey.

So ended a quaint and typically English country railway. Yet after 62 years, when *Ringing Rock* made the last ramshackle journey from Selsey to Chichester, the days of 'The Tram' are not forgotten. Many recall the line with affection, bringing back childhood memories of sunny, happy September days when they jumped out of the train to pick blackberries while the staff tried to repair the ailing engine. It was a time when life proceeded at a more gentle pace and, for the Selsey line, arrivals on time took second place to the personal service of its customers. Happy 100th Birthday, 'Selsey Snail', you will be remembered always!

Chapter 9: From Emperors to Evacuees — special trains in West Sussex

The arrival of the railway set the ordinary working man free from the constraints and boundaries of village life for the very first time. For some a trip to the local town on market day must have been a fascinating experience with the hustle and bustle of the traders, the throngs of people and the various sideshows. What a contrast to the sleepiness and tranquillity of the village with its pub and isolated shops! For others the railway was the start of a new life, be it in the new developing towns far away from the agricultural community, or perhaps the start of an epic journey to a new beginning in the developing countries of Canada or Australia, away from the class-ridden society of England. Either way, life in the country was never quite the same, for the railway gave ordinary people the ability and opportunity to travel and to broaden their horizons.

On Sunday, 18 October 1859, eight days after the opening of the Mid-Sussex Railway from Horsham to Petworth, the line saw its first excursion train. Nearly 100 people travelled from Petworth to Sydenham to view the Great Exhibition for the sum of 3/6 which included admission into Crystal Palace. The *West Sussex Gazette* reported that 'they returned to their homes much delighted and satisfied with their trip.'[1] A matter which was deplored by a local minister, but enthusiastically supported by the editor of the paper, for 'it gives those, who only have a rest on one day of the week, an opportunity of visiting friends at a distance.'[2] The following Sunday another excursion was run to the seaside at Brighton – the excursion trains of the railways retained their

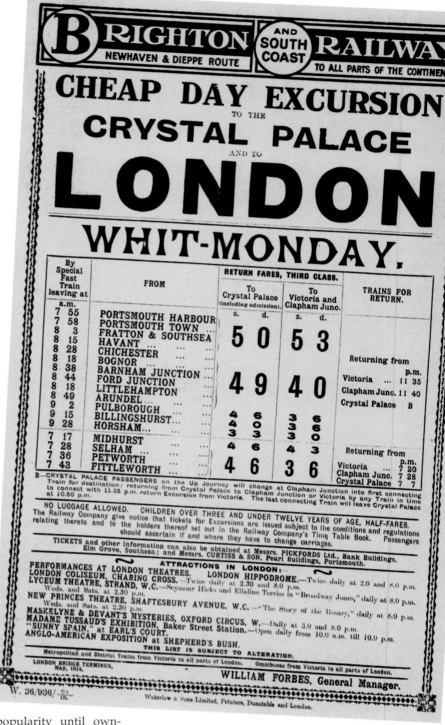

popularity until ownership of a motor car became widespread.

The Petersfield to Midhurst section of the line was not opened until 1 September 1864 by the London and South Western Railway Company. Within seven months of its opening the line was to witness one of the most notable events in the railway history of the county. On 2 April 1865, the radical politician, Richard Cobden, the man celebrated as the popular hero behind the Repeal of the Corn Laws, died in London.

One of a family of 11 children, he was born in 1804 of yeoman stock, in the tiny and impoverished hamlet of Dunford near Midhurst. He made his fortune as a calico printer in Manchester before turning to reformist politics and the philosophy of free trade.

With John Bright, he led the Anti-Corn Law League to success in 1846, abolishing the protective duty on corn which had artificially inflated the price of bread. A man who refused to compromise his beliefs, who rejected slavish allegiance to a party and who declined Cabinet office in the interests of independence. Ultimately, he saw his vision of international peace come closer to reality through his successful negotiation of the Anglo-French Commercial Treaty in 1860 which reduced tariffs on trade.

113. Left: *LBSCR poster for a June 1914 excursion from West Sussex stations to the Crystal Palace and Victoria.*

114. Right: *Richard Cobden, MP.*

115. Below: *The funeral procession for Cobden at Cocking causeway, 1865.*

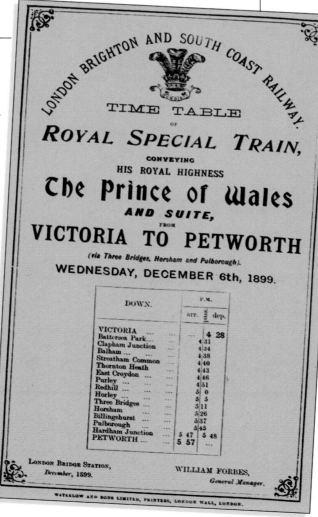

London, Brighton & South Coast Railway.
General Manager's Office.
London Bridge Station. S.E.

TELEGRAPHIC ADDRESS:-
"COASTLINE,
LONDON."

In your reply please
quote this reference.

A. 5978   November 30th   1899.

Dear Sir,

In reply to your letter of the 20th instant, I am
arranging for a special train as under to run on Wednesday next
from Victoria to Petworth for the conveyance of H. R. H. the
Prince of Wales:-

                    Victoria,   dep.   4. 28. p.m.

                    Petworth,   arr.   5. 57. p.m.

As regards decorations I am consulting the Prince's
Equerry as to this but as it will be dark when His Royal Highness
arrives I am afraid we can do very little in this direction.

                    Yours truly,

Hubert E. Watson, Esq.,

        Estate Office,

            P E T W O R T H.

Arrangements for the royal train to run
from Victoria to Petworth on 6 December
1899.

116. Above: *Letter from the General*
Manager of the LBSCR to Petworth House.

117. Right: *The LBSCR's special train*
notice.

Described by a recent biographer
as the most important backbencher of
his time, his death was accompanied
by mourning which transcended all
shades of political opinion and all
ranks of society. *The Fun* magazine
on 15 April 1865 wrote: 'Since the
death of Sir Robert Peel England has
sustained no such loss as she now
suffers in the early and unexpected
death of Richard Cobden. Few men
whose views have met with so
much opposition have left with so
few enemies.'

Cobden's wish was to be buried
beside his son in the churchyard at
West Lavington, near Midhurst. It
had been announced that a special
train would leave London for

Midhurst on the day of the funeral. The
officials of the LSWR thought that about
50 persons would take the special train.
However, deputations from the most
important towns in the manufacturing
districts arrived in London and required
places on the train. On the morning of the
'special' there were 600 passengers and
the train consisted of no less than 21 first-
class and four second-class carriages.

The train staff of inspector, driver, fireman and guards were supplied with com-
plimentary mourning of crêpe hat-bands
and black gloves. Superintended by W.M.
Williams, Traffic Manager of the line, the
train left Waterloo at 9.40am for Midhurst
with every seat taken.[4] The *West Sussex*
Gazette reported that 'it was about twelve
o'clock when the train arrived at Midhurst – containing the greatest number of
carriages ever disgorged at the station.'[5]

A large deputation from Midhurst
headed the funeral procession which was
estimated by the local press to consist of
between 3,000 to 4,000 people. When it
reached the church, 12 of Cobden's closest
friends including John Bright and Glad-
stone carried the coffin.

The national press gave the funeral
extensive coverage, with
black borders and columns
of eulogy. It was indeed an
elaborate and spectacular
occasion and one in which
the railway had fulfilled a
central role.

It was not until towards
the end of the century that
other important trains – particularly those patronised by
royalty – ran on the local lines
around Chichester. Queen Victoria had made her first train
journey on the Great Western
Railway back in 1842, and yet
she never travelled to
Portsmouth for the trip to
Osborne House on the Isle of
Wight by the LBSCR – for her, it
was the LSWR. She disliked
Brighton where she had been
publicly insulted and therefore a
railway including this name was
not to be used.

Her eldest son, the Prince of
Wales, had no such qualms. In
1897, in his mother's Diamond
Jubilee Year, the LBSCR built
him a complete train. It was very

Going off the rails

beautiful with carriages all in varnished and gold-lined mahogany with deeply arched clerestory roofs. Lighting was electric and, in accordance with royal wishes, there was no corridor as he did not wished to be disturbed while travelling.

The royal train was a frequent visitor to the local lines around Chichester. Both as Prince of Wales, and later as King, Edward VII was a frequent visitor to the Goodwood Races and the West Dean Estate. For Goodwood Races the most convenient station was Drayton on the main west coast line just beyond Chichester – it is believed that the King would not use Chichester as the cathedral had refused to ring the bells on one occasion. Although Singleton, on the Chichester-Midhurst line, was used as a station for ordinary traffic to Goodwood Races, especially for the unloading of horses from Newmarket, the King only used Singleton station when he visited his friend William James who owned West Dean House. The 8,000-acre estate also became a popular venue during the pheasant shooting season and, complete with a splendid coat-of-arms in full heraldic colours on the front and sides of the locomotive, the royal train was often seen in Singleton station.

The first visit was made to West Dean in 1895 following the rebuilding of the house. Thereafter, and until his death in 1910, Edward VII and Queen Alexandra stayed at West Dean in preference to Goodwood House 'be it for shooting, the racing or to partake of that particular Victorian and Edwardian phenomena, week-ending. West Dean thus became one of the main social focal points for the smart set known as the Marlborough House Set, that retinue of friends that trailed around in the wake of the Prince and Princess of Wales.'[6] For the next 15 years these visits gave Singleton the reputation of being the royal station visited more times by the royal train than any other on the LBSCR. [7]

Singleton station was certainly not a typical country wayside halt. It was a very elegant building with platforms built on the side of a hill. Down below was the booking hall, ladies rooms, and the largest gentlemen's toilet block ever constructed for a country station. Also built on the lower level, the station master's house was occupied between 1895-1900 by William Odd. The platforms were reached by means of a covered way leading to a subway from which the stairs led up to the platforms. Situated on the downside platform was a magnificent refreshment room with a marble counter. Both platforms had waiting rooms. There were also a number of sidings to accommodate the racecourse traffic which included many special trains of horseboxes. To facilitate the easy departure of trains, Singleton also possessed a 40-foot diameter turntable, used to turn the engines of incoming trains.

With so many engines calling during race weeks, the station was equipped with water-cranes for replenishing the engines and a pump house, with a steam engine, to pump the water from the station's own supply into the water tank.

Phil Norrell grew up in Singleton and was appointed junior porter at the station in 1938. He well remembers the washbowls being set in one-inch thick marble. He was told that when royalty visited, a long length of red carpet was rolled up which went down from the platform steps through the subway and out to the entrance so they could join their carriage for the short journey to West Dean House.

It was not until July 1899 that the new LBSCR royal train made its first appearance at Singleton. In December of that year, the Prince of Wales visited Lord Leconfield at Petworth for a two-day pheasant shoot. Mrs W. Labbet of Addiscombe recorded how Granny Clarke outwitted the station protocol:

It was in 1899 when my mother was a little girl that there was great excitement because the Prince of Wales was coming to the station. He was going to visit Lord Leconfield. The station was painted and cleaned as never before – even the chocolate machines had a new coat of paint. All the children from the station cottages

118. The LBSCR royal train conveying King Edward VII, about to depart from Singleton station c 1906, and headed by 'B4' class 4-4-0 No 60 Kimberley.

opposite were allowed to go on to the station to stand at one side as their fathers were porters or station staff. This didn't apply to my mother. Although Granddad Clarke worked for the railway, he was a ganger on the line and so his children were not allowed on the platform.

The other fortunate children made sure they showed her their clean, white and starched pinnies and their best Sunday clothes, telling her and her younger brother that they were going to see the Prince.

Granny Clarke however told them to go down to the bottom of the garden and climb on the bank there: this made them only a few feet from the line and about eye-level to the train windows.

My mother can remember the Royal Train shining as it rounded the bend and slowed up on its approach to the station. There was the Prince in the compartment and my mother and her brother waved for all they were worth and he turned round, lifted his hat and smiled at them.

She was so close she could see the colour of his eyes, she says. When he arrived at the station, he walked across the red carpet inside the station and out to a waiting horse and carriage quite quickly and the other children hardly had a chance to see him![7]

An official visit was made to Midhurst on 13 June 1906 when the King and Queen arrived by the Royal Train to open the new sanatorium which had been known locally as the King's Sanatorium. Following the opening it was called the King Edward VII Sanatorium, Midhurst.

The King had been impressed with the sanatorium at Falkenstein near Frankfurt which he had visited while staying with his sister, the Empress Frederick of Kronberg. He therefore decided on his succession to build a sanatorium with money put at his disposal to help those sick with tuberculosis.[8] At that time the disease was rife and thousands of people died every year, many of them in their youth.

According to contemporary reports on the day of the opening the town of Midhurst was quite transformed with every part of the royal route decorated with flags and bunting proclaiming loyal greetings. 'The railway station had been decorated profusely by the LBSCR and the station, together with the courtyard, were policed by the company and no one but those receiving their Majesties and the Guard of Honour of the 2nd Vol. Batt. Royal Sussex Regiment were allowed inside.'[9]

'Punctually at four o'clock the Royal Train steamed into the station, a glimpse of the gaily decorated engine being caught through the garden attached to the station master's house. Their Majesties were conducted down a red carpeted slope placed

against the carriage door and were received on the platform by the Duke of Norfolk, who was attired in the gorgeous scarlet uniform of a Lord Lieutenant, the Duchess of Norfolk and other local dignitaries.' So reported the *Midhurst Times* of 15 June 1906.

After a few moments' delay the royal party walked through the booking hall to the station door where they boarded the royal carriage. To the sound of cheering crowds and the peal of the church bells the King and Queen commenced their 3½mile journey to the Sanatorium where 100 local schoolchildren greeted their arrival by the singing the National Anthem. There the King and Queen had a guided tour lasting approximately three hours, and the King expressed his pleasure at opening such a magnificently situated building.

The most historic royal train ever to pass through Chichester through Ford Junction, Arundel, Pulborough and thence to London was Queen Victoria's funeral train. It was ironic that while alive she refused to travel on the LBSCR but that her final journey to her place of rest should be over the South Coast line at the request of the new King, Edward VII. More bizarre was the manner of the journey.

On 18 January 1901, a press bulletin announced that the Queen was ill at Osborne House, on the Isle of Wight. Edward, Prince of Wales, together with the German Emperor travelled to Portsmouth Harbour in the royal train and went over to the island to be at her bedside.[10]

Going off the rails

Queen Victoria died on 22 January. On 1 February, her coffin was taken on board the Royal Yacht, *Victoria and Albert* for passage across the Solent to Royal Clarence Yard, Gosport. In his official work, *City of Portsmouth Corporation Records 1837-1927*, Mr W. G. Gates states that 'As the Royal Yacht entered the harbour, the last gleams of the winter sun shone forth upon the anchorage, the sky for a few minutes glowed red as the sun set, and the grey mist veiled the ships anchored in the Solent.'[11]

On the day of the funeral, Saturday, 2 February, Victoria Station was closed to the public and ordinary traffic between 9am and 11pm in preparation for receiving the royal train, the advertisements and placards were removed and parts of the station structure cleaned-up. The journey was to begin on the LSWR with the train being attached to a Brighton locomotive at Fareham.

Operating difficulties caused the carriages of King Edward's LBSCR train to be reversed into the platform and, according to the prepared seating plan, the coaches were the wrong way round. This was much to the annoyance of the royal and distinguished mourners, including the Kaiser. By the time the mourners had taken their seats – a process made more difficult in view of the lack of an internal corridor – the train pulled out of Royal Clarence Yard eight minutes behind time. Fortunately, the King was waiting in London for it was well-known that he disliked unpunctuality. [12]

There was a further delay on changing the engines at Fareham with Brighton 'B4' class 4-4-0 No 54 *Empress* coming on to the train. The pilot engine, also a 'B4', No 53 *Sidar*, was sent off in advance. By the time the funeral train was ready a further two minutes' time had been lost. On the footplate of the train engine were the LBSCR's Locomotive Superintendent, R. J. Billinton, with his Outdoor Locomotive Superintendent, J. Richardson and Driver Walter Cooper and Fireman F. W. Way. Richardson told Driver Cooper that for heaven's sake he was to make up some of the time at all costs as the new King would be livid if kept waiting at Victoria. [13]

The old Queen had always insisted that no train in which she travelled should ever exceed 40mph. Driver Cooper did as instructed and the Queen's mortal remains found themselves travelling at 80mph on the flat between Havant and Ford. To Victoria, a top speed of 92mph was then reached down Holmwood bank. With such speeds, quite unbecoming for the ultimate Victorian funeral, the train reached Victoria station two minutes early. The German Kaiser was so delighted with the high-speed journey that he sent an equerry to congratulate the driver and fireman. The King was, at that point, none the wiser and completely unruffled. This was not to last.

From Victoria Station, the coffin was conveyed on a gun-carriage through London to Paddington Station of the Great Western Railway for the last stage of the journey to Windsor. Before departure of the train, the King was heard to say to the Emperor, 'Come along, hurry up, we are

122. **Above:** *LBSCR 'B4' 4-4-0 No 54* **Empress** *which hauled Queen Victoria's funeral train from Fareham to Victoria on 2 February 1901. Note the funeral drapes and snow.*

123. **Right:** *Southern Railway poster warning of service reductions associated with the running of evacuation trains.*

20 minutes late already!' On arrival at Windsor the hawsers provided to haul the gun-carriage had frozen up and the horses had become restive in the intense cold. Communication cords had to be taken from berthed GWR coaches to enable seamen to haul the gun-carriage. [14]

King Edward VII made further visits to West Dean in 1904, 1906 and 1909. On 6 May in the following year the King died. Although the James family were on good terms with the new king, George V, he did not share his father's passion for racing or shooting. So, when Edward died, the Marlborough Set with its passion for weekending at West Dean also came to an end. Two years later, William James died and that ended the era of the royal trains to Sussex [15].

Between 1939 and 1945, the railways were crucial to the war effort and transported raw materials, armaments and forces personnel. One operation, imperative for the future of the country and very rarely acknowledged, was the evacuation of children just before the outbreak of World War II. By the end of September 1939, nearly 42,000 had arrived in West Sussex, including mothers and babies, children and their teachers.

Going off the rails

They arrived at one of the 12 chosen railheads around West Sussex. Pulborough was one such railhead which expected to receive 1,773 children. These railheads were a vital key to the whole evacuation plan, from the receipt of children to their dispersal throughout West Sussex.

'Big boys don't cry!' James Roffey recalls his teacher's admonition to boys in his class showing signs of becoming apprehensive or, even worse, beginning to cry at the looming prospect of being evacuated from London to the countryside. [16]

In August 1939, with war on the horizon, the schools in London had been reopened to make final preparations for the evacuation of children.

For a number of years the government had been planning an evacuation in the event of war as it was believed that massive air-raids would be launched upon London and other major cities as soon as war was declared, so making road and rail traffic very difficult. To avoid the chaos and panic, the children were to be sent away in advance.

James Roffey was eight years old at the time. With his brother John, one year older, he went to his sister's school, the Peckham Central Girls School. Parents could decide whether younger children should be evacuated with an elder brother or sister and, if so, they would go with their school.

Every day he set off for school with his brother and sister, each child taking with them a packed lunch, a changed of clothing, nightclothes, toothbrush and toothpaste, soap and towel. All these things were to be carried in a suitcase or strong knapsack. There was no room for teddy-bears or dolls which would have helped many of the children with prolonged homesickness. In addition each child carried a gas-mask.

There were frequent practices of evacuation drill with the children being formed into a long crocodile and marched round the playground. At some schools the children were even marched down to the local railway station and back again.

Parents had known about the evacuation for months, being urged by the government to 'Send them to Safety', yet they would not know the departure date until their child failed to return home from school, or in going to the school to meet them the parents would have found only the destination notice of the school population affixed to the gates. For this reason, many mothers used to gather outside school at playtimes to see whether the children had left for the country. It was rumoured that the departure date was being kept a secret because it was feared the Germans might bomb the trains carrying the evacuees and so induce mass panic.

Each child had been given a stamped postcard addressed to their parents which was to be sent home on arrival with the name and address of their foster families, together with a mes-

EVACUATION
OF
WOMEN AND CHILDREN FROM LONDON, Etc.

FRIDAY, 1st SEPTEMBER.
Up and Down business trains as usual, with few exceptions.
Main Line and Suburban services will be curtailed while evacuation is in progress during the day.

SATURDAY & SUNDAY.
SEPTEMBER 2nd & 3rd.
The train service will be exactly the same as on Friday

Remember that there will be very few Down Mid-day business trains on Saturday.

SOUTHERN RAILWAY

sage saying that they had arrived safely. No other arrangements had been made for billeting officers, or for the schools to notify parents where their children had been placed.

In schools all over London, on Friday, 1 September 1939, school bells rang for what might have been another evacuation drill. In playgrounds something new happened. Teachers went round tying brown cardboard luggage labels on to each child, upon which had been written the child's name and that of the school. Instead of marching round the playground, the school gates were flung open and, clutch-

ing bags and suitcases, children marched into the busy streets to commence a new life: for some, a wonderful time, but for others years of misery never to be forgotten – The Evacuation had begun!

That day, 600,000 children, together with their teachers and helpers, were moved on special trains out of London. Railwaymen who should have been off-duty were at their depots waiting for instructions. For the next four days, the railway timetable on the Southern Railway was suspended between 8am and 5pm for the movement of the 225 special trains. To assist the passage of children being evacuated by bus, no traffic was allowed to re-enter London along nine major routes.

On the gates of Peckham Central Girls School, the notice stated that the school population had gone to Pulborough and Fittleworth in West Sussex.

With so many children to be evacuated it was impossible for every school to use the main London termini and therefore each school had been instructed to use a local railway station. Peckham Central Girls school had to depart from Queens Road station which was approximately a mile from the school.

By the time the children had reached the station on this sunny September day the earlier excitement was beginning to wane. Children struggled with bags and cases as they climbed the steps up to the station platform where the train had not yet arrived.

Eventually, the train arrived, made-up of old Southern Railway carriages with single compartments, i.e. with a corridor and no toilets. As children do, they surged forward to obtain a window-seat while brothers and sisters tried to keep together. Then the train departed and, as James Roffey recalled, 'No one thought for one moment that most of us would be away for many years and that some families, mine included, would never again be fully reunited.' [17]

The sprawling suburbs gave way to green fields and cows and sheep, but for the children the journey was slow and tedious with many checks at signals. With children hot and clearly anxious about their new lives, the lack of toilet facilities was an acute problem. John Kelly of Herne Hill, south London, well remembers the difficulty. He was seven years old at the time and was evacuated with his sister's school to Horsham. After two hours on the train he badly needed to 'go' and had to tell his sister that he couldn't hold on any longer. John remembers that 'two of the girls then held me up to an open window while the rest all laughed. I was acutely embarrassed but it was either that or wet my trousers.' [18] His train arrived in Horsham at 3.30pm, having departed at ten o'clock in the morning. One little chap in John Roffey's compartment was not so lucky and had an accident.

The train conveying James, John and sister Jean eventually stopped at a station. They had no idea where they were because there were no station names: all place-names had been taken down or painted over on Government instructions. The porters came along opening all the doors and shouted to the occupants to get out. All the children were then marshalled in Pulborough station's hot station yard.

Facing the evacuees were rows of temporary lavatories. At last, relief for the weary travellers. Though individual cubicles had been formed from canvass over a wooden frame, each with a wooden seat and a shiny bucket underneath, they were all open-fronted and few of the children would use them saying, 'We may be busting to go but we are not using those with everyone gawping at us.' [19] At the station the Women's Institute were present and the Boy Scouts were at tables issuing every evacuee with a carrier-bag containing food.

Gladys Gent of Pulborough remembers the day the evacuees arrived: 'One incident I can remember was of the torment of my father. He was a permanent way inspector on the railway and was helping the station master at Pulborough with all the children who arrived off the train and were waiting for their new families to collect them. Suddenly, there was an air-raid warning. Fortunately it was a false alarm, but at the time it was very frightening.'

'The special train brought-in hundreds of children to the small country station of Pulborough. They filled the platforms and the area outside, there was little or no shelter for them from the hot sunshine: certainly not from bombs or machine-gun bullets. There were no air-raid shelters. The carnage that could have been caused by an attack is too frightening to think about.' [20]

Even the government feared heavy air-raids on Britain before war was declared, in the hope of forcing an early peace settlement. The special evacuee trains were seen as a prime target because of the devastating effect upon public morale if children had been killed.

The Southern Railway performed a extremely complex operation moving 42,000 evacuees to West Sussex and there would doubtless have been difficulties. When the first schools arrived at the railway stations with fewer children than expected, changes had to be made to prevent trains running half-empty. In some cases, trains were cancelled but this led to overcrowding and with so much extra traffic on the railways delays became worse as the evacuation continued throughout the weekend.

Following their arrival at the railhead the children were put on to buses for their eventual destinations. Even though a large number were relocated to Petworth and Fittleworth they were transported from Pulborough by bus; the railway service was not used, probably because buses would still have had to be provided because of the distance of these stations from the places they purported to serve.

In John Roffey's case, he was transported to the Pulborough village school where all new arrivals were inspected for head-lice, by a nurse with a metal comb dripping with disinfectant, followed by a mouth inspection while holding the tongue down with a wooden stick. Then it was soon 'cattle market time' with foster aunts and uncles looking over the children and some being very selective. According to James Roffey 'it was said afterwards that some of them only wanted strong, quiet children who looked as though they were capable of farm or housework.' [21]

This was not always the case. After a few false starts, James and his brother went to live with Mr and Mrs Birchell who kept a shop near the railway station. His sister was billeted up the road and, later on, his brother lived with Mr and Mrs Deadman at Ferrymead Cottage.

Living near the station James became a good friend of the goods porter who regularly came into the Birchell's shop for a cup of tea. Although a proper village shop selling a full range of groceries, ice cream, cigarettes and confectionery, it also possessed a tea-room in the back garden. It was

very popular with people who had a cup of tea while they waited for a bus or train.

'The good porter', as he called himself, would call out 'strong cup of tea with lots of sugar for a good porter!' [22] when he came into the shop and James would help him with the unloading and sorting of all the parcels and items which arrived in boxvans which had been shunted into the station's goods bay. They were then delivered to a wide radius from the station on one of the lorries of Mr Pullin, the local carrier.

The railway station became one of his favourite places, especially after he had made friends with another evacuee who had been billeted with the station master and his wife. Both boys had free run of the station, provided they behaved themselves and didn't go anywhere dangerous. There were visits to the signalbox, although it was completely against railway regulations, and the boys had to crouch down whenever a main line train went through – in case an inspector was on board.

The motor-train service to Midhurst was known by the locals as the 'Midhurst Boat Train' because when the River Arun was in flood everyone could see the little train puffing its way along an embankment apparently surrounded by water. At times, it was actually *in* the water because a section of the line near Fittleworth station would sometimes become flooded by the River Rother.

The line was used by many pupils of Midhurst Grammar School who caught the 8.20 train in the morning and arrived back in Pulborough at 5.09pm. Running eight times a day in each direction the train was always on the move and, according to James Roffey, made far more noise than any of the electric trains. 'As it approached Pulborough station it always gave off numerous whistles and shrieks, and when it stopped at its side platform there would be a loud whoosh of released steam. Then it had to be shunted across the lines to the down sidings, where it waited until a main line train had been cleared from the station.' [23]

James Roffey enjoyed his time at Pulborough and wrote 'although in the early 1940s Pulborough was still primarily a rural village there were always plenty of things going on to keep small boys interested. By comparison London was quite dull.' [24]

Undoubtedly, country life was a shock for many evacuees. From living in a mod-

Going off the rails

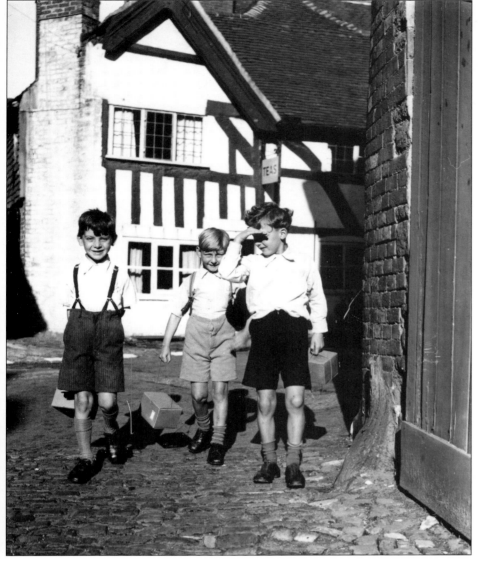

ern brick-built house with electricity and indoor sanitation, many children moved to old country cottages without electricity and whose toilets were outside and merely comprised a bucket. No wonder parents were puzzled when reference was made to 'stinging nettles got my knees on the way to the lavatory.' [25] Lighting was usually provided by a single oil-lamp while the only light in the bedroom was a candle.

However, food – of major importance to growing boys – was far more plentiful in the countryside than in the towns. Mr Reg Hough of Lightwater who billeted with Mr and Mrs Kenward at Foxhill, near Petworth, records that the generous quantities of food available did not result from frequent visits to International Stores, the largest of the grocers in Petworth, but from the constant and on-going planning. 'Large sections of the garden would be devoted to sowing potatoes so that their crop ensured that potatoes were available throughout the year. So it was with every crop.' [26]

Fruit was also in plentiful supply provided by the use of 'Kilner jars' of which the Kenward's store cupboard contained no less than 300. In Mr Hough's own words, 'this resulted in quite different styles of meals. Before being billeted at Petworth, I cannot recall ever having been provided with spotted dick, suet pudding, or steak and kidney pudding, and certainly my London meals would never have contained such a high percentage of fruit when one had a sweet... Before going to Petworth, I doubt if I had ever seen a gooseberry.' [27]

Margaret Smith (née Petty) of Nunhead has fond memories of the evacuation:

I was 13 years old in 1939 and lived in Camelot Street, near the Old Kent Road and went to Leo Street School. I can remember going off that day with my belongings in a pillow-case. I had a younger step-cousin with me who I had to look after. When we arrived at Pulborough we were assembled...... and we finally ended up with a Mrs Bartlett (Aunt

Eileen) and her sister Miss Saxby (Aunt Linda) at a house called 'Sunningdale' in Lower Street.

I have fond memories of my time there; I loved the country; the River Arun ran at the bottom of the garden and I was allowed to fish there. I remember the flooding when the water came halfway up the garden..... We were treated kindly and bought dresses and Wellington boots and fed well.

We seldom saw Mr Bartlett. He worked in the bank in the village. I remember they used to have musical evenings and he had a deep voice singing *On the Road to Mandalay*, while his wife played the piano. I had only been used to my mother tinkling on the piano, *Lily of Laguna* and *Knees up, Mother Brown* but we were too polite to laugh. It was a completely different way of living to what we knew. [28]

It is not the intention of these few pages to investigate in depth the experiences of the evacuees. Indeed, their stories are worthy of a whole book. Given the fear of aerial bombing, evacuation seemed a logical step in 1939, its wisdom subsequently confirmed by the casualties and deprivations endured by Londoners during the Blitz.

Yet, even in West Sussex, the children were not out of danger, and after Dunkirk the vulnerability of the South Coast saw some London evacuees transferred inland. A number reported strafing by enemy planes, and in 1941 bombing raids led to the evacuation of West Sussex schoolchildren to the Midlands. A year later, on 29 September 1942, came the tragedy at Petworth when 28 children aged 7-12 and two school teachers were killed in the bombing of the Boys' School.

For many evacuees their time in West Sussex changed their outlook on life. James Roffey, for instance, became a country lad and yearned to be back at Pulborough following his return to London. Many kept in touch with their foster families while other evacuees never left Sussex. Some children chose to stay in the country and were helped by their foster parents who looked upon them as their own. For others, they had no home to return to as all their relatives had been killed.

It is easy to become sidetracked from

125. *London schoolchildren at Billingshurst station, on their way to country homes in West Sussex.*

the special evacuation trains to the plight of the evacuees but the stories are so many, personal and varied that some mention must be included of their lives once the trains had delivered them to West Sussex. Perhaps the recollections of William Story of South London provide a suitable conclusion to the account.

I was an evacuee and left London on 1 September 1939 from Waterloo station to be taken to the village of Redford, near Midhurst in West Sussex, where I lived with the same family for about four years. I was ten years old and a pupil of St Alnan's School, Walworth. I was well cared for by my foster parents and enjoyed a happy time – but for the fact of being separated from my family.

I had three brothers, one of them considerably older than me. He stayed in London but the other two were evacuated, one going to Somerset with St Paul's School, Walworth. The other, who was only three, was taken to Mentmore Towers in Hert-

fordshire. It has remained a mystery to me as to why we had to be separated and can only assume it was due to lack of co-ordination during what must have been a traumatic time for all the parents and the authorities.

Although it was done for the best intentions it created many problems, I did not see my brothers until five years later, and only saw my father once while I was away. I did not see my mother until I came home in 1944. Although we lived together again we were never to regain our family closeness.

I am now the only survivor of the family and often wonder what it would have been like if we had all been able to keep together during what I regard as a very important part of our lives. [29]

The local lines around Chichester witnessed a variety of special trains from those conveying racehorses to the Goodwood Races to King Edward VII's resplendent royal train of the early part of this century. These were in marked contrast to the plight of the evacuees during World War II – a progression from the joyful to the sad.

126. *The exterior of Pulborough station in the late 1960s.*

Going off the rails

Chapter 10: 'Years of cheerfulness and friendship'
— the Petersfield-Pulborough passenger service

'Once a year, on a Saturday afternoon, our mother, father, my three sisters and I went to Petersfield, a distance of nine miles, to shop for bargains in the market, to see the crowds, to listen to the Salvation Army band and to buy fish'. So wrote Mavis Budd in her book *Dust to Dust*.

She continued:

Buying the fish was the main reason for going. There was a stall on the market, owned by a fishmonger from Portsmouth, locally known as 'Lovely Grub', and there was no fish in the world to compare to the fish he sold. Our annual feast of cod from this stall was an event we all looked forward to for weeks and looked back on with great satisfaction.

Catching the train was a chancy business because we had to walk nearly three miles over the common to the station, and in the last desperate minutes before leaving Mother *always* discovered things which *had* to be

127. An all too common sight on the West Sussex branch lines – a one-coach train, in this case a motor-train worked by an ex-LSWR 'M7' 0-4-4T. This view dates from July 1954 and shows a Petersfield-Midhurst service at Elsted.

done. Also, the dog seemed to detect the mounting urgency and whined to be let out, or else rushed about the garden and refused to be brought in.

However, we always reached the station in time, and generally with some to spare. Mother, who was the family leader in all things bought the tickets, while Father pottered about in the station yard, looking at whatever there was to look at, and probing about among the wagons and farm equipment which lay about.

The station was small and really much less like a railway station and much more like a smallholding. There were flourishing vegetables on the banks and wherever there was earth to grow things in. Chickens roamed the line. Goats were tethered in the sidings. Lines of washing hung along the platform at the far end, and garbled voices of ducks came from the back of the waiting room.

We hadn't been waiting long before the bell clanged. The hens

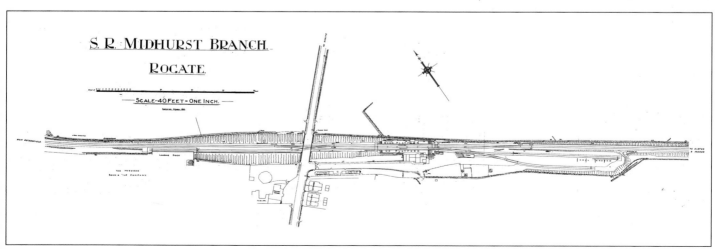

128. Official drawing of Rogate station, surveyed in 1914. Note the loading dock for traffic from the Nyewood Brick & Tile Co.

129. *The former LSWR station at Midhurst which closed in 1925. This shows the former platform side.*

clucked and fluttered with panic, while the ducks set up a long chorus of disturbance.

'That means she's left Midhurst' said Mother. 'Now you can begin to watch for her.'

We stared down the line to where it curved away out of sight in the trees. We were all anxious to be the first to see the puff of smoke from the engine ... But somehow ... we all managed to see it at the same time. .... then suddenly the train curled out from the trees and raced towards us while the creatures scattered in all directions.

In the carriage there were four window seats and it really didn't mat-

Midhurst carriers:

130. Below: *I. L. Stent, 'Coal, corn and forage merchants'.*

131. Below right: *J. Hillier, Easebourne Dairy.*

ter which one we each had. Mother then let down both windows, as low as they'd go saying there was no air at all and she'd never survive the journey if there wasn't some ventilation.

She was right about there being no air in the carriage, it was hot and stifling, and you could taste the flavour of tobacco smoke and other people.

The seats were upholstered with dark-red material which was rough and pricked through our clothes and against our bare thighs. They were hard seats, narrow and rigid, and it was not easy to settle comfortably on them.

Then the train began to move and for the first time since we started to get ready for the trip I could relax.

Here was a typical journey on the Midhurst to Petersfield route in the 1920s. It is probable that travel on the line remained very much the same until the closure notices appeared.

Let us return to Mavis Budd for the family's return trip after buying the cod from 'Old Lovely Grub', listening to the

Salvation Army band, obtaining red jelly sweets from Woolworth's, a visit to the baker's, purchasing Grandfather's liniment and Aunt Georgie's braid. After a panic for the train it was found steaming slightly in the station and the family scrambled aboard and waited.

Mother said, 'If I'd known there was going to be all this time to wait I'd have had a look at the second-hand books. They might have had some Edgar Wallace............

The train continued to wait. Our parents asked each other what on earth happened. Both answered that they didn't know, but someone ought to go and find out. Father got out. We heard him shout 'Oi', to someone, then after a few minutes, he was back, grinning and muttering 'he might have known'.

'The engine's gone off without the carriages', he said. 'It's on its way back, but the porter doesn't think it'll be here for another half-hour.

So we continued to sit and wait, and it was every bit that half-hour before we recoupled and on our homeward journey.

So it seems that this branch had similar incidents to those on the Selsey Tram. As with Selsey Line's Tram the 'Petersfield Bumper' (every country branch in the land seemed to christen its train with the name Bumper) was run for the benefit of its customers. Staff were always considerate and young mothers were grateful for the help with prams which could be accommodated in the guard's van. Mrs Strugnall living at Nyewood had cause to remember a visit to her grandparents at Petersfield with her first baby. Just as she was about to board the train for the return

132. *Rogate station, looking towards Petersfield, in 1905.*

journey home, the driver, whom she remembers as Sandy, asked 'Where's the baby?' The baby and pram were hastily retrieved from outside the shoe-shop and the train which the driver had held, departed two minutes late.

For mothers with young infants living in small villages the railway made journeys possible – without it they would not have gone anywhere. Baby and pram could be pushed to the station and then put aboard the train. Even if the journey was just seven miles to the nearest town it enabled young married women to obtain items not available in the village shop and allowed them to have a life beyond the same four walls of home.

Mr J. Merritt of Headley Down also remembers the kindness of the staff when travelling through the picturesque Sussex countryside. During the war he had been posted from Halifax to Tunbridge Wells for six months and obtained 48-hour leave. Returning to his parents home in Easebourne, near Midhurst, from barracks in Tunbridge Wells, from a colleague at the army camp he had managed to hire a dress uniform with peaked cap instead of wearing the ill-fitting battledress. Having changed at Three Bridges for a train to Pulborough, and then at Pulborough for the Midhurst train, he settled down for the journey home. As most people do, he put his head out of the window to view the Sussex scene and take in the air whereupon his peaked dress cap blew off. The monetary consequences of this incident would be quite severe.

In a bit of a fluster Mr Merritt mentioned the incident to the porter at Midhurst, who said he would pass the mes-

sage through and asked him to come to the station next day to see whether they had any luck. Upon Mr Merritt's arrival at the station the following day, he was presented with his dress hat. Such was the service of the staff who had tramped the line to find the peaked cap.

Further up the line at Rogate, Commander Bird RN had fond memories of the line. Living in Nyewood he commuted to the Admiralty for two years and possessed the last season ticket on the line. Although the station was called 'Rogate for Harting', and was situated in the parish of Harting, it was also a stone's throw from Nyewood. Commander Bird could time the start of the day by the railway. The sound of the engine puffing its way towards Rogate meant that he should soon be out of the front door where a short walk over the bottom field brought him to Rogate station for the motor-train service to Petersfield, then an electric train to London.

Friendliness of the staff was another memory. Once, some of Commander Bird's horses got on to the line and the train chased them in fits and starts all the way to Elsted station. There they left the line and found their own way home. His wife had gone in pursuit

133. *Joan Gibbs contemplates today's dereliction at Rogate station.*

of the horses but on their return journey from Midhurst the staff on the train stopped to give her the latest news.

Being a season ticket-holder did have its advantages. Commander Bird recalled that on one bitterly cold day, when the electric service from London was subject to long delays, he had arrived in Petersfield two hours late to find his steam train connection to Rogate long since departed. Imagine his astonishment to find the train still in the bay. When he asked why the train had been held he was told, 'Well, you are a season ticket-holder!' Needless to say, his arrival was met with relief by the other passengers who could have been home sometime previously.

Between 1944 and 1947 'Rogate for Harting' station was run by Joan Gibbs, née Hill. Joan had come from a family with a long history of railway service. Her grandfather worked on the LSWR while her father had joined the LBSCR and was a platelayer on the local lines. Her brother had joined the locomotive department and was a driver from Guildford locomotive shed.

Among her earliest memories were those of her father being out all hours, especially at night during the weekends, when track was being relaid. Home was a railway cottage at Nyewood, adjacent to Rogate station, and as a young girl Joan would walk along the track at Rogate

picking cowslips and primroses. There was no danger as she knew the times of the trains and when it was safe to walk by the line.

During World War II men were being called up and three jobs became vacant at Rogate, Elsted, and Midhurst stations. Joan applied and went up to Redhill with two other girls, Joy Uckfield and Audrey Carter, for an exam. Joan came out top and was allocated to Rogate, while Joy was posted to Elsted, and Audrey to Midhurst.

Joan Gibbs was the only paid staff at the small country station of Rogate which came under the control of the station master at Midhurst, Mr Gent, who came out on a weekly check to see that all was in order. Joan Gibbs remembers him as a very fair man but he liked everything carried out properly, in true railway service tradition. When he was on board the train the drivers would often blow the engine's whistle on the approach to Rogate as a warning that an official visit was to be made. Naturally, Joan was given a uniform, consisting of navy-blue trousers and jacket which had brass buttons, white blouse, black tie, black shoes, and a peaked cap. Of the uniform Joan recalls 'it was much nicer than they wear today'.

Work started at 8am and the station was opened up ready for the first train from Midhurst at 8.20. Tickets were issued and collected. One early arrival from Midhurst would have been Ron Treagus who delivered papers in Rogate for W. H. Smith and Sons. The busiest day for passengers was on Saturdays when a

number of people travelled to Petersfield for shopping.

Following the arrival and departure of the first train, general station duties were carried out until the sound of the daily goods could be heard as the engine puffed its way into Rogate. Some drivers would blow the whistle after leaving Elsted, and also whistle before coming into the station. When the train came to a standstill the crew would tell Joan how many wagons were to be shunted off. She would then go up into the signalbox and pull the point lever and the crew would uncouple and shunt the appropriate wagons into the siding, and collect the empties.

The train would go on to deliver materials to the Nyewood brickworks which had its own siding beyond the station where the village road bridge crossed the line. Coal was brought in, and bricks taken out.

Each day Nine Elms would be telephoned with details of trucks required for the transport of freight for the following day, and how many empties had to be collected. At sugar beet time there was considerably more traffic and Joan recalled no matter how many trucks she ordered for Messrs Silk, Challen, Davey and Bates, who were local farmers, they always required more when the produce was delivered to the station.

134. BR notice announcing the withdrawal of the Pulborough-Petersfield passenger service.

Munday's had a timber yard adjacent to the station and sent out a lot of timber. Corn was another commodity which was also dispatched. For every truck sent out a label displaying its destination was attached and, on delivery, the consignment was entered into a ledger. The charges for the goods were calculated by railway clerk, Mr Whale of Lavant, on his weekly visit. The railway was essential to the village shops which received the majority of its stock by train. Occasionally, a coal wagon would be shunted off into the station siding but normally coal for the Rogate neighbourhood would be delivered to Elsted.

Joan Gibbs did all station jobs, including sheeting the wagons with tarpaulins. There was one exception, as she recalls 'The only job I didn't do was to clean the gentlemen's toilets – they sent out a man from Midhurst to do both Elsted's and Rogate's. My father was very proud of me and used to help me at the end of the day with moving heavy loads such as sacks of flour after he had finished his ganger duties on the line. He looked after the stretch of line between Rogate and Petersfield and there was not a weed in sight.'

Once Joan became used to the work she found it easy and then time could be

135. The last day of regular passenger services at Midhurst in February 1955, and out of Midhurst Tunnel ahead of a train appeared a fine horse!

Going off the rails

spent tending the station garden. It was boarded with whitewashed stones and was always full of colour with spring and summer flowers. The last train to arrive was the 6.50pm but by this time Joan had locked up the station and the guard on the train would attend to the tickets.

Joan, known as 'Copper Knob' because of the brightness of her red hair, left Rogate in 1947 when men returning from the War required their old jobs back. But memories of those days of the friendliness of the passengers and life in the railway cottage are still vivid and looked upon as a good period in her life.

As with the earlier closure of the Chichester to Midhurst line, falling passenger traffic and road competition sealed the fate of passenger services on the Petersfield-Pulborough line. British Railways claimed that it was losing £31,000 a year on the service. The final day came in February 1955. In complete contrast to the Chichester line where passenger services were withdrawn without a murmur or a 'memorial' send-off, Midhurst and Petersfield stations witnessed more people than ever when the final day came on 5 February 1955.

Midhurst station was the centre of attraction for hundreds of enthusiasts and sightseers. Had they used the railway more they might not have been witnessing the last passenger train journey. Even the uniformed town band, playing rousing tunes, greeted the trains from Petersfield and Pulborough.

The demand for tickets had been the largest for many a year, only Bank Holidays in days before World War I had witnessed such crowds. Every train both ways was crowded all day and the demand for tickets was so great that at Midhurst the large stocks dwindled away. All single and ordinary return tickets and blank tickets were issued, and finally staff had to write out 'blanks'.

One of the last to book his tickets to Pulborough on the last train was Mr H. A. Chave. He was station master at Midhurst from 1933-1942 and was in charge of stations on the Chichester to Midhurst line when both Phil Norrell and Vic Clayton were running Singleton. According to the

West Sussex Gazette on 10 February 1955 Mr Chave said that there was talk about closing the line in the 1930s and the 'heads' had a conference about it at Lavant station. 'I told them, you have not properly opened it yet'.

Earlier on that last day the 1.59pm from Pulborough was late. Officials on the platform looked towards the tunnel in the hope of seeing the train. Suddenly, a white horse emerged at the trot and proceeded down the track with guard Mr J. Hutchinson who had chased the horse from Selham! Then came the train. The horse was headed-off and eventually caught and restored to its owner.

All too soon, the evening came with the approach of the final services. The train came in from Petersfield with the three coaches and their corridors packed with people. With over 200 people on the platform, the cheering and shouting faded away and then the Last Post was sounded by Mr J. Pett of the Midhurst Band. The guard, Mr J. Hutchinson, waved his flag. To the stirring sounds of *Sussex by the Sea*, long, shrill whistles and the blast of fog detonators, with Driver F. Goldsmith at the controls, and Fireman G. Howse, the 8.20pm pulled out of Midhurst for Pulborough and entered the tunnel for the very last time.

There were similar scenes for the departure of the Pulborough train when it had been sent on the last stage of its journey to Petersfield. The driver for the Petersfield train was R. Fears and the engine was fired by J. Myers, both of Guildford, with L. Horwood as guard.

The last day of services, 5 February 1955

139. Top: *Passengers pose in a doorway of one of the typically elderly coaches used on Pulborough-Petersfield trains.*

140. Above: *A banner is strung on the bunker of the engine hauling the last train.*

141. Right: *The guard of the last train from Midhurst waits with his lamp while the station master looks on.*

142.
The last ticket issued at Midhurst on 5 February 1955 was never used and retained as a souvenir.

Both trains having departed from Midhurst, 14 year-old Mary Taylor, daughter of porter-clerk, Mr C. Taylor, switched-off the station lights. After a final look round, Station Master, Mr J. B. Dymond locked the main entrance door for the last time.

In special honour of the final day's services, the train used the main line platforms at Petersfield, and when it pulled in ready for the last run through to Pulborough scores of people were waiting to board it.

After the long shrill of the engine's whistle, prompt on 7.48pm the train moved forward to the blast of fog detonators which were the station staff's contribution to the excitement of the final run. As the locomotive steadily accelerated to 40mph, excited shouts came from the swaying carriages as every wayside dwelling was passed.

As an acknowledgement to the last train, cottage and house curtains were thrown back. Torches, candles even, were waved behind the windows as the train went by with smoke drifting back over the carriages to the purring beat of the exhaust. At Rogate and Nyewood, a score or more of villagers welcomed the train with a rousing cheer while only two cheering souls were at Elsted station. Then it was on to Midhurst to the banners and cheering crowds, through Selham, Petworth, Fittleworth, and finally into Pulborough station.

The train from Midhurst made steady progress on its final leg to Petersfield. However, just before it was due to join the main line, it came to a grinding halt. It waited and the seconds turned to minutes, followed by the appearance of heads from windows. Then, through the night air came the roar of a passing London to Portsmouth electric express. Soon all was quiet once more, then signals clanked and the train completed its last journey.[2] The end had truly arrived. For the very last time people climbed out of the carriages – carriages which had seen generations of children from their first journey in prams to the independence of teenage years on the 'Petersfield Bumper'.

143. *It's 6 February 1955 and the day after the last public services the 'Hampshireman' rail tour special comes to Midhurst.*

A number of people went to the locomotive seeking the autographs of the driver and the fireman. Then it was all gone and, apart from the memories, the line might not have existed for all those years.

The feeling of the staff about the closure is exemplified by this letter from a guard on the Midhurst branch line, Mr Les Horwood of Emsworth. It was published in the *Midhurst, Petworth and District Times* on Friday, 11 February 1955.

The letter was headed – 'To the Nyewood and district residents':

I cannot let this day go by without conveying my sincere thanks to you all, for the kindness shown to me on Saturday on a very sad occasion in my career as guard on your branch line. I must say I felt a great wrench, when I signalled with my lamp, that last train from Rogate station on Saturday, and said those cheerios to you all, and signed those tickets and autograph books. Although I have been with you all only six years on our little run between Rogate and Petersfield and sometimes from Rogate to

144. *The last passenger train of all to run to Midhurst was a railtour whose passengers have spilled over the track and platforms to photograph 'Q' class 0-6-0 No 30530 on 18 October 1964.*

Midhurst, they have been years of cheerfulness and friendship which I will always remember, even whether it was with the adults or the children and their mothers.

I have always tried to keep a family feeling among you, and treated you all alike. Civility and friendliness cost nothing, but can mean much to the giver and receiver.

You will all know my opinion of this drastic closure of the line, and how much I hoped it would never come, now it has happened it remains to live, and hope, for the return at some future date.

On the following day a railway enthusiasts' ten-coach excursion special named the 'Hampshireman', and pulled by two ex-LBSCR Class 'E5x' tank engines Nos 32576 and 32570, travelled over the Petersfield-Midhurst-Pulborough and Meon Valley Lines. About 250 people were aboard and the train stopped for about ten minutes at Midhurst station. Three of the passengers were unlucky. They forgot to reboard the train before it left.

The final passenger train at Midhurst was another excursion, one jointly organised by two railway societies. It ran on 18 October 1964, hauled by an ex-Southern Railway 'Q' Class locomotive No 30530.

Goods continued on the Midhurst to Pulborough line, but falling traffic brought about the closure of the goods yard at Selham and Fittleworth in May 1963. A goods train continued to run three times a week, and during the final months, mainly coal trucks for Corrall's Petworth depot.

On 20 May 1966, the last train travelled from Pulborough to Petworth where commemorative detonators where placed on the track in recognition of the final train. One hundred and seven years of railway history had been brought to a close.

145. *The track had been removed by the time this photograph was taken of Midhurst station.*

Chapter 11: Bombs and washout on the Chichester-Midhurst line

Mention has been made already that, during World War II, Singleton and Cocking Tunnels on the Chichester-Midhurst line were used for the storage of wagons containing naval ammunition – mines, torpedoes and shells. West Dean Tunnel remained clear so that the daily goods train could continue to serve Singleton. The ammunition wagons for Cocking arrived from the Midhurst end and those stored at Singleton came from the Chichester end of the line.

Singleton Tunnel was straight and, according to Vic Clayton, 'you could see the horseshoe of light at the other end'. The tunnel accommodated 100 wagons, either

146: *The recovery in February 1952 of the 'C2x' class goods engine*

147. *Humdrum may be....a sugar beet train at Lavant in the 1950s.*

box vans or open wagons sheeted with tarpaulins. Wagons were stabled to within 100 yards of either end of the tunnel.

Although the storage of the ammunition wagons was supposed to be a secret, Vic Clayton recalls that the wind blew loose the tarpaulins letting him see the spikes projecting from the mines. In fact, most local people knew that ammunition was stored in the tunnels. In his radio broadcasts the Nazi propagandist 'Lord Haw-Haw' announced on the radio that the Germans would bomb the tunnels and blow the whole place to smithereens. They tried one night but let loose their bombs on West Dean Tunnel instead and so little damage was done. As the cutting started some way back from the tunnel-mouth it was very difficult to bomb. For any chance of success a bomb would have had to entered through the tunnel-mouth – a virtual impossibility.

According to Vic, placing the ammunition trains made the railway staff nervous, not least the train crews. The scheduled goods train brought up a couple of ammunition wagons attached at 10 in the morning. The train crew would prepare the train ready for the return to Chichester, and then place the other wagons in the tunnel. While Phil Norrell was at Singleton the tunnels were guarded by the Pioneer Corps based at a camp at nearby Littlewood Farm. During Vic Clayton's time the army guard was billeted at the *Horse and Groom* Pub at Singleton and a detachment of Coldstream Guards were also billeted at the station.

When it was time for wagons to be removed from the tunnel a small tank engine would come up the line from Chichester with a guard's brake van in tow. On board there was a driver, fireman, pilot guard, and a Navy representative who came from Cocking. Arrangements for the storage of ammunition at Cocking were dealt with by Midhurst station.

At Singleton the engine would run round the brake van and push it to the tunnel. Instructions as to how many wagons were required came from the Admiralty through Chichester station. If the last wagon was needed then all the wagons had to taken into Singleton yard, and then shunted back into the tunnel.

Vic Clayton remembers the guards – Bill Marsh, George Hurst, Bill Lillywhite and Dave Power. There was one who had

148./149. Above and right: The recovery in February 1952 of the 'C2x' class goods engine which went into the washed-out culvert between Singleton and Midhurst.

no problems during a daytime turn but at dusk or at night-time didn't want to go to the tunnel to shunt the wagons. This chap stayed in the office to get the engine crew's supper ready – at lunchtime, eggs were cooked on the shovel over the firegrate of the engine.

One night, a local policeman knocked on Vic Clayton's door and summoned him to the station. Up he went on his bike, without any lights because of the blackout, and on arrival telephoned Chichester station. The message was that a particular wagon was required and its location was known by a list. As it was near the end of the rake of stored wagons this meant moving 98 of them to get to the remaining two.

Vic recollects that the written regulation was that only 10 wagons could be moved at one time, so the operation to shunt out and back would take hours. Even with 10 wagons the small tank

engines had to puff to shift the wagons loaded with mines and to get a run up the gradient the locomotive had to make a start down at West Dean Tunnel.

On this particular night there was a beautiful full moon but the ominous sound of bombers overhead on their way to bomb London. Bill Marsh, the guard, said to Vic: 'We aren't going to get up there eight times with 12 wagons at a time, we'll take a few more.' 'Be it on your head', replied Vic.

Removal of the wagons was no problem: 20 could be withdrawn at a time but putting them back proved a different matter altogether. Having extracted the two nominated wagons and placed them into the dock at Singleton, the rest were stabled

Going off the rails

in the siding. With the bombers high above, the wagons returning to storage were shunted back. All of a sudden, a shout went up from Bill. 'Vic get up here – quick'. Vic recalls: 'I went out of the office and found that the sides of the embankment alight because the little tank engine had been chucking out hot cinders because it was overloaded. Quick as a flash, I got a bucket of water and chased after the engine with a stirrup-pump towards the tunnel to put out the embankment fires.'

The engines did not stay in the tunnel; it was far more dangerous once trains had left. On one occasion, Phil

Norrell was on duty when 25 wagons had been removed, but Chichester station refused to accept the train as a midnight air-raid was in progress.

With the departure of the ammunition trains, normal working was resumed, with the daily goods between Chichester and Midhurst. This working ceased abruptly in 1951. Bognor passed fireman, George Howess has good reason to remember the event. On Monday, 19 November 1951, he and his driver, Fergus (Fred) Bunker of Hove, left Bognor with a locomotive for Chichester to pick up the daily goods train for the trip up to Midhurst.

The weather was typical for November in 1951, quite different from today. In the 1950s and early 1960s there would be days, even weeks, during the autumn when it would rain and rain day in, week out. It had been pouring with rain all weekend and was still wet when the crew coupled the locomotive to the wagons and picked up the staff at Fishbourne signalbox on the start of the journey up the line. On such days, extra unofficial activities such as shooting game were not considered. The main aim was to keep dry. The normal routine of dropping-off and picking wagons at Lavant and Singleton was carried out and now came the journey to Midhurst.

The downhill approach round into Midhurst was on a horseshoe-shaped curve and the station could be seen through the trees. George Howes just happened to be on the driver's side of the engine when he looked down. In his own words, 'I'd never seen so much water down there – it was like a river.' He crossed back to the fireman's side of the engine but as they were on a curve he couldn't see anything. On his return to his mate's side he took another look, saw that there was no bank supporting the rails and jumped, followed by his driver. 'We both jumped off the wrong side, but luckily enough the trucks stayed on the track otherwise they might have come over on us.'

The engine carried on until the track collapsed under its weight and buried its smokebox in the mud at the bottom of the gully. The tender shot straight up in the air and filled the cab with coal. Subsequently this caught fire and in turn set alight the anthracite coal from the crushed wagon behind the tender.

George Howes had landed on level ground and was unhurt but Fred Bunker had dropped down the bank, got wet up to his knees and had to hobble up from the bottom. George recalled 'It was still very cold and not very nice and we were lucky we got off. If we'd stayed we would have both been killed. The engine had a full head of steam and we were frightened that if it had dropped into deeper water then it would have exploded'. The guard, Albert Betterton of Littlehampton, also jumped clear and was unhurt.

Both driver and fireman walked back up the line to be met by a policeman riding a bike between the track. At the *Greyhound* public-house the signalman was telephoned and notified of the accident. It

RAILWAY BRIDGE WASHED AWAY BY FLOODS

Engine Crashes Into 30-Foot Gully

SCHOOL MASTER FLYING TO NORTH AFRICA

AN eight-truck goods train carrying sugar beet, put the Midhurst to Chichester goods line out of order this week when the engine crashed into a 30-foot deep

Child In S...

A VERDICT adventure the Midhurst day afternoo Ian Robert son of a farmer, who swoller

150. *Back in service after its mishap 'C2x' No 32522 continued at work for British Railways until the autumn of 1961 and here is seen at Midhurst.*

was a very dull and foggy day and the steam from the engine was blowing across the road. As the two men were approaching the station two ladies accosted them and complained bitterly of the noise and the damp, steamy mist. Midhurst and Petworth Fire Brigades turned out in full force and Midhurst Ambulance stood by as there was a distinct possibility of the locomotive exploding.

On arrival at the station the crew were soon besieged by reporters, but the crew could not say anything until the matter had been reported to the railway Inspectorate. The event made local news and the crew had a lucky escape which is personified in the words of late Fred Bunker as recalled by his fireman. 'If we'd been killed I would never have had my first Christmas with my baby.' Fred had just become a father and it is a reminder that railway

work had its dangers in which other unfortunate railwaymen paid with their lives.

It seems that the culvert running underneath the bank had been unable to cope with the water which in turn had pushed the bank away. The aftermath of this event was that the coal surrounding the engine kept burning for a couple of weeks. Attempts to recover the engine using a crane failed as every time the crane approached the scene the bank gave way. Eventually, the locomotive was extracted by removing the embankment for several hundred yards and laying a length of track along which the engine, former LBSCR Class 'C2x' No 32522, was winched out.

The engine was sent for repair at Brighton in February 1952. George, who subsequently fired on No 32522, thought it was better than before it had been put down the gully!

From time to time, there were hazardous events such as the washout that derailed the Midhurst goods and, more exceptionally, the drama associated with storage of the naval ammunition. That said, daily routine on these rural railways was usually humdrum and changed little during the time they served West Sussex.

151. *After closure of the line, Singleton Tunnel was fitted with doors.*

Going off the rails

Chapter 12: Going off the Rails?

The demise of the rural railways in West Sussex lasted nearly a half-century, from the closure to passenger traffic of the Chichester-Midhurst line in 1935 to the departure from Lavant in 1991 of the last gravel train to Drayton. Now operated again by private companies, passenger services remain between Portsmouth and Brighton, and down the Arun Valley. What however is the legacy of the departed lines?

There are tangible reminders. In other parts of Britain, evidence of the trackbeds, stations and earthworks of some lines is hard to find. That is not the case in West Sussex. Of the intermediate stations along Chichester-Midhurst line, all have survived. Cocking has been lavishly converted into a private dwelling. For some time Singleton was the headquarters of a vineyard but is a now a shadow of its former self. The tunnels cannot be easily obliterated, nor the deep and expensive cuttings through the chalk downs.

Of the grand station at Midhurst, with its beautiful moulded stone window-frames, nothing remains and a housing estate has been built on its site. Somewhere underneath there lies the station subway, full of rubble but with the railings still intact and the Portland stone steps still being trod by the spirits of passengers of long ago.

On the route west from Hardham Junction, the station buildings survive at Fittleworth and Petworth and both are flourishing in their new roles. Selham station building is still standing although somewhat dilapidated. West of Midhurst, Elsted station has been obliterated and its site is occupied by modern factory units. Rogate

152. *Track-lifting in progress.*

remains but is sadly vandalised. One pair of railway cottages next to the station drive remain, and both are occupied.

Somewhat ironically, the Chichester-Midhurst line provides more to remind the onlooker of the railway past, as if this expensive 'white-elephant' has tried to provide some justification for its relatively brief working life. Chichester's residents heard the Lavant-Drayton gravel trains for the last time during 1991 and the track between Fishbourne Crossing and Lavant was removed two years later. In 1994, West Sussex County Council purchased the trackbed between Chichester and Lavant. With substantial funding from English Partnerships,

a cycle/pedestrian path known as 'Centurion Way' was constructed on the old route, to become a popular and delightful cycle-path and country walk.

For all the investment made in the area's railways something worthwhile remains for the use of future generations.

At the time they were operating what did the lines serving Petworth, Midhurst and intermediate points contribute to West Sussex?

There is no doubt that the railway helped to liberate country-dwellers. Horizons were extended, if no more dramatically than to convey a family to buy fish in Petersfield, as so vividly recalled by Mavis

Going off the rails

Budd (Chapter 10). The railway transported local products further afield, notably milk, bricks, timber and sugar-beet. It brought coal, newspapers – and weekenders, royal and less exalted – to rural Sussex.

The railway provided mobility but this was not necessarily accompanied by accessibility. That was not entirely the railway's fault. Major landowners had considerable influence in West Sussex and chose – as exemplified by the Earl of Egmont – to ensure that the railway was kept out of sight from their fine homes. The ordinary men and women suffered as a result because the stations at Petworth, Midhurst and Arundel were some distance from the towns they served, as the *West Sussex Gazette* commented in the late 1850s when the railways serving these towns were under construction. Not only the landowners were to blame for the routes taken by the railways. In their desire to minimise costs the railway promoters tried to avoid bridging rivers, as was the case on the approach to Petworth from the east, and to reduce earthworks, with the result that gradients were more severe.

Eventually, the inconvenience of the

153. Above left: *Into the shadows – nostalgia for the steam-hauled trains of rural Britain. Working a 'C2x' 0-6-0, Driver Fred Bunker and Fireman George Howes of Bognor shed approach Selham in 1950.*

154. Left: *Rogate station still largely complete but without track.*

155. Below: *Fittleworth station building, converted to a dwelling.*

stations told against the railway. For so long, people had little option but to walk miles to and from their local station. As soon as bus services developed in West Sussex, they were used in preference to the railway because they picked up passengers from village centres and took them where they wanted to go, to shopping streets and places of work.

The story of railways in West Sussex might have been different had Parliament approved the construction of the Guildford, Chichester and Portsmouth line proposed in 1845. Then Midhurst would have been located on a main line. Possibly the major landowners played a role in forestalling the proposed railway. Other than on aesthetic grounds, it is difficult to understand why they were so concerned to keep the railways at arm's length when it would have benefited their estates and fortunes considerably. Elsewhere in Britain landowners were certainly more responsive. It would be interesting to identify the backers of the Mid-Sussex, and the Mid-Sussex & Midhurst Junction companies and their standing vis à vis the aristocratic landowners.

Given the less than conveniently-sited stations, infrequent services and slow timings for through journeys to Portsmouth, London and further afield, passenger services on the lines serving Petworth and Midhurst probably only survived as long as they did because of the onset of World War II, and the subsequent nationalisation of the railways in 1948.

Having electrified both its main lines between London and Portsmouth, the

Southern Railway arranged its Petersfield-Pulborough passenger service to provide a basic two-hourly timetable. By then, it was probably too late to reverse the decline of this service although in its 1946 proposals the Southern contemplated electrification of the line between Hardham Junction, Midhurst and Petersfield.[1] The poor standard of roads in the area was another reason for the railway service surviving as long as it did.

Whatever the value of the railways to the local population, the concept of public service was important, particularly in a national context. After the outbreak of World War II, the Chichester-Midhurst line awoke from its tranquillity to serve a new role, as a repository for naval munitions. The paradox is that the line's expensive tunnels through the South Downs at last came into their own. In contrast, a telling point was made as to the remoteness of stations from villages when those children evacuated to West Sussex from the capital detrained to buses at railheads such as Pulborough rather than travelling throughout by train to Petworth or Fittleworth.

A real sense of public service was inculcated in employees by railway companies. Poorly paid they might be, but railwaymen (and women, too) took a pride in their occupation and in working as a team. Guard Les Horwood of Emsworth was probably speaking for many of his colleagues when, as quoted in Chapter 10, he wrote to the local newspaper to say 'I have always tried to keep a family feeling among you, and treated you all alike'. The feeling was that the railway was a public service, always to hand even if there was a handful only of regular users.

Compared to other occupations there was a measure of job security on the railway but as traffic declined from the 1920s, jobs were shed in West Sussex. Jack Tulett provides evidence of that when talking of his time at Fittleworth station (Chapter 5).

Although they may have been employees of a large undertaking, and ultimately a national one, the railwaymen and women were part of their local community, took part in its social activities, and drank in its pubs. They were country people, as adept at bagging pheasants as filling-in forms for the Southern Railway. That sense of community is perhaps underlined in local feeling for the Selsey Tram, despite its failings and eccentric timekeeping. After all, for long enough

CENTURION WAY *Chichester - Lavant*

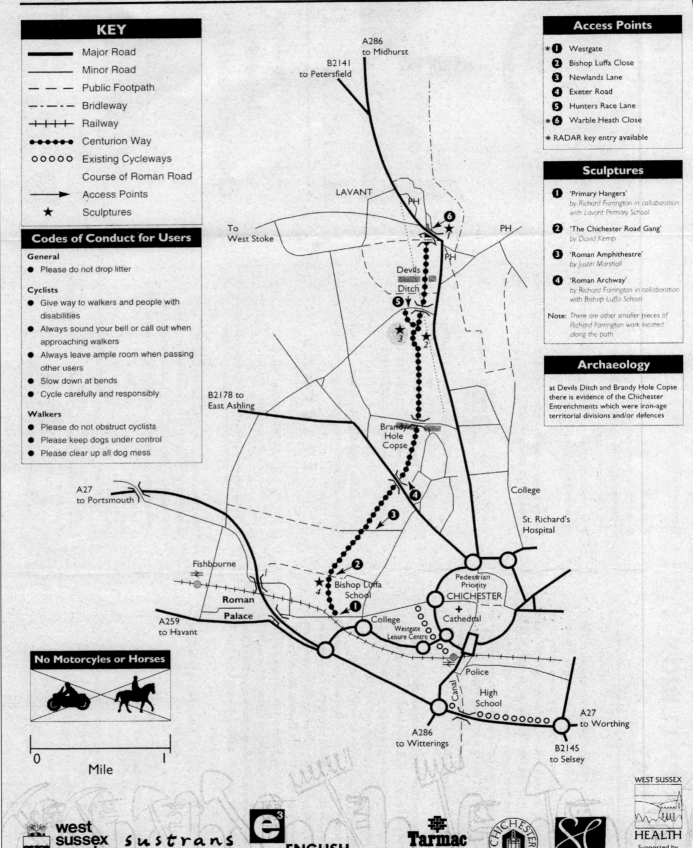

KEY

▬▬▬	Major Road
────	Minor Road
─ ─ ─	Public Footpath
─ · ─ ·	Bridleway
+++++	Railway
●●●●●	Centurion Way
○○○○○	Existing Cycleways
	Course of Roman Road
➔	Access Points
★	Sculptures

Codes of Conduct for Users

General
- Please do not drop litter

Cyclists
- Give way to walkers and people with disabilities
- Always sound your bell or call out when approaching walkers
- Always leave ample room when passing other users
- Slow down at bends
- Cycle carefully and responsibly

Walkers
- Please do not obstruct cyclists
- Please keep dogs under control
- Please clear up all dog mess

Access Points

- ✱**❶** Westgate
- **❷** Bishop Luffa Close
- **❸** Newlands Lane
- **❹** Exeter Road
- **❺** Hunters Race Lane
- ✱**❻** Warble Heath Close

✱ RADAR key entry available

Sculptures

- **❶** 'Primary Hangers' *by Richard Farrington in collaboration with Lavant Primary School*
- **❷** 'The Chichester Road Gang' *by David Kemp*
- **❸** 'Roman Amphitheatre' *by Justin Marshall*
- **❹** 'Roman Archway' *by Richard Farrington in collaboration with Bishop Luffa School*

Note: *There are other smaller pieces of Richard Farrington work located along the path*

Archaeology

at Devils Ditch and Brandy Hole Copse there is evidence of the Chichester Entrenchments which were iron-age territorial divisions and/or defences

No Motorcyles or Horses

0 —————— 1
Mile

WEST SUSSEX
HEALTH
Supported by
West Sussex
Health Promotions

west sussex county council

sustrans
ROUTES FOR PEOPLE

e³
ENGLISH PARTNERSHIPS

Tarmac
Quarry Products

CHICHESTER

SOUTH·EAST ARTS

156. Left and above: *The Centurion Way leaflet.*

157. Below: *A new use for one-time railways - a scene on Centurion Way.*

Selsey's fishermen relied on the Tram to take their highly perishable catches to market. Its reliability cannot have been too suspect.

In time, changing social influences and needs had their effect. People were less inclined to walk two or three miles to the station, wait in a draughty gas-lit Victorian station and board a train that had changed little from the days before World War I. The railway belonged to the past and to a more spartan life-style, one associated with oil-lit, weatherboarded cottages, devoid of a bathroom or an indoor lavatory. Journeys to school of the sort stoically endured by Philip Hounsham, and recounted in Chapter 3, became increasingly unacceptable. More recently, parents have become fearful for the security of their children for reasons that were unimaginable 50 years ago.

The basis of change was more fundamental. In place of a slower, less demanding pace of life, people wanted even greater mobility and accessibility, both of which could be provided by the car. The number of private cars doubled between 1953 and 1960, and doubled again in the next decade.[2] The railway was increasingly chosen for longer journeys only, and then much less frequently.

Until the 1950s, enough goods traffic

on these lines dwindled from the 1920s, as Jack Tulett pointed out in his reminiscences of working at Fittleworth station (Chapter 5). It is easy to overlook the disadvantages of inconveniently located stations or infrequent services. While the passing of the Chichester-Midhurst passenger service attracted little attention in 1935, 20 years later the ending of the Pulborough-Midhurst service brought out numbers of local residents, most of whom, in all probability, had not used the train in years.

There is a depth of feeling about the Victorian steam railway that has proved strong enough to support the development and enhancement of what are nowadays known as the heritage railways. The Bluebell Railway has preserved part of one of the former LBSCR's rural branch lines, and its stations are similar in style to those on the Chichester-Midhurst line. So although the rural railways of West Sussex are now represented by no more than fading memories and collections of archive material, thanks to the Bluebell and other heritage railways it is possible to experience once more the sights and sounds of the steam-worked country branch line.

Going off the Rails has attempted to present some first-hand experiences of those who worked on and used the West Sussex country railways, and to explain the history of the area's railways in a wider social and economic context. We hope that it has gone some way to record their life and times in a way that also pays tribute to the human dimension.

159. *An imaginative use for railway artefacts.*

remained to justify the retention of the lines to Midhurst and Petworth. To some extent, it was a matter of convenience because the local coal merchant had traditionally operated from a depot in the station yard. As households changed from a reliance on coal to electric, oil or gas heating, this staple traffic declined sharply. Builders' merchants similarly tended to be based in goods yards.

The other influence was of changing patterns of distribution which were dependent on road. In West Sussex, there were insufficient sources of bulk traffic for which the railway was better suited, except for sugar-beet and gravel, both of which moved by block train. In place of less efficient local manufacturers who had sent their output by train, there was now more centralised production away from rural areas and served by road hauliers.

The decline of the West Sussex rural

railways was inevitable, and reflected what was happening elsewhere in Britain.

The railway is unlikely to become a general carrier again, operating from numerous wayside stations. The national railway network no longer has the facilities to provide countrywide distribution, but it is possible that there might be a limited number of regional freight break-bulk depots, served by rail. Passenger traffic densities are unlikely to justify new railway construction in West Sussex but we might well see greatly enhanced services along the coast line between Brighton, Chichester and Portsmouth, perhaps with connecting bus services.

Looking back at the rural railways of West Sussex, inevitably there is nostalgia for picturesque lines running through attractive countryside. We are prone to be sentimental about past ways of life. Traffic

160. *The site of Selsey East Beach station in 1997.*

References

CHAPTER 1

1. J. Howard Turner, *The London Brighton & South Coast Railway*, ii, 28, 29, 79, 80.

2. Ibid. ii, 29, 30, 79 et seq.

3. Ibid. ii, 85, 91.

CHAPTER 2

1. Bradshaw's April 1910 Railway Guide.

2. J. Howard Turner, *The London Brighton & South Coast Railway*, (Batsford 1978) ii, 85.

3. Ibid, ii, 86.

4. *A Regional History of the Railways of Great Britain*, H. P. White, ii, 1st Edition, (Phoenix House 1960) 106.

5. J. Howard Turner, *The London Brighton & South Coast Railway*, iii, 58 et seq.

6. Edward Griffith, *The Hundred of Manhood and Selsey Tramways* 2nd Edition, (Edward Griffith 1968), 3-5.

7. E. L. Ahrons, *Locomotive & Train Working in the latter part of the Nineteenth Century*, v, (Heffer, 1953) 64-5.

8. Gervase Hughes, 'British Express Train Services in 1898', i, in *Railway Magazine* March 1961, 163-164.

9. Bradshaw's April 1910 Railway Guide.

10. London & South Western Public Timetable 7 June-30 September 1914.

11. C. Hamilton Ellis, *The Trains We Loved*, (Allen & Unwin, 1947) 29.

12. Bradshaw's July 1922 Railway Guide.

13. C. F. Klapper, *Sir Herbert Walker's Southern Railway*, (Ian Allan, 1973) 121.

14. *Locomotives of the LBSCR* D. L. Bradley, ii, (RCTS 1972) 20.

15. M. J. Overbury *Traffic on a Branch Line*, in *The Brighton Circle*, 15 (1989).

16. M. J. Overbury *Traffic on a Branch Line*, in *The Brighton Circle*, 15 (1989).

17. Norman Harvey, 'Steam Working on the Mid-Sussex Line', in *Railway World* June 1960, 165-166.

18. Bradshaw's July 1938 Railway Guide.

19. Edward Griffith, *The Hundred of Manhood and Selsey Tramways*, (2nd Edition, 1968) 46.

20. C. F. Klapper, *Sir Herbert Walker's Southern Railway*, (Ian Allan, 1973) 208.

CHAPTER 4

1. 1871 and 1951 Census returns. WSRO

2. D. L. Bradley, *Locomotives of the London Brighton & South Coast Railway*, i, (RCTS 1971) 24.

CHAPTER 5

1. B. Hart, 'Fittleworth – a Sentimental Journey' in *British Railway Journal*, (1987), 198

2. Ibid

3. Ibid, 200

4. Ibid

5. Ibid, 201

6. J. Northrop Moore, *Edward Elgar, The Windflower Letters*, (Clarendon Press, 1989), 183

7. B. Hart, 'Fittleworth – a Sentimental Journey' in *British Railway Journal*, (1987), 201

8. J. Northrop Moore, *Edward Elgar, The Windflower Letters*, (Clarendon Press, 1989), 202, 203

9. Ibid, 208

10. Ibid, 210

11. Ibid, 211

12. Ibid, 244

13. Ibid, 254

14. *West Sussex Gazette* 21 September 1995

15. F. Osborne, *A Life on the Iron Road*, WSRO MP 2214

16. Ibid

17. J.Tulett, 'Fittleworth Station From 1915', in *Petworth Society Bulletin*, No 38, (1984) 20-24

CHAPTER 7

1. David St John Thomas, *The Country Railway*, (David & Charles, 1976), 26

2. M. J. Overbury, 'Traffic on a branch line', in *The Brighton Circle* 15, (1989), 122

3. A. Hemans, in *The Brighton Circle*, 15, (1993), 106

4. F. Rich, *Yesterday Once More – A Story of Brighton Steam*, (P. E. Watts & Associates, 1996), 66

5. Chichester and Midhurst Railway Extension to Haslemere, *West Sussex Gazette*, 27 April 1865

6. *West Sussex Gazette*, 8 September 1864

7. *West Sussex Gazette*, 18 October 1866

8. Council Minutes, 25 July 1890, WSRO WOC/CCl/1

9. Council Minutes, 6 February 1891, WSRO WOC/CCl/2

10. Council Minutes, 1 May 1891, WSRO WOC/CCl/2

11. M. Cruttenden, 'Singleton. The Station and its Stationmasters', in *The Brighton Circle*, 19, (1993), 72

12. Ibid, 'The Lavant View', 74

13. *West Sussex Gazette*, 4 July 1935, Letters to the Editor by a Shareholder

14. Ibid, 11 July 1935

CHAPTER 8

1. Eric Coates, *Suite in Four Movements*, (Heineman, 1953), 20

2. Ibid, 210

3. *West Sussex Gazette*, 23 May 1963

4. *Daily Mail*, 13 March 1924

5. E. Griffith, *The Hundred of Manhood and Selsey Tramways*, (2nd Edition, 1968), 11

6. Copy Letter, F. Sanden Street to H. Phillips, Selsey Tramway, 31 May 1912, WSRO Raper 210

7. Letter H. Phillips, H.M. & ST Co. Ltd. to F. Street, London, 18 May 1912, WSRO Raper 210

8. Copy Letter, Kerr Stuart to Messrs F. Street & Co. Ltd., 19 February 1912, WSRO Raper 210

9. Copy Letter, F. Sanden Street to Henry Phillips, 23 May 1912, WSRO Raper 210

10. Copy Letter, H. F. Stephens to H.G. Phillips, 29 May 1912, WSRO Raper 210

11. Copy Letter, H. F. Stephens to Kerr, Stuart, 5 June 1912, WSRO Raper 210

12. Copy Letter, F. Sanden Street to H. G. Phillips, 13 June 1912, WSRO Raper 210

13. Extract from Minutes of Directors Meeting, 20 June 1912, WSRO Raper 210

14. Copy of Letter, Kerr, Stuart to H.G. Phillips, 24 June 1912, WSRO Raper 210

15. Extract from Minutes of Special Meeting of Directors, 3 July 1912, WSRO Raper 210

16. E. Griffiths, *The Hundred of Manhood and Selsey Tramways*, (2nd Edition 1968), 32

17. Ibid, 23

18. Ibid, 47

CHAPTER 9

1. *West Sussex Gazette* 27 October 1859 from Worthing Reference Library, Railway Newspaper Cuttings File

2. Ibid

3. *West Sussex Gazette* 8 September 1864

4. *Illustrated London News* 15 April 1865

5. *West Sussex Gazette* 13 April 1865

6. P. Jerrome and Jonathan Newdick, *Time Out of Mind*, (The Window Press, 1982), 101

7. M. Cruttenden 'Singleton. The Station and its Stationmasters', in *The Brighton Circle*, 19, (1993), 69

8. S. E. Large, *King Edward VII Hospital*, (Phillimore & Co. Ltd., 1986), 2

9. *West Sussex Gazette*, 13 June 1906

10. C. Hamilton Ellis, *The Royal Trains*, (Routledge & Kegan Paul 1975) 80

11. W. A. Wilcox and Charles E. Lee, 'Queen Victoria's Funeral Journey', in *The Railway Magazine* (March 1940)

12. C. Hamilton Ellis, *The Royal Train*, (Routledge & Kegan Paul, 1975), 81

13. Ibid

14. W. A. Wilcox and Charles E. Lee, 'Queen Victoria's Funeral Journey', *The Railway Magazine*, (March 1940), 137

15. M. Cruttenden, 'Singleton. The Station and its Stationmasters', in *The Brighton Circle*, 19, (1993), 72

16. James Roffey, *Big Boys Don't Cry*, WSRO MP 3974, 9

17. Ibid, 14

18. Ibid, 241

19. Ibid, 19

20. Ibid, 212

21. Ibid, 21

22. Ibid, 82

23. Ibid, 84

24. Ibid, 85

25. Ibid, 24

26. Reg Hough, 'Recollections of an Evacuee (2)' in *Petworth Society Magazine*, 76, (1994), 20

27. Ibid, 21

28. James Roffey, *Big Boys Don't Cry*, WSRO MP 3974, 228,229

29. Ibid, 223

CHAPTER 10

1. Mavis Budd, *Dust to Dust*, (J. M. Dent & Sons Ltd, 1966), 7-9

2. Ibid, 11

3. *West Sussex Gazette*, 10 February 1955

4. Ibid

5. *Midhurst Petworth and District Times*, 11 February 1955

6. Ibid

7. *Evening Argus*, 21 May 1966 and *West Sussex Gazette*, 26 May 1966

CHAPTER 11

1. *Midhurst Petworth and District Times*, Sat 24 November 1951

CHAPTER 12

1. Report of the Committee on Proposed Extensions of Electrification, February 1946. RAIL 648/124 at the Public Record Office.

2. See Table 42, *Transport Statistics Great Britain 1966-1976*, HMSO, 1978

Index

Going off the rails